THE LAST BEST HOPE OF EARTH

Abraham Lincoln and the Promise of America

Yours truly
A. Lincoln

Mark E. Neely, Jr.

THE ———————————
LAST BEST HOPE
OF EARTH

Abraham Lincoln and the
Promise of America

Harvard University Press
Cambridge, Massachusetts, and London, England

The Huntington Library
San Marino, California

Illinois State Historical Library
Springfield, Illinois

1993

Frontispiece: Photograph of Abraham Lincoln, taken by Alexander
Hesler in Springfield, Illinois, June 3, 1860. Courtesy of the
Louise and Barry Taper Collection.

This book is printed on acid-free paper, and its binding
materials have been chosen for strength and durability.

Library of Congress Cataloging in Publication Data

Neely, Mark E.
  The last best hope of earth : Abraham Lincoln and the promise
  of America / Mark E. Neely, Jr.
    p. cm.
  Includes bibliographical references (p.) and index.
  ISBN 0-674-51125-5
  1. Lincoln, Abraham, 1809–1865. 2. Presidents—United States—
  Biography. I. Title.
E457.N49 1993
973.7′092—dc20   93-22863
  [B]   CIP

Foreword

The title of this volume, and of the 1993–1994 exhibit at The Huntington Library it serves as a companion publication, is taken from Abraham Lincoln's message to Congress in December 1862. He closed his speech with the following eloquent passage: "We know how to save the Union. In giving freedom to the slave, we assure freedom to the free—honorable alike in what we give, and what we preserve. We shall nobly save, or meanly lose, the last best hope of earth."

In mounting what is arguably the largest and most comprehensive exhibit of original Lincoln materials ever undertaken, our intention is to provoke thoughtful contemplation of the Lincoln legacy, especially his vision of America as a land of opportunity and a government based on democratic ideals. The American experiment survived the tests of Civil War and the assassination of a President, but succeeding generations have had to contend with new threats to freedom, and the goal of social justice remains elusive. We are still called upon to rededicate ourselves to the "unfinished work" of those who fell at Gettysburg; we are still called upon to work for a "new birth of freedom." Lincoln's words still resonate.

The exhibit represents an unprecedented collaboration between The Huntington Library and the Illinois State Historical Library, and draws as well upon the extensive personal collection of Lincolniana amassed by Louise and Barry Taper. It consists of more than two hundred rare pieces, including original letters and documents written by Lincoln, personal possessions of the sixteenth President and his family, as well as a rich variety of contemporary photographs, prints, broadsides, political campaign

memorabilia, and other artifacts, some of which are pictured in this vol-
ume. The exhibit is co-curated by Thomas F. Schwartz, curator of the
Illinois State Historical Library's Henry Horner Lincoln Collection, and
John Rhodehamel, curator of American historical manuscripts at The
Huntington. They have been advised by James M. McPherson, Henry
George Davis Professor of History at Princeton University, who has served
as the chief scholarly consultant.

The exhibit was made possible by a major grant from the National
Endowment for the Humanities, with additional support from Nestlé
USA, Bank of America, ARCO Foundation, The William and Flora
Hewlett Foundation, The Sever Institute, Union Bank of Switzerland, and
the H. Russell Smith Foundation. We are grateful for their support, and
for Professor Neely's superb biography, which will be read long after the
last visitors depart and the manuscripts are put away.

William A. Moffett
Director of The Huntington Library

Preface

Had Abraham Lincoln died in the spring of 1860, on the eve of his first presidential nomination, he would be a forgotten man. Whatever made Lincoln's life memorable in history occurred in the brief but eventful time between the summer of 1860 and the spring of 1865, and those years provide the principal focus of *The Last Best Hope of Earth*. Strangely, that crucial half-decade has been rather neglected in recent works on Lincoln. Instead, Lincoln's private life as son and father, as husband and friend, and even his psychology have been probed and dissected. The rise of psychohistory, the emphasis in women's history on the nineteenth-century family and domestic scene, and the turning inward of the "me generation" of the late twentieth century have all played parts in directing interest more toward Lincoln's early, intimate home life.

But Abraham Lincoln was not a great romantic. He did not experience remarkable religious passion. He was not a speculative thinker. He was not given to introspection. Or if he was, he never talked about such subjects or left revealing documents or telltale letters to suggest such a dramatic private or inner life. As his law partner, who sat in the office with him day after day for sixteen years, remarked, Lincoln was the "most shut-mouthed man" he ever knew. In his public life, on the other hand, Lincoln dealt almost daily with war and peace, slavery and freedom, nationalism and rebellion, as well as progress and poverty. He spoke on all these subjects eloquently, and he acted decisively. The text of this book treats Lincoln's presidency at length, and that is as it should be, surely. The focus is on his political life throughout, for, whatever we may think of political parties today, Lincoln knew that "the man who is of neither party, is not—cannot be, of any consequence."

Professor James McPherson's brief essay defining the focus of the landmark 1993–1994 exhibition of materials relating to Abraham Lincoln at The Huntington Library helped assure concentration on the grander topics of public life: politics and war. I owe him a special debt for suggesting that proper weight be given Lincoln's role as "war President." Other important influences on this book include G. S. Boritt's *Lincoln and the Economics of the American Dream*, Reinhard Luthin's *The Real Abraham Lincoln*, and James G. Randall and Richard N. Current's *Lincoln the President*.

I am grateful to several people in the making of this book. Aida Donald, Editor-in-Chief of Harvard University Press, invited me to write this text and criticized drafts, and Robert C. Ritchie, Director of Research at The Huntington Library, joined with the Press early to create a companion book to The Huntington's exhibit. Susan Wallace, my peerless manuscript editor, oversaw the project from its initial stages through a bound book. Marianne Perlak and Jill Breitbarth of the Press designed an elegant volume. The illustrations for the most part are selections from the exhibit at The Huntington Library. Many items from the Collection of Louise and Barry Taper appear in that exhibit and, through Mrs. Taper's generosity, in this book as well. I am also grateful to Ruth E. Cook of The Lincoln Museum, Fort Wayne, Indiana, a part of Lincoln National Corporation, for permission to include works in that collection.

My brother Wright, my wife Sylvia, and my old friend Frank J. Williams read the manuscript and offered valuable criticism without ever discouraging me. Matthew Warshauer, a graduate student in American Studies at Saint Louis University, checked quotations for accuracy and volunteered helpful suggestions on the text as well. For the sake of readability, I have occasionally altered terminal punctuation, spelling lapses, or initial capitalization in quoting original sources.

Mark E. Neely, Jr.
St. Louis, June 1993

Contents

Illustrations follow pages 54, 118, and 182

CHAPTER ONE

Peculiar Ambition

H istorians are forever doomed to ignorance about the early life of Abraham Lincoln. His modesty, combined with a reluctance to recall the harsher details of his impoverished youth, made Lincoln reticent about such subjects even among friends. He did not write an autobiography or keep a diary. The circumstances of his early youth, spent in rural poverty with illiterate parents and other mostly uneducated relatives and neighbors, meant that there were few persons available to record the humble milestones of this life. No one knew he would become a great man, least of all Lincoln himself, who at one critical juncture seriously weighed the choice between becoming a lawyer or a *blacksmith!* Many years later, after his death, Lincoln's old law partner, William H. Herndon, conducted a sort of oral history, interviewing and corresponding with old settlers and relatives and associates of Lincoln. Unfortunately, in many instances decades had passed since the interviewees had known Lincoln, and the fame that had come to him since those early times made people prone to exaggerate their importance in his life.

Given the meager record, it is remarkable how much has been written on the subject of Lincoln's youth. Lincoln himself once warned a would-be biographer that his early life could best be summed up in the words of Gray's elegy as the short and simple annals of the poor. What has driven biographers and historians to go beyond that has varied from age to age. While Lincoln was still living, politicians and others saw in his life inspirational power, particularly for young people. Here, to borrow a phrase coined by Henry Clay, was a genuinely "self-made man." Writers attempting to formulate simple lessons for American youth from the great man's life naturally focused on his early years for examples. Later, historians removed from Lincoln's era by a generation and seeking more analytical than inspirational descriptions of his life were fascinated by America's rapidly disappearing frontier and looked to Lincoln's experience in backwoods Kentucky and Indiana and on the unbroken prairies of Illinois as a contributor of special attributes of character. Today, the influence of psychology on historians who write biography often dictates a focus on the subject's formative years. Whatever the reasons, the result has been rather too much focus on Lincoln's early life at the expense of the important presidential years.

Abraham Lincoln was born on February 12, 1809, in a log cabin on a farm in Hardin County, Kentucky. He was the second child and first son of Thomas Lincoln and Nancy Hanks Lincoln. Later she would give birth to another boy who would die in infancy. The Lincoln family history, which has proved more important to historians than it was to the Lincolns, who did not know much of it, followed patterns of migration typical of a great mass of Americans. The first Lincoln came to Hingham, Massachusetts, from England during the Great Puritan Migration of 1630–1640. Succeeding generations followed the Allegheny Mountains to Pennsylvania and then further south to Virginia and from there westward to Kentucky. Abraham Lincoln's grandfather, also named Abraham Lincoln, was killed by Indians—"not in battle, but by stealth," as his famous grandson recalled from family stories— while laboring to clear a farm in the wilderness. The sudden family tragedy left Thomas, the President's father, "a wandering labor boy" who "grew up litterally without education." The documentary record for the maternal side of Lincoln's family is so spare that we can tell almost nothing about Nancy Hanks or her people.

Modern categories of social class are made primarily for industrialized societies, and Lincoln was born too early to fit such categories. His family might be described as yeoman farmer. For generations the Lincolns had been living in the back country.

Class made more difference in the South than in the North, perhaps. Because Thomas Lincoln was not of the planter class, his son did not grow up to be like his political idol, Henry Clay. The great Kentucky politician in his younger years was a gambler, a lover of race horses, and a duelist; one biographer calls him a "hedonist" who imported Madeira and sherry by the cask. Although he was the son of a Virginia Baptist minister, Clay became an Episcopalian late in life. Clay owned slaves. Lincoln grew up to become a teetotaler who did not use tobacco. He lacked a vengeful nature and, though he became muscular and developed into an able wrestler, escaped the frontier's familiar reliance on violence. He did not even like to hunt. His parents were Baptists in religion and not defenders of slavery.

Slavery formed part of the landscape of Lincoln's earliest youth. When Abraham was two years old, Hardin County held 1,007 slaves (there were 1,627 white males in the county above the age of sixteen). Some of Lincoln's kin who wanted to get ahead in Kentucky society became slaveholders. Nancy Hanks's guardian had owned three slaves. Lincoln's great-uncle Isaac owned dozens of slaves, and his uncle Mordecai, Thomas Lincoln's brother, was also a slaveowner. Thomas wanted to get ahead in life, too, but he took another route. As a sometime common laborer, he had to compete for wages with slaves who were rented out by their masters, and as a member of the local Baptist church, he was a parishioner in a religious body formed by persons who had seceded from other churches out of opposition to slavery.

The route Thomas and Nancy eventually chose was the road to Indiana. Restless "wandering" in search of fertile land to which he could make good legal claim characterized Thomas's most productive years. His son grew suspicious of geographical mobility ever after: Abraham Lincoln moved twice in his adult life, in 1831 out of his father's home and in 1837 out of the dying town of New Salem, Illinois, before it became truly dead. Many years later, when Lincoln's stepbrother, John D. Johnston, expressed a wish to sell his Illinois farm and move to Missouri, Abraham advised against it: "If you intend to go to work, there is no better place than right where you are; if you do not intend to go to work, you can not get along any where. Squirming & crawling about from place to place can do no good." But Lincoln retained for the whole of his life the family's early dislike of slave society.

Slavery, according to Abraham's recollections, was one of the reasons that Thomas left Kentucky, but the main reason lay in difficulties with land titles encountered every time he tried to better himself by purchasing a farm. Thomas was trying to get ahead, and therein lies one of the problems with the term "yeoman." It has too much of a fixed image about it, as though these modest farmers were sturdily ambitionless and satisfied with respectable subsistence farming. Thomas sought improvement restlessly, for a time, and he raised a son in whom ambition became, in the words of William H. Herndon, "a little engine that knew no rest." True, part of Abraham's ambition was to escape his father's lot, but it would be wrong to make of his unsuccessful father a caricature, an amiably lazy southern poor white.

Thomas's ambition was thwarted by the legal system. Kentucky was a crazy-quilt of overlapping land claims, and uncertainty of title drove many a farmer from the state. If one lived in the part of the Bluegrass State that the Lincolns did, a good place to go was nearby Indiana because it fell under the Federal Land Ordinance of 1785. That meant that land could be purchased from the national government, which had surveyed it in great mile-wide squares subdivided into smaller squares; land titles were more secure. When Abraham was seven, the Lincolns moved westward to Indiana, to the Pigeon Creek community near the Ohio River in the southwestern corner of the state.

It was a move backward in terms of civilization, for Indiana, which became a state the year the Lincolns moved there, was still "an unbroken forest" with "bears and wild animals" all about. This is where Abraham Lincoln grew up, where he learned to read and write, and where he developed his irrepressible sense of humor. Such an environment had to be defied if one were to accomplish anything in life.

"There was absolutely nothing to excite ambition for education," he recalled. The wilderness could not be held completely at bay by even the strongest, the most humorous, the most ambitious, and it left in Lincoln a tragic view of life.

The earliest Lincoln documents come from Indiana, fugitive pages from a sum book in which the boy practiced arithmetic and writing. If the pages suggest youthful diligence, they also betray an irreverent streak and a somewhat darker outlook than sentimentalists later described in this period of his life. "Abraham Lincoln / his hand and pen / he will be good but / god knows When," he wrote. He also wrote, "Abraham Lincoln is my name / And with my pen I wrote the same / I wrote in both hast and speed / and left it here for fools to read." The boy was already attracted to melancholy verse as well: "Time What an emty vaper / tis and days how swift they are swift as an indian arr[ow] / fly on like a shooting star the present moment Just [is here] / then slides away in h[as]te that we [can] never say they['re ours] / but [only say] th[ey]'re past." He was seventeen years old when he wrote those words.

Who saved these haunting fragments of the ignorant teen whom no one yet suspected of potential for greatness? His stepmother did. Nancy Hanks Lincoln died in 1818 of "milk sickness," a disease, common on the frontier, contracted by drinking the milk of cows that had eaten poisonous white snakeroot. The boy was only nine. About a year later, Thomas returned to Kentucky and brought home a new wife and mother, a widow named Sarah Bush Johnston. She was illiterate, too, but she defied the stereotype of the evil stepmother. No one in all the vast Lincoln literature has an unkind word to say about her. She apparently came to like Abraham better than her own progeny, and he apparently came to like her better than he liked his own father. Sarah Bush Johnston Lincoln saved the boy's copybook and gave it to Herndon when he contacted her for an interview about her famous stepson.

Little else survives to illuminate the events of Lincoln's formative years in Indiana. He had less than a year's formal education, and that came "by littles" in wretched schools with unenlightened schoolmasters. Lincoln recalled that when he came of age, he "did not know much." He could read and write and solve algebraic equations. He could not spell well or speak with polished grammar, and he did not know geometry. But he did know that life was hard.

Lincoln was large for his age, and his father handed him an ax to hack away at the Indiana wilderness from very early years on. Death grew familiar. First there had been his little brother's death, then his mother died in Indiana, and later his older sister died in childbirth. Lincoln had his own brush with death when a horse kicked him in the head while he ground grain at a mill, rendering him unconscious. When he came to, he finished the sentence he had started when the horse kicked him.

In 1830 the Lincolns moved westward again, this time to Illinois, seeking fertile soil and freedom from milk sickness. Abraham went with them but left his father's roof for good soon thereafter. The young man had few skills, little education, and no prospects. Evidently he simply desired to leave agriculture and his father. They hardly ever saw each other again.

Wanting to get ahead in life, Abraham was attracted to commerce, such as it was on the frontier. In 1828, while still in Indiana, he was hired to help the son of a merchant take a load of produce by flatboat to Louisiana. The youths had to "trade along the Sugar coast," and while doing so they were attacked by seven men bent on killing and robbing them. The tough Indiana youths fought them off, weighed anchor, and escaped. Lincoln remembered that the attackers were black.

In the spring of 1831 Lincoln and some of his relatives took a canoe on the swollen Sangamon River to Springfield, where they constructed a flatboat to carry cargo once again to New Orleans for a small-time merchant named Denton Offutt. Offutt had the twisted ingenuity sometimes associated with the frontier entrepreneur. He got the idea that the thirty-odd hogs to be carried on the boat could best be driven to it if the hired hands sewed the hogs' eyes shut. In fact, the animals could not be driven anywhere blind, and Lincoln and his companions had to tie them and carry them on board. When Lincoln became

President thirty years later, old Offutt wrote to let his former employee know about his secret method for training horses—by using phrenology to understand them. Offutt saw promise in Lincoln and hired him to run a store and a mill in New Salem, Illinois, after he returned from New Orleans.

In March 1832 Lincoln declared himself a candidate for the Illinois House of Representatives. Only a few months before he had been "friendless, uneducated, penniless," but he was going to give politics a try. He studied grammar to prepare for it, and his first published communication to voters, Lincoln's first platform, printed in the local newspaper, the *Sangamo Journal,* showed considerable skill.

Lincoln had nothing to fear from the leveling currents of Jacksonian democracy in American politics. He could in all honesty tell the voters that he "was born and . . . ever remained in the most humble walks of life." He had "no wealthy or popular relations to recommend" him. His case was "thrown exclusively upon the independent voters of this county." Lincoln added, "Every man is said to have his peculiar ambition," and he had "no other so great as that of being truly esteemed of my fellow men." There was more than Uriah Heep demagoguery to this candidacy, however.

Lincoln's turn to politics followed from recent personal experiences. He had been forced, with his fellow would-be employees of Offutt, to purchase a canoe when flooding made overland travel to meet their boss impossible. Then low water and drifted debris delayed their flatboat journey when the boat hung up on a mill dam at New Salem. Offutt's store had been delayed in opening, perhaps by the slow transit of goods to stock it. Such frustrations of personal enterprise and ambition demanded political solutions, large public projects. Americans called them "internal improvements."

Association with Offutt and resolve to overcome the deprivations of his youth had given him a developer's outlook, and Lincoln in fact offered himself to the voters as a sort of expert on internal navigation. He applied his personal experience of the preceding year, on flatboats and watching millraces, to the questions of the day and announced himself an advocate of "internal improvements" to benefit "the poorest and most thinly populated countries." No one had studied the river more closely than he, Lincoln asserted, and he argued that improving the Sangamon for navigation seemed possible and was the only practical course, however alluring the idea of railroads, with their invulnerability to seasonal variations in weather. He also denounced usury and spoke in support of education. The document was free of bombast. It was dignified, on the whole, and generally grammatical. But it did not say what the program would cost or how the money should be raised.

Finances were getting to be a personal problem, too, as Offutt's store was near failure. Lincoln decided to enlist in the militia for the Black Hawk Indian War in April 1832. American armies were democratic in those days, nearly everyone being imbued with the idea that the New World's citizens had to be treated with respect for their independence and could not be made soldiers by harsh discipline as the hopeless peasantry of Europe could (an idea Lincoln retained when he became commander in chief). Officers were customarily elected, and Lincoln became captain by vote of his men, mostly neighbors from the county. The vote surprised him but pleased him immensely. It made him think that his political career might really succeed.

Lincoln did not come home a war hero. In fact he never saw a hostile Indian or fired a shot in anger. On the campaign he did once protect a friendly Indian who strayed into camp from being killed by the soldiers in blind frontier fury. After being mustered out, Lincoln had his horse stolen and had to walk much of the way home, traveling also by canoe.

Thus poor transportation contributed to Lincoln's political undoing in 1832. He arrived home too late in the summer to conduct an extensive campaign, and Sangamon County was one of only two Illinois counties with substantial population, over 8,000 voters in this election. That put Lincoln, "young and unknown" as he was, at a considerable disadvantage. In the voting to choose four representatives, he ran eighth in a field of thirteen, gaining 657 votes (the top vote-getter got 1,127).

Without employment or prospects, too uneducated to become a

lawyer but too smart to want to become a blacksmith, Lincoln made an important decision: he decided to stay put. Moving elsewhere would not improve on his modest stock of learning, and he was already willing to work. Most of his neighbors had voted for him. He had a base to work from if he could find a way to make ends meet until the next election. This pattern would persist in Lincoln's life. He would find himself diverted in even-numbered years by the demands of politics, and in odd years he would work hard to make up the loss of income.

He decided to become a partner in a general store with a man named William F. Berry. They went deeply into debt, the store closed, and then Berry died in 1835, leaving the unsophisticated Lincoln liable for all the partnership's debts (which he eventually paid). Lincoln had become postmaster in 1833, an office too insignificant to make it matter that his politics did not square with those of the administration in power at the time, Andrew Jackson's Democrats. He also became deputy surveyor for the county.

Lincoln ran again for the state legislature in 1834, this time, apparently, as an avowed anti-Jackson candidate. He won and came within fifteen votes of being the top vote-getter in the county. The election campaign brought him into association with John Todd Stuart, a leader of the people opposed to Jackson who would soon form Illinois's Whig party. Stuart encouraged him to study law and lent him the necessary books. Toward the end of the year he left for his first legislative session in the state capital at Vandalia.

Lincoln entered politics before he chose a profession or married. It was his first love. He did not go to Vandalia to enhance his prestige and attract more law clients back home. Nor had he grown up in a station in life where he was expected to lead or to take on such offices as trappings of his rank in society. Lincoln went because he needed employment and because he sought political solutions to his personal problem of lack of economic opportunity. He did not seek the solution, as some did, through corruption or favoritism; he sought it through statesmanship, that is, cooperative effort to bring to Sangamon County and to Illinois internal improvements (now called infrastructure). Transportation came first to Lincoln's mind back in 1832, after all his delays in high and low water, but credit (usury) was not far behind, and when he got to Vandalia, he began to respond to wider issues. Lincoln voted for state support for building the Illinois and Michigan Canal to connect Illinois via the Great Lakes with the Erie canal and even ocean-going commerce. (In his first platform he had said that the "public utility of internal improvements" had been "verified to a demonstration"—doubtless a reference to the famously successful Erie canal.) He voted to incorporate a state bank, as the Second Bank of the United States was under attack by the Democrats in Washington and its charter was expiring. He also advocated distributing to Illinois at least 20 percent of the proceeds from the sale of public lands located within the state.

Lincoln's later fame arose from issues of liberty and equality, and historians and biographers attracted to Lincoln because of those issues have generally been impatient with his early political career, occupied as it was with canal companies, bank stock subscribers, and builders of toll bridges. Nor have Lincoln's admirers always been comfortable with his choice of profession, the law, and the clients such as railroad executives he came to associate with regularly. The Whig party, Lincoln's choice, has not fared particularly well in the works of modern historians. But the problem lies with the historians as much as with Lincoln or the other Whigs. From the closing of the frontier in the 1890s to the modern ecological movement, American intellectuals have often been in revolt against industrialism and vaguely sympathetic to pastoralism. Lincoln fought his entire political life *for* industrialization, and there was not a pastoral bone in his body. His consorting with stock-jobbers and note-shavers, boosters and developers was not an alliance of convenience, necessary to promote his serious career in pursuit of liberty and equality and Union. The developers' program *was* his serious career, his life-work until the 1850s, a deeply felt attempt to solve the problems of his deprived youth.

Lincoln clung to most of the program for his entire life and, though respectful of other beliefs and interests, had trouble understanding why anyone would oppose it. In his first published platform, back in

1832, Lincoln said, "There cannot *justly* be any objection to having rail roads and canals, any more than to other good things, provided they cost nothing." Railroads and canals were in his era undeniably "good things," and he would have been as baffled by anyone who did not desire them as he was later by those who, in order to defend slavery, questioned the principles of liberty and equality set down by Thomas Jefferson in the Declaration of Independence. Such things were axiomatic with him, ingrained by personal experience as much as by party indoctrination.

Though Lincoln felt sincerely the need for these programs for economic development of the West, they were not original with him. He appropriated ideas from Henry Clay and from the Whig party. Clay called his program of protective tariffs and internal improvements the "American System," an ingenious label that wrapped the whole package in the flag. Indeed, it became one of the most important statements of American nationalism to emerge from the nineteenth century. Though not the only source of Abraham Lincoln's profound and stubborn nationalism, it was an important one.

Formulated while Lincoln was a teenager and widely publicized as he reached political age, the American System might best be understood as a response to the near defeat of the United States in the War of 1812 and to the near prostration of the economy after the Panic of 1819. Clay, emphasizing what modern economists would call comparative advantage, foresaw a great nation in the New World united by harmoniously complementary regional economic specialization. The primary element was a protective tariff to shelter infant manufacturing establishments until the United States boasted enough industrial might to become secure in war and to provide a domestic market in the form of urban workers hungry for the products of American farms. Such a platform appealed especially to New England, with its developing mills, and to the Northwest, with its foodstuffs. To get those agricultural products to market, the government would have to encourage the building of internal improvements, a transportation network to knit the country together in commercial harmony. The South's river systems gave it a more "natural" economic network, but the Northwest in particular craved transportation to markets. Money from the sales of public lands, redistributed to the states, could provide much of the funding. Clay supported the establishment of a Bank of the United States to provide a sound national circulating medium to facilitate commercial transactions.

One of the problems of the American System, for Clay as a politician with national ambitions, was that it did not offer much to the South. The South stood to gain only by a modest domestic market for cotton in New England mills. On the other hand, tariffs would impede the region's foreign trade and make its imported manufactures more expensive, while its agricultural products—staple crops for the world market like tobacco and cotton—would not benefit by the increased demand to feed American urban workers. Clay became known as a southern man with northern principles. Lincoln did not bother himself with the problem, for his ambitions were as yet confined to one small part of the Northwest—Sangamon County, Illinois.

Sangamon County apparently contained many people who saw things the way Lincoln did, but the rest of the state did not, at least not enough ever to form a majority at election time. In that sense, Lincoln did make the wrong choice of party: being a Whig in Illinois doomed him to an insignificant political career because the state's voters turned out to be preponderantly Democratic, and the Whigs could never elect a governor or senator. Unmindful of that circumstance, some have mistakenly seen Lincoln's early political career as a failure. In fact, he rose quickly to prominence in the party, and a term in the U.S. House of Representatives, which Lincoln eventually gained, was as high as any Illinois Whig ever went. Up to 1848 only one Whig, John Todd Stuart, gained election even to two terms in Congress.

By 1836 Lincoln's self-confidence was soaring. He ran again for the state legislature, this time with an almost breezy letter to the newspaper announcing his candidacy and platform. "I go for all sharing the privileges of the government, who assist in bearing its burthens," he wrote. "Consequently I go for admitting all whites to the right of suffrage, who pay taxes or bear arms, (by no means excluding females).'' He vowed to represent those who voted against him as well as those who voted for him, and he promised to be guided by his constituents' will when he could know it, his own judgment otherwise. Such statements came as close as Lincoln ever did to voicing the doctrine of instruction, the idea that an elected representative must vote as instructed by constituents. Later he would show himself distrustful of it. He also advocated "distributing the proceeds of the sales of the public lands to the several states, to enable our state, in common with others, to dig canals and construct rail roads, without borrowing money and paying interest on it." He explained that he would vote Whig in the presidential election (he had not divulged his presidential preference to the voters in 1832).

Lincoln returned to the legislature in Vandalia, where he led the Sangamon delegation to victory in moving the state capital to Springfield. He also worked hard for a large internal improvements scheme: a north-south trunk railroad and an east-west one, with half a dozen spurs to communities whose importance (or whose representatives in the legislature) could not be ignored. Illinois would borrow money to pay for these and other works such as roads and river improvements. The package, with bipartisan support, passed in 1837, and workmen started digging all over the state.

Abraham Lincoln's earliest surviving speech, seldom quoted, comes from the same internal-improvements session of the Illinois legislature in Vandalia. Lincoln rose to speak in the House against a resolution to inquire into the affairs of the State Bank of Illinois. The subject makes the speech's lack of reputation understandable: from the Age of Jackson on, probes into the affairs of banks have been fairly popular in American politics. If lawyers have been perennially unpopular in American history as a group, bankers have surely been even less popular, and when they were closely connected with the government, as in the case of the Second Bank of the United States and the State Bank of Illinois, they seemed less attractive yet. But Lincoln's speech advocated *shielding* the bank from investigation.

Lincoln knew how to appeal to the passions of the multitude. He characterized the proposed inquiry into dealings in the bank's stock as a feud among capitalists, irrelevant to Illinois' real interests. An investigation would cost the government money, of course, and Lincoln said, "These capitalists generally act harmoniously, and in concert, to fleece the people, and now, that they have got into a quarrel with themselves, we are called upon to appropriate the people's money to settle the quarrel." Thereafter, Lincoln neatly refuted each allegation in the resolution, asserting flatly that the bank had served the people well and had "doubled the prices of the products of their farms, and filled their pockets with a sound circulating medium." He charged that only politicians questioned the bank's work, and the source of complaint explained much: "Mr. Chairman, this movement is exclusively the work of politicians; a set of men who have interests aside from the interests of the people, and who, to say the most of them, are, taken as a mass, at least one long step removed from honest men. I say this with the greater freedom because, being a politician myself, none can regard it as personal."

In a statement that lay near the heart of his faith in the efficacy of a banking system for providing capital and a sound circulating medium, Lincoln added, "Whatever the Bank, or its officers, may have done, I know that usurious transactions were much more frequent and enormous, before the commencement of its operations, than they have ever been since."

The Democrats, Lincoln asserted, were attempting to conjure up an image of the bank commissioners' involvement in "a mass of corruption." Here lay the central political problem in many a Jacksonian debate. Democrats thought connections between government and business were inherently corrupt and would unfairly benefit a few at the expense of "the people at large." Whigs like Lincoln thought the people at large benefited enough from having capital for loans and a reliable currency that there could be no cavil with some benefiting more than others within the system.

Amidst these partisan events, there arose in the assembly a question about slavery. Abolitionism, a newcomer to American reform movements this decade, was meeting ferocious and violent resistance from white people in both the North and the South who felt threatened by changes in the racial order. From Massachusetts to Illinois, mobs attacked abolitionists and antislavery meetings. Several states circulated resolutions condemning abolitionist agitation and forwarded them to Illinois. A resolution condemning abolitionists, asserting that the Constitution sanctioned slavery and that it was wholly a state matter, and declaring the illegality of abolishing slavery in the District of Columbia was introduced in the Illinois General Assembly. Lincoln was one of only six men to vote against it; seventy-seven others voted for it.

At the end of the session Lincoln and one other Whig representative entered a protest into the record, saying that "the institution of slavery is founded on both injustice and bad policy; but that the promulgation of abolition doctrines tends rather to increase than to abate its evils." They also stated their belief in the power of Congress to abolish slavery in the District of Columbia, though they admitted it "ought not to be exercised unless at the request of the people" of the District. It may have been a further sign of his growing confidence that Lincoln decided to buck the majority to condemn slavery. Or maybe he could not bear to let any statement in support of slavery pass without comment on the obvious evils of the institution. Eight months and four days later a mob in Alton, Illinois, across the river from St. Louis and less than seventy-five miles from Springfield, killed Elijah Lovejoy, an abolitionist newspaper editor, and threw his press into the Mississippi.

Less than three months after the Lovejoy incident Lincoln delivered a speech that has consistently attracted the attention of historians and biographers, who generally agree that it was Lincoln's first distinguished speech. In fact, it has proved more fascinating the further it recedes in time, so that it is now the focus of intense scrutiny and, among writers on Lincoln, one of the half-dozen best known and most closely examined texts. This is attributable more to the obsession of our age with psychology than to the speech itself; many modern writers find it psychologically revealing. Other factors have aided its modern reputation. The speech is about liberty and Union and not about banks and tariffs. It is not overtly partisan, for Lincoln's forum was not the disputatious state legislature but the Young Men's Lyceum of Springfield, a self-improvement society that necessarily eschewed political partisanship in quest of broad membership.

Lincoln's speech, entitled "The Perpetuation of Our Political Institutions,"addressed the problem of the motivation to perpetuate the work of the country's founders. They were a "hardy, brave, and patriotic . . . race of ancestors" who accomplished a heroic task. Merely to transmit the fruits of their work through the generations hardly seemed to require similarly heroic virtues. Once established, the United States was difficult to destroy. Protected by physical isolation from foreign conquerors like Napoleon, the country could now die only by "suicide." The problem, as Lincoln saw it, was to link heroic ambition to the unheroic goal of perpetuating what the geniuses of old had created.

There is undeniable sophistication in Lincoln's statement of the problem, couched in the language of the romantic era with its preoccupation with genius and creativity. The young politician, on the eve of his twenty-ninth birthday, had reached a stage of self-conscious ambition. On the brink of a third term in the legislature and considerable responsibility in his new law firm, he was no longer, as he stated in his first political platform back in 1832, accustomed to "disappointments." But he knew now that politicians had interests separate from the people's, that he was himself a politician, and that the people knew it.

Lincoln thought that he could now see distressing signs that the field was ripe for a man of great ambition to reap a fatal harvest in the young republic. Sinister opportunity beckoned in "the increasing disregard for law which pervades the country." He had been worrying about this for over a year and had mentioned the "lawless and mobocratic spirit . . . abroad in the land" in his speech about the bank the preceding winter. He apparently saved as proof items from the press over the year.

The frightening wave of antiabolition violence offered many examples, but Lincoln studiously avoided linking violence to one cause alone. Moreover, he admitted that most of the victims were "obnoxious," and he included among the targets of mobs people like gamblers as well as sympathetic martyrs to free speech. Even so, every act of vigilante justice was to Lincoln another step toward detaching the people from law and the Constitution, the institutions that ultimately guaranteed the liberties of the people.

The possibility that some demagogue might exploit mob spirit seemed to Lincoln a real danger. With cities, counties, rivers, and mountains already named for the heroes of the Revolution, the "field of glory" was "harvested, and the crop . . . already appropriated." But "new reapers" would inevitably "arise." The "ruling passion" of the ambitious genius as well as the passions of the people in the days of the country's founding had been "smothered and rendered inactive" by united effort "directed exclusively against the British nation." Now the common enemy was departed, but towering ambition and the people's passions remained. The former, Lincoln said, "thirsts and burns for distinction; and, if possible, it will have it, whether at the expense of emancipating slaves, or enslaving freemen."

Lincoln proposed remedies that made this perhaps the most con- servative speech he ever gave. "Let reverence for the laws," he said, "be breathed by every American mother, to the lisping babe, that prattles on her lap—let it be taught in schools, in seminaries, and in colleges;—let it be written in Primmers, spelling books, and in Alma- nacs;—let it be preached from the pulpit, proclaimed in legislative halls, and enforced in courts of justice. And, in short, let it become the *political religion* of the nation." Lincoln embraced rationality rather than the familiar conservative institutions of religion, family, or prop- erty as the country's salvation. "Passion has helped us but can do so no more," Lincoln warned. "It will in future be our enemy. Reason, cold, calculating, unimpassioned reason, must furnish all the materials for our future support and defence."

Ambition, as much as unimpassioned reason, continued to play a large role in Lincoln's life, especially in the next decade. He was reelected to the General Assembly on August 6, 1838, with the highest total given any of the seven representatives elected from giant San- gamon County. In 1839 like many other alert Whigs, Lincoln began to work hard to win the upcoming presidential election for his party, scenting opportunity in the economic woes of the ill-starred Democratic administration of Martin Van Buren. Lincoln took the smooth high road, with speeches on complex economic matters, mainly central banking. But Lincoln did not neglect the bumpier low road, drafting organizational plans and urging vigorous partisan effort to equal the fabled vote-getting ability of the Democratic party.

Lincoln's distinction as a political figure was that he united vote-getting skills and canvassing energy with genuine political substance and vision. For most of his career in Illinois politics, the substance was the Whig vision of economic development of the West. Organizing and energizing a mass electorate required skills not universally shared or admired within the Whig party. The Democrats' skill at attracting the votes of immigrant Catholics, for example, bred in some Whigs aggressive anti-Catholic and nativist sentiments. Lincoln recognized political realities without deriving ugly partisan prejudices from them. Foreign-born voters in Illinois, many of them Irish Catholic common laborers who worked on the internal improvements the Whigs were so enthusiastic about, generally went for the Democrats. If elections could be timed to occur when those roving Democratic voters were not working in the district, all the better, thought Lincoln. But Lincoln remained throughout his long career in politics untainted by advocacy of exclusionist, nativist, or anti-Catholic policies, something that could not be said about all his associates.

Enthusiastically supporting Whig presidential candidate William Henry Harrison, Lincoln drafted a circular marked "confidential" that he sent to county organizers. There was nothing in it beyond exhortations to work for the party and to encourage others to do so in turn, but Democrats managed to get copies of the document and published it as if it were scandalous, mostly on the strength of its being marked "confidential." Though not scandalous, the circular was unusual, for Whigs had lagged behind Democrats in the matter of tight political organization in the state. "*They* set us the example of organization; and we, in self defence, are driven into it," Lincoln explained. Political passions ran unusually high. Simeon Francis, editor of the Whig newspaper in Springfield and of the special Whig paper for the Harrison campaign statewide, scuffled with Stephen A. Douglas in the street over an alleged slur printed in the paper.

Little wonder passions were aroused. Americans were in the process of constructing the most broadly based and skillfully managed political parties in the world. These vote-getting organizations, created entirely outside the Constitution (indeed, those who drafted that old document would have been horrified to see them), would raise political enthusiasm and consciousness to the greatest heights in the world. Voter turnout reached 80 percent in 1840, and it remained consistently high in Lincoln's political era. He was in part a creator of that system and certainly an eager and skilled participant, a creature of the system. It would be difficult to think of a more thoroughgoing democrat than Abraham Lincoln, a man against whom charges of Whig elitist conservatism always had a hollow ring.

Lincoln's role as enthusiastic organizer in the Whig party gained him enemies. For a time he thought the party would not select him as candidate for the legislature again in 1840, but his well-developed skill at making "stump speeches," as they were called, made him useful for the Whig ticket in the county. In that role he appealed to voters' higher instincts by urging sane central banking practices, and to their lower instincts by attempting to embarrass Van Buren for inconsistent support of the War of 1812 and "for allowing Free Negroes the right of suffrage" in New York (in fact, Van Buren had worked to restrict the extent of black suffrage).

Lincoln gained reelection, but this time all the Whigs in the Sangamon district got about the same number of votes—a sign of party discipline and organization. Harrison won the national election, and Lincoln showed himself to be a far cry from a ruthless spoilsman. "I am," he wrote to John Todd Stuart, "as you know, opposed to removals to make places for our friends." But he remained an enthusiastic Whig partisan and a believer in organization for political victory, and he did suggest a few who ought to be turned out of office and a few to replace them.

Lincoln clung to the Whig platform but shifted emphasis. The internal improvements scheme had been buried "without benefit of clergy" with the state's financial collapse in 1837, and the bank issue was fading as well. Now he pushed tariff increases, which he advertised as promising many benefits: they would "prevent excessive importations of goods, and excessive exportations of specie; . . . create a Home market for agricultural productions; a Home demand for the skill and industry of our people; . . . raise revenue enough to relieve the nation from debt and to support the government, and so to foster our manufactures as to make our nation PROSPEROUS in PEACE and INDEPENDENT in War." As usual, he was well prepared to deal in closely reasoned arguments above the sloganeering of party platforms.

In 1843 he drafted a campaign circular to be sent from the Whig State Committee, urging two policies with which he was now closely identified: protective tariffs for the nation and the convention system for nominations to office in the state. Lincoln argued that either taxes or tariffs were necessary for the support of the government; that tariffs, collected in larger amounts in fewer transactions and locations, required fewer government officers for collection; that "the burthen of revenue falls almost entirely on the wealthy and luxurious few," who paid tariffs on imported "fine cloths, fine silks, rich wines, golden chains, and diamond rings," while "the man who contents himself to live upon the products of his own country, pays nothing at all." Thus "house . . . barn, and . . . homespun" of the "laboring many" were not "perpetually haunted and harassed by the tax-gatherer."

As for the convention system, it had become the centerpiece and symbol of the organizationally minded Whigs, who were determined not to let the party become a permanent minority in the nation after the disappointments of President Harrison's death and the succession of Vice President John Tyler, whose policies satisfied few Whigs. The problem was that to many old Whigs, embracing nominating conventions constituted an abandonment of principle. Back in 1835 as their party was initially forming, Whigs in the Illinois Senate endorsed Hugh Lawson White for President and declared that "every man who is eligible to the office of president has an undeniable right to become a candidate for the same . . . without the intervention of caucuses and

conventions." "We disapprove," they added, "of the convention system attempted to be forced upon the American people by the Van
Buren party, and believe it to be destructive of the freedom of the
elective franchise, opposed to republican institutions, and dangerous
to the liberties of the people." Nominating conventions doubtless had
no such effect, but the important point is that many of Lincoln's fellow
Whigs thought they did. "Whether the system is right in itself,"
Lincoln wrote defensively, "we do not stop to enquire; contenting
ourselves with trying to show, that while our opponents use it, it is
madness in us not to defend ourselves with it."

In advocating the convention system, Lincoln was not necessarily
promoting a device to further his personal career within the party; at
any rate, he failed to control the next district convention in 1843 and
saw his now burning ambition to go to Congress falter when his friend
Edward D. Baker gained the nomination. Lincoln had been working
to run for Congress for some time. On February 14, 1843, he wrote
a political associate, "Now if you should hear any one say that Lincoln
don't want to go to Congress, I wish you as a personal friend of mine,
would tell him you have reason to believe he is mistaken. The truth
is, I would like to go very much." In the ensuing district nominating
convention Lincoln's candidacy was weakened among organized
Christians because it was rumored that he was a "deist" and "had
talked about fighting a duel." He was labeled, however unlikely the
charge may seem, as "the candidate of pride, wealth, and arristocratic
family distinction." The religious problem would arise again.

Lincoln's determined identification with efficient party organization
apparently was hurting him, too. He "got thunder" as his "reward"
for writing the district address for 1843. It also hurt him indirectly in
a way, for the stirring of political passions by efficient party organizations had led to a rash of dueling, Lincoln himself being challenged
in 1842 by James Shields, a Democrat. In the masculine culture of
American politics, Lincoln could not afford to decline, but he had no
taste for such violence. He proposed absurdly unheroic conditions for
the duel in the hope of avoiding it. As the challenged party, he had
the choice of weapons and opted for cavalry broadswords, a huge

advantage for the 6′4″ Lincoln over his shorter opponent. Seconds patched up the dispute at the last moment.

Lincoln remained ambitious but patient. He could wait a long time for what he wanted, three years in the case of a seat in Congress. He struck a bargain, apparently, with two other able Whigs in the district: they would take turns running for the congressional seat. Baker would not run again in 1844; John J. Hardin would be the Whig candidate then; and in 1846 Lincoln's turn would come. Meanwhile, he had to work at the law. He was, as he said himself on July 4, 1842, "so poor" and made "so little headway in the world" that a month's idleness undid a year's profits.

Lincoln was active in the 1844 presidential canvass, speaking in Illinois and southern Indiana in support of Henry Clay. He took a prominent place at a public meeting that denied any connection between the Whig party and recent riots against Catholic immigrants in Philadelphia. He drafted the resolutions of the state Whig convention, putting "foremost in importance" among the party's principles "that of providing a national revenue by a tariff of duties on foreign importations, so adjusted that while it will yield no more than is necessary for an economical and efficient administration of the federal government, will at the same time afford equal protection and encouragement to every branch of American Industry."

Clay lost to James K. Polk in a close election, but Lincoln continued to work unabated for the success of the party and to gain the Whig nomination to Congress in 1846. Hardin provided the main hurdle to the nomination. Baker was persuaded to withdraw in accordance with the agreement; he was after all a friend of Lincoln's. The able and ambitious Hardin, though, wanted to return to Congress. Lincoln was loyal Whig enough, modest enough, and a shrewd enough judge of ability to admit, "I know of no argument to give me a preference over him, unless it be 'Turn about is fair play.'" Hardin attempted to gain the nomination by changing the nominating process from Lincoln's convention system to one more nearly resembling a Whig primary election, but not allowing candidates to campaign outside their own county—a great advantage to Hardin, who had been to Congress and was therefore better known across the district than Lincoln. To his credit, Lincoln proved willing to adopt the measures that appeared more democratic in Hardin's proposal, but others he balked at. He preferred the old convention system.

Both men feared splitting the party in this district, the only one the Whigs could count on winning, and eventually Hardin withdrew, and Lincoln gained the nomination. The Democrats chose Peter Cartwright as their candidate. Lincoln had faced the Methodist circuit rider and politician before, in his first race for Congress, and that experience, or the trouble Lincoln had had with religious groups at the 1843 Whig convention, suggested to the parson an issue to use against Lincoln: infidel religious beliefs. Lincoln was eventually forced to deny the charges in a handbill published on July 31, 1846, less than a week before election day.

The handbill is among the most important sources for Lincoln's religious views, for it was the only time he explained them in public, and he rarely spoke of them in private. He admitted that he was "not a member of any Christian Church," but maintained that he had "never denied the truth of the Scriptures" or "spoken with intentional disrespect of religion in general, or of any denomination of Christians in particular." He also admitted that "in early life" he "was inclined to believe in . . . the 'Doctrine of Necessity'—that is, that the human mind is impelled to action, or held in rest by some power, over which the mind itself has not control." He had given up arguing for that view more than five years earlier. He added that he could not himself "be brought to support a man for office, whom I knew to be an open enemy of, and scoffer at, religion," because that would injure the feelings and the morals of the community.

The charge apparently did not hurt Lincoln much. He beat Cartwright handily, the Democratic vote falling off much more from the previous election (a presidential election year) than the Whig. Lincoln later remembered the election almost fondly as a rather quiet time, without the rancor he experienced in his later contests as a Republican when the issue of slavery embittered politics.

He seems not to have had much inkling that the issues were brewing that would cause this rancor. In fact, he had told an abolitionist in 1845, "Individually I never was much interested in the Texas question. I never could see much good to come of annexation; inasmuch, as they were already a free republican people on our own model; on the other hand, I never could very clearly see how the annexation would augment the evil of slavery. It always seemed to me that slaves would be taken there in about equal numbers, with or without annexation. And if more *were* taken because of annexation, still there would be just so many the fewer left, where they were taken from . . . I hold it to be a paramount duty of us in the free states, due to the Union of the states, and perhaps to liberty itself (paradox though it may seem) to let the slavery of the other states alone; while, on the other hand, I hold it to be equally clear, that we should never knowingly lend ourselves directly or indirectly, to prevent that slavery from dying a natural death—to find new places for it to live in, when it can no longer exist in the old." Abraham Lincoln did not in 1845 think of slavery as a pressing political problem. He apparently did not yet think there was an aggressive "slave power," an active political movement dedicated to preserving or expanding slavery in the United States. Otherwise, he would have been disturbed at the prospect of the addition of another slave state, whatever the actual distribution of slave population, for the new state would give the slaveholding interest greater representation in Congress.

Nor did he foresee that the Mexican War would become a rancorous and troubling issue. Somehow, Lincoln seemed more aware of the personal meaning of his election than the political and public one. He had at last realized his "peculiar ambition," insofar as it was embodied in a term in the U.S. Congress. Three years of managing and working, without scheming or muscling aside opposition, had brought success. But among other things, a curious American electoral practice conspired to make the prize seem anticlimactic for Lincoln. Elections in the nineteenth century were not nearly as standardized in their timing as now. Except for the presidential contest every four years, elections occurred at times determined by the states without any consultation with one another. At almost any moment in the country, somewhere, there would be an election or a campaign going on. For any single Congress, states held their elections over a period of sixteen months, ranging from August of the even-numbered year to November of the odd-numbered year before the opening of the first session of the new Congress in December. Illinois held its election the earliest, and Lincoln therefore faced a sixteen-month wait for the opening of the Congress to which he had been elected. In October 1846, he told his old friend Joshua Speed, "Being elected to Congress, though I am very grateful to our friends, for having done it, has not pleased me as much as I expected."

The rest of the experience proved anticlimactic as well. Lincoln was nervous before rising to speak in Congress the first time but found it to be about the same as speaking in court back in Illinois. As a Whig during a Democratic administration, he had little influence on patronage, and franking documents and answering constituents' letters grew tedious at times. He felt lonely much of the time. He was "never quite satisfied."

While Lincoln had waited for months for Congress to open, other Whigs across the country who would become his colleagues ran their campaigns. They usually took stands against the Mexican War, which began in earnest after Lincoln's election. By the time Congress convened, on December 6, 1847, active fighting had ceased, but no peace was concluded. On the 22nd Lincoln introduced a series of resolutions demanding to know the exact "spot" on American soil where the spilling of American blood at the hands of Mexican attackers had started the war. Lincoln and everyone else in Congress knew where the "spot" was: the point was that it lay in territory claimed by both Texas and Mexico and was not, by Whig (and Mexican) reckoning, on American soil at all and thus did not constitute justification for starting the war. On a resolution of thanks to a victorious American general he voted for an amendment declaring the war "unconstitutional and unnecessary." Lincoln gave a formal speech on the war on January 12, 1848. He was in the company of most congressional Whigs in his antiwar beliefs.

Such ideas made his law partner back in Springfield, William H.

Herndon, uneasy, and Lincoln felt compelled to explain the mainstream Whig position to him. Lincoln knew the unhappy fate of the old Federalist party after its opposition to the War of 1812, and he had been careful to vote supplies for the soldiers in the field. The Whigs constituted a loyal opposition, but they were otherwise opposed to the war. They criticized its origins and purpose but not its manner of prosecution, which was brilliantly successful and conducted by Whig generals to boot (Zachary Taylor and Winfield Scott). Herndon, Lincoln shrewdly reasoned, took a constitutional position never assumed by the President, who had maintained simply that the first shot had been fired on American soil. His law partner was apparently arguing that "if it shall become *necessary, to repel invasion,* the President may, without violation of the Constitution, cross the line, and *invade* the teritory of another country; and that whether such *necessity* exists in any given case, the President is to be the *sole judge.*" Lincoln's answer was:

> The provision of the Constitution giving the war-making power to Congress, was dictated, as I understand it, by the following reasons. Kings had always been involving and impoverishing their people in wars, pretending generally, if not always, that the good of the people was the object. This, our Convention understood to be the most oppressive of all Kingly oppressions; and they resolved to so frame the Constitution that *no one man* should hold the power of bringing this oppression upon us. But your view destroys the whole matter, and places our President where kings have always stood.

Lincoln rarely sought rigorous consistency in doctrine; he usually sought the politically possible. The war may have been one "of conquest" and unjustly begun, but Lincoln was not entirely opposed to retaining some territory won by conquest from Mexico in the war. Most westerners were expansionists, and Lincoln was not about to ignore such sentiments. He had no wish, however, to acquire territory "so far South, as to enlarge and agrivate the distracting question of slavery." He suggested holding on to all of Texas above the Rio Grande, New Mexico, Utah, and California somewhat south of its modern border with Mexico. He was not eager to acquire all that territory, but he recognized "a sort of necessity of taking some." It constituted about half of Mexico.

Slavery remained as yet merely a "distracting question" for Lincoln, but being a member of Congress forced him to take more notice of it. He voted several times for the principle of the Wilmot Proviso, which would have excluded slavery from any territory acquired as a result of the war. He drafted a bill to abolish slavery in the District of Columbia, adhering to the beliefs he had expressed in the Illinois legislature over ten years earlier. He would declare free all children born to slave mothers after January 1, 1850. Masters who manumitted their slaves would receive compensation from Congress, the freeborn blacks after 1850 would serve apprenticeships to their current masters, members of Congress temporarily resident in the District were exempted, and the whole scheme was contingent upon the approval of the District's white voters. In the end he could not round up enough support to make it worthwhile to introduce the bill. He voted for another member's bill that would only abolish the slave trade in the District of Columbia.

Lincoln faced more sectional questions, but they were not crowding his political agenda. More singleminded antislavery men were beginning to see slavery's perversion of America's mission. They saw the Mexican War as a southern conspiracy to expand slave territory (slavery was illegal in Mexico). Lincoln did not. He said that he "did not believe with many . . . fellow citizens that this war was originated for the purpose of extending slave territory." It was, rather, "a war of conquest brought into existence to catch votes." President Polk, embarrassed by settling the Oregon boundary dispute with England at a line far to the south of what people in the northern states wished, went aggressively for Mexican territory instead, according to Lincoln.

Lincoln retained his interest in the old Whig program. In fact, he thought the question that was "verging to a final crisis," the policy whose "friends must now battle, and battle manfully, or surrender all," was the question of internal improvements, not slavery. After President Polk vetoed a bill for river and harbor improvements, Lincoln delivered a speech arguing that the constitutional issue had been settled long ago and making his accustomed case for utility and practical fairness. "No commercial object of government patronage can be so exclusively *general, as to not be of some peculiar local* advantage; but, on the other hand, nothing is so *local,* as to not be of some general advantage," he said, pointing to the Navy as an example; its benefits were undeniably general and yet it was "of some peculiar advantage to Charleston, Baltimore, Philadelphia, New-York and Boston beyond what it is to the interior towns of Illinois." To the idea of having the states fund internal improvements by tonnage duties, Lincoln responded with characteristic humor:

> The idea . . . involves the same absurdity of the Irish bull about the new boots—"I shall niver git em on" says Patrick "till I wear em a day or two, and strech em a little." We shall never make a canal by tonnage duties, u[n]til it shall already have been made awhile, so the tonnage can get into it.

Likewise, the slavery question did not hinder Lincoln's focus on the other major preoccupation of his congressional term, helping to make Zachary Taylor, a Louisiana slaveholder and Whig, the next President of the United States. Lincoln gave a long and amusing speech in Taylor's behalf in Congress (to be franked to constituents as a government-subsidized campaign document). And during the congressional recess in 1848 he campaigned for Taylor in New England.

Lincoln had long since relinquished any ambition to run for reelection to Congress, in obedience to the spirit of his own agreement forged in 1843: there were plenty of other able Whigs to run. (In this he proved wrong: Stephen T. Logan, the next candidate, ran so inept a campaign that the Whigs lost the seat in the 1848 election.) Lincoln was ready to go home. When an old friend wrote him near the end of his term, Lincoln answered, "Out of more than three hundred letters received this session, yours is the second one manifesting the least interest for me personally."

Taylor won election, however, and Lincoln worked mightily to gain a patronage appointment he thought due him as an early and energetic

Taylor supporter: Commissioner of the General Land Office. He did not get it, and what he did get, an offer of the governorship of the Oregon Territory, he refused to accept.

Instead, Lincoln devoted himself to his law practice as he had never done before, and he began to lose interest in politics.

CHAPTER TWO

Republican Robe

Lincoln's return from Congress seems almost a symbol for turning away from the public and toward the private side of life. Though he wanted a political reward from the Taylor administration—a sure sign that political ambition still burned in him—he would not go to Oregon. Probably that was not a matter of the governorship's being beneath him. Other Whigs with frustrated careers in Illinois went west—Edward Baker, for example, who eventually became a senator from California. Lincoln probably did not go because of his wife and family; the adjustment for them would be too difficult.

Like many other episodes, this one offers inadequate evidence from which to judge the impact of personal life on Lincoln. His domestic circle in general offers nothing very interesting to the modern reader. He lived the life of a bourgeois Victorian; it makes rather dull reading for twentieth-century taste, but Lincoln never complained.

Abraham Lincoln's private life is not directly accessible to historians. Though outwardly affable and far more amusing than most American public men in that earnest age of evangelical piety and Victorian respectability, Lincoln was reticent about his personal affairs. He was not introspective enough to keep a diary nor enough of a believer in his own destiny to retain the materials for autobiography. The legacy of Lincoln's parents is substantially lost because of their illiteracy and his silence.

Ambition was often at odds with Lincoln's patrimony. He wanted to leave his father and all he seemed to stand for: illiteracy, migration in search of economic security, and back-breaking agriculture. But Thomas Lincoln also may have given his son an antislavery outlook and political leanings toward Whiggish views, though his son never said so.

On his own, Lincoln had trouble meeting the right young women in part because his frontier manners were slow to catch up to the standards prevailing in the circles to which his political gifts early gave him access. He was also unlucky in love. His first purportedly serious relationship, with Ann Rutledge, whom he knew in New Salem, ended in 1835 when she died at the age of twenty-two.

Although it is difficult to appreciate from the perspective of twentieth-century America with its informality, Lincoln's manners and poverty interfered with a successful love life. Mary Owens, a young woman from Kentucky who visited New Salem and whom Lincoln courted in 1837 and 1838, noticed that Lincoln was no "gentleman" when, out for a ride on horseback with friends, the party came to a "bad branch" of water. The other men were "very officious in seeing that their partners got over safely," but Lincoln rode ahead without "looking back to see" how Miss Owens got along.

Lincoln almost missed his chance to marry Mary Todd, of Lexington, Kentucky. She met Lincoln when she came to Springfield to visit her sister in 1839. They were soon engaged, but the engagement was broken on January 1, 1841. The reasons are unknown, but the fact that Mary's sister, Elizabeth, and brother-in-law, Ninian Wirt Edwards, regarded Lincoln as a "rough" man surely did not help.

Lincoln was terribly depressed afterward and seriously distracted from his work. For the first time he showed a poor attendance record in the state legislature. The couple reconciled and were married on November 4, 1842. Marriage to a Todd may have been an advantage for his career in the long run, but in the short run it almost surely was not. Association with that family and with Edwards left Lincoln open to accusations of elitism. Edwards was a silk-stocking Whig uncomfortable with popular democracy if ever there was one, and the family connection likely formed the basis of the charges leveled at Lincoln at the Whig convention in 1843.

Abraham and Mary's first son, Robert, was born in 1843. Edward Baker Lincoln was born in 1846 but died in 1850. The Lincolns soon thereafter conceived another son, born at the end of the year and named William Wallace. In 1853 their last son was born. They named him Thomas after Lincoln's father, who had died two years earlier; the boy's nickname from infancy was "Tad." Neither Lincoln's father nor his stepmother, Sarah, ever met Lincoln's wife or any of their children, though Sarah outlived her husband, her stepson, and two of the grandchildren. After Lincoln left the log cabin, he never wanted to look back. He married a woman who had attended finishing school and spoke French, and he sent his firstborn to Exeter Academy in New Hampshire and to Harvard University.

The two younger children were not so educationally advantaged. Eddie's death had been traumatic for the Lincolns and accelerated the penchant of both parents (neither of whom had enjoyed a happy childhood) to strive to make their children's lives pleasanter. The result was a lack of parental restraints on the younger children and little enforcement of an educational program.

Marriages of proper Victorians offer little in the way of evidence of closeness except the births of children. By that standard, the Lincolns' marriage appears sound, and suggestions to the contrary—that, for example, Mary's bad temper proved a severe trial for Abraham—mostly come from the hostile collected recollections of William Herndon. He hated Lincoln's wife and may have led his witnesses a bit in dealing with the subject of Lincoln's marriage. In modern times, the children of famous people have often offered interesting reminiscences of their family life, but only Robert among Lincoln's children lived to a ripe old age—he died in 1926—and he shared his father's habits of reticence, believing fiercely in privacy.

Lincoln loved his wife and children, but historians have not always found them as lovable. Mary Todd Lincoln grew materialistic and complaining, the younger boys spoiled and undisciplined. Robert became cold and lacked the common touch of his father. The family simply did not share all the qualities that have led historians to praise Lincoln: good political judgment, open-mindedness, forgiveness, dedication, and irrepressible good humor.

Lincoln's professional life remains surprisingly inaccessible to the historian as well, though the problem in this realm is largely archival. The documents from Lincoln's legal practice are only now being systematically gathered from Illinois court houses, and because of two peculiarities of the nineteenth-century legal system, they yield information grudgingly. First, below the appellate level, there were no courtroom stenographers, and without transcripts it is impossible to know what happened in the courtroom unless the trial was sensational enough to be covered by newspapers. Second, the legal system of Lincoln's day was bound by antique terms (like *de homine replegiando*) and obscure forms and procedures long since discarded. Until more specialized studies are made of these arcane legal practices, it is not safe to hazard many conclusions about Lincoln's life as a lawyer.

We do know that Lincoln was admitted to the bar in 1836 and quickly became John Todd Stuart's law partner. In 1841 that partnership dissolved, and Lincoln formed a new firm with Stephen Trigg Logan, a better lawyer than Stuart, from some reports. When Logan's son was old enough to practice, Lincoln left the firm to make way for him and in 1844 took a younger man, William Henry Herndon, as partner. Lincoln was a diligently successful lawyer, and if, as is the case with most practitioners, he left no mark on the law, he nevertheless became a lawyer's lawyer, participating in over 330 cases before the Illinois Supreme Court. He was involved in more than a dozen state Supreme Court cases in 1853 but only five in the exciting political year 1854. Not even the most interesting sort of appellate work could wean Lincoln from politics.

The passage of the Kansas-Nebraska Act in 1854, perhaps the most explosive piece of legislation ever passed by a U.S. Congress, so alarmed Lincoln that he reentered a path that led away from his home, from Illinois, and from the narrow political horizons that were his lot because of the limited appeal of the Whig party. Although the Mexican cession had injected the issue of slavery expansion into American politics in the form of the Wilmot Proviso, probably most Americans considered the question resolved by the sectional Compromise of 1850, which admitted California to the Union, among other measures. The ill-conceived Kansas-Nebraska Act, mainly the handiwork of Illinois Senator Stephen A. Douglas, sought to organize politically a crucial part of the national domain lying within the old Louisiana Purchase. Nebraska Territory, as it was called, lay entirely above the 36°30′ latitude established a generation before in the Missouri Compromise as the dividing line in the Louisiana Purchase lands between free soil to the north and possible slave territory to the south. The urgency to provide a permanent government for the immense Nebraska Territory, which stretched from present-day Oklahoma to the Canadian border, stemmed in part from the acquisition of the Mexican cession. A railroad was needed to connect the eastern states with California and the West. Douglas had no personal desire to disturb the old Missouri Compromise settlement, but he did feel a burning mission to get on with settling the continent and spreading American freedom. The Pacific coast was settled rapidly because of the discovery of gold in California, and there now existed an enormous unorganized hole in the heart of the republic.

The slave states were not eager to encourage the creation of necessarily free states in Nebraska Territory. To resolve the impasse, Douglas invoked the formula devised for the Mexican cession, called "popular sovereignty," by which the citizens of the territory would decide for themselves whether to let slavery in or not. The old Missouri Compromise restriction now became "inoperative." The large territory was divided into two areas, Kansas and Nebraska.

Lincoln expressed outrage at the passage of the Kansas-Nebraska Act, and a few months later returned to the stump in support of the candidacy of the incumbent Whig Richard Yates for Congress. Lincoln said he was mainly "anxious . . . that this Nebraska measure shall be rebuked and condemned every where," but of course none of his actions can be entirely divorced from personal political ambition, for Lincoln almost immediately became a candidate, too—for the state legislature. He used his skills as a stump speaker to spread arguments already developed by antislavery politicians like Salmon P. Chase of Ohio, who, long before the time of the Kansas-Nebraska Act, had already been shocked by what he regarded as the aggressions of the "slave power." Lincoln's personal contribution lay more in the eloquence of his statements than in his originality.

Political circumstances in Illinois now promoted Lincoln's success as much as they had hindered it in the past. The disarray of political parties offered Lincoln practical hope of electoral victory, something the Whig party had not been able to do for some time. Opportunity alone did not dictate his political views, but most of what he said about political questions arose not from reflection in his study but in speeches on the stump. It is therefore never a simple matter to answer questions about Lincoln's views on slavery, race, the Constitution, or nationalism. Lincoln's ideas cannot be accurately described without specifying the time in his life when he held the view in question; his racial policies, especially, changed dramatically in the space of a very few years.

And yet Lincoln did have political values that he held for most or all of his political life. About a year before his death he could say, for example, "I am naturally anti-slavery. If slavery is not wrong, nothing is wrong. I can not remember when I did not so think, and feel." He had a consistent antislavery record, but the degree to which he acted upon his views varied with political circumstance.

Lincoln was likewise consistent in his views on nationalism. Thus when he eulogized Henry Clay at the time of his death in 1852, Lincoln, in describing Clay's patriotism, avoided unthinking flag-waving:

Mr. Clay's predominant sentiment, from first to last, was a deep devotion to the cause of human liberty—a strong sympathy with the oppressed every where, and an ardent wish for their elevation. With him, this was a primary and all controlling passion. Subsidiary to this was the conduct of his whole life. He loved his country partly because it was his own country, but mostly because it was a free country; and he burned with a zeal for its advancement, prosperity and glory, because he saw in such, the advancement, prosperity and glory, of human liberty, human right and human nature.

This was an important idea because the life of the nation and the life of slavery had long since become mutually sustaining, and politicians were now constantly being accused by their adversaries of willingness to sacrifice the life of the one to the other. Like Clay, Lincoln loved his country partly because it was his country but mostly because it was a free country. And Lincoln repeatedly said so even when it was not politically expedient.

Whereas most of Clay's eulogists, speaking in the aftermath of the Compromise of 1850, celebrated the Great Compromiser's Union-saving measures, Lincoln put more stress on the slavery issue. He warned "against a few, but an increasing number of men, who, for the sake of perpetuating slavery, are beginning to assail and to ridicule the white-man's charter of freedom—the declaration that 'all men are created free and equal.'" These reactionary ideas sounded "strangely in republican America," Lincoln said. "The like was not heard in the fresher days of the Republic."

Beginning in 1854, Lincoln explained to voters in Illinois his reading of recent events in light of the American past and the values given the republic by that heroic generation of founders he had described in his address at the Young Men's Lyceum back in 1838. He explained that in the republic's "better days" most Americans who were not themselves slaveholders, with a personal economic interest in the institution, disapproved of slavery as a moral, social, and political evil. The republic's founders had scrupulously avoided mentioning the word "slavery" in the Constitution. Their document quietly sanctioned the peculiar institution in order to gain the national union essential to the safety and strength of the republic, but they looked forward to the day when slavery would disappear from America. Northerners like Lincoln had assumed that slavery had been put on the road to "ultimate extinction" a generation before by the country's founders at first and later by the Missouri Compromise. They were startled from their complacency by the Kansas-Nebraska Act, which reopened territories in the West to the possibility of slavery's introduction, more or less by local option. The country appeared to be going morally backward, continuing the retrograde course Lincoln had noticed in his eulogy of Henry Clay two years earlier.

To Senator Douglas and his followers, popular sovereignty had two prime virtues. First, it was democratic and thus embodied the traditional American solution to political problems. It left the question to the (white) people to decide—and to those (white) people most affected by the question, the ones who lived in the territory. Second, it was practical. The West had to be settled. America's mission was to expand freedom. Popular sovereignty would take the slavery debate out of Congress, where the constant arguing, shouting, and posturing over which side would benefit stalled American progress and prevented new territories from being organized and new states from entering the Union.

Lincoln saw it differently. The only practical effect of the measure was to allow slavery the possibility of expanding where it had once been forbidden—once and for all, many northerners thought. To expand slavery was to expand the most undemocratic institution on earth. It would call into question America's commitment to republicanism and seriously undermine belief in the assertion of the Declaration of Independence that "all men are created equal."

Lincoln's argument, which may seem unanswerable today, was in its own day politically vulnerable on at least two scores. First, it was sectional and threatened the continuing existence of the Union. Second, the time and manner in which slavery was to end were not specified, and whites were threatened by the lack of a program to deal with slaves after they became free black men and women.

Lincoln did not believe the first problem really existed. He thought of himself as a nationalist, and he did not think the South likely to attempt to secede from the Union because of the policies he championed. Lincoln sincerely believed that his own policy began with the very origins of the republic and especially in the ideas of equality expressed by Thomas Jefferson, who had written the defining assertion that all men are created equal. Jefferson had also urged restriction of slavery in the Northwest Territory. "Thus," Lincoln said in a speech at Peoria, on October 16, 1854,

> with the author of the declaration of Independence, the policy of prohibiting slavery in new territory originated. Thus, away back of the constitution, in the pure fresh, free breath of the revolution, the State of Virginia, and the National congress put that policy in practice. Thus through sixty odd of the best years of the republic did that policy steadily work to its great and beneficent end. And thus, in those five states [formed from the Northwest Territory], and five millions of free, enterprising people, we have before us the rich fruits of this policy. But *now* new light breaks upon us. Now congress declares this ought never to have been; and the like of it, must never be again . . . That *perfect* liberty they sigh for—the liberty of making slaves of other people—Jefferson never thought of; their own father never thought of; they never thought of themselves, a year ago . . . Oh, how difficult it is to treat with respect, such assaults upon all we have ever really held sacred.

Lincoln maintained that he was no radical introducing something new and disturbing to the unity of this heretofore happy republic; Douglas and the Democrats were doing that. "Let no one be deceived," Lincoln warned. "The spirit of seventy-six and the spirit of Nebraska, are utter antagonisms; and the former is being rapidly displaced by the latter."

There was as much personal passion as political craft in Lincoln's arguments now. The Peoria speech was his first great speech, better than any he would give in the famous Lincoln-Douglas debates four years later. He spoke of "sacred" beliefs and he expressed "hate." This was a new tone for him.

> The *declared* indifference, but as I must think, covert *real* zeal for the spread of slavery, I can not but hate. I hate it because of the monstrous injustice of slavery itself. I hate it because it deprives our republican example of its just influence in the world—enables the enemies of free institutions, with plausibility, to taunt us as hypo-

crites—causes the real friends of freedom to doubt our sincerity, and especially because it forces so many really good men amongst ourselves into an open war with the very fundamental principles of civil liberty—criticising the Declaration of Independence, and insisting that there is no right principle of action but *self-interest*.

Lincoln asserted with genuine conviction that he was patriotic. "Nebraska is urged as a great Union-saving measure," Lincoln acknowledged.

> Well I too, go for saving the Union. Much as I hate slavery, I would consent to the extension of it rather than see the Union dissolved, just as I would consent to any GREAT evil, to avoid a GREATER one. But when I go to Union saving, I must believe, at least, that the means I employ has some adaptation to the end. To my mind, Nebraska has no such adaptation . . . It is an aggravation, rather, of the only one thing which ever endangers the Union. When it came upon us, all was peace and quiet . . . In the whole range of possibility, there scarcely appears to me to have been any thing, out of which the slavery agitation could have been revived, except the very project of repealing the Missouri compromise.

Lincoln's policy in fact made few gestures toward saving the Union except for avoiding criticism of southerners' motives; it simply put the blame for arousing disunion feeling on the opposing party and largely ignored southern threats of disunion.

All of Lincoln's ideas about the slavery controversy were already present at Peoria, and he did not improve on the combination of moral arguments and nationalism in any of his speeches later in the 1850s:

> Our republican robe is soiled, and trailed in the dust. Let us repurify it. Let us turn and wash it white, in the spirit, if not the blood of the Revolution. Let us turn slavery from its claims of "moral right," back upon its existing legal rights, and its arguments of "necessity." Let us return it to the position our fathers gave it; and there let it rest in peace. Let us re-adopt the Declaration of Independence, and with it, the practices, and policy, which harmonize with it. Let north

and south—let all Americans—let all lovers of liberty everywhere—join in the great and good work. If we do this, we shall not only have saved the Union; but we shall have so saved it, as to make, and to keep it, forever worthy of the saving. We shall have so saved it, that the succeeding millions of free happy people, the world over, shall rise up, and call us blessed, to the latest generations.

Eloquent and unanswerable as such a formulation of American nationalism seems today, it should not be forgotten that to most white southerners Lincoln's doctrines were best described as sectionalism rather than nationalism. Consigning the doctrines of southerners to the rubric of sectionalism while describing Lincoln's views as nationalism is to condemn southerners by semantics alone. To call them sectionalists marks them as illegitimate in an age of nationalism. Historians like David Potter have urged an evenhandedness in appraising such ideas by suggesting that both southern and northern ideas were sectional, and the two sections were vying for control of the federal government in Washington. It would be very difficult to characterize the Republican party as anything but a sectional party, offering nothing to the white South and, in the speeches of most party members, making political capital of antisouthernism. Abraham Lincoln was a good Republican, and his ideal of nationalism looked forward to an American nation based entirely on northern free-soil principles.

Lincoln's vagueness about the eventual "extinction" of slavery, which betrayed the second political vulnerability of his doctrine, was perhaps the most intellectually dishonest part of his platform. Neither he nor any other anti-Nebraska politician much wanted to deal with the question of race. They did so only to the degree that Douglas and the Democrats, through mean-spirited, demagogic race-baiting, forced them.

Lincoln was necessarily limited here by two considerations. First, the intellectual assumptions of white society—from scientists to political thinkers and clergymen—about black people assigned them to an inferior and degraded position in the human race. Lincoln did not escape these assumptions, though he said as little on the subject as possible. Second, the mass of white people were bitterly prejudiced, and political realism demanded a circumspect approach. Abolitionists, though no longer routinely physically attacked on the streets, were still generally despised. Lincoln continued to avoid them, and when the time came in 1862 to end slavery, he did not call his greatest document the "Abolition Proclamation." Moreover, he had a healthy practical respect for the seemingly ineradicable racial prejudices of ordinary white people, which no politician could afford to ignore.

Illinois offered Lincoln a clear object lesson in the vehemence of white racism and its political consequences. In 1831 the legislature passed a law requiring a free black person wishing to settle in Illinois to post $1,000 bond guaranteeing his good behavior while in the state. At the time Lincoln was making less than $150 a year himself: he could not have paid such a bond and neither could most black people. That was the point: it effectively constituted exclusion from the state. Yet that apparently insurmountable barrier did not satisfy Illinois' white voters, who offered an even more dramatic lesson while Lincoln was a member of Congress. The new Illinois constitution of 1848 contained an article forbidding blacks to enter the state to settle at all. Submitted to the people separately from the rest of the constitution, the black exclusion clause carried by a thumping 50,261 votes to 21,297; Sangamon County voters went for it by a wider margin, 1,483 to 418. Lincoln was in Washington at the time and did not vote.

For a candidate for public office to speculate on the social consequences of the aftermath of slavery among such voters might constitute political suicide: freed slaves would presumably be free to move north and put pressure on Illinois to end its black exclusion. Lincoln apparently did not think about it much, but when he did, in the 1850s, he was led to an old idea: colonization. At its core lay the notion of encouraging emancipation by sponsoring the emigration of freed blacks to another continent. It was a profoundly racist dream, rooted in an inability to imagine a biracial future for America if the black race were free, and wholly unrealistic about the rate of natural increase of African-Americans on the North American continent.

These ideas were not new in 1854. In 1852 Lincoln celebrated

Henry Clay's presidency of the American Colonization Society in his eulogy. Endorsing the idea that blacks would take to Africa from their New World experience "religion, civilization, law and liberty," he applied the sort of biblical language he would later use in describing the end of slavery and said:

> Pharoah's country was cursed with plagues, and his hosts were drowned in the Red Sea for striving to retain a captive people who had already served them more than four hundred years. May like disasters never befall us! If as the friends of colonization hope, the present and coming generations of our countrymen shall by any means, succeed in freeing our land from the dangerous presence of slavery; and, at the same time, in restoring a captive people to their long-lost father-land, with bright prospects for the future; and this too, so gradually, that neither races nor individuals shall have suffered by the change, it will indeed be a glorious consummation.

In 1853 Lincoln addressed the local meeting of the American Colonization Society. He agreed to do so again the next year but had to cancel. He spoke to the organization in 1855 as well. Neither of these addresses survives, and Lincoln's specific thinking on the subject remains unknown. The accident of their failure to survive has probably helped Lincoln's reputation in modern times.

Whatever the vulnerabilities of Lincoln's policies, his presentation of them was effective. The Quincy *Whig,* for example, termed one of his 1854 addresses "one of the clearest, most logical, argumentative and convincing discourses on the Nebraska question to which we have listened." Logical argument and convincing discourse even when spiced with the new-found passion may not have been enough to equal the highest ambitions. To aim for high office a politician must stir the passions of the electorate too. The voters of Lincoln's day did not generally share his racial moderation. Lincoln would make his arguments more powerful yet by focusing even less on race and developing a new argument when he aimed deliberately at the U.S. Senate in 1858.

On November 7, 1854, Springfield voters elected Lincoln to the

Illinois House of Representatives. When the results were all in, it was apparent that an anti-Nebraska Whig might realistically hope for election to the Senate. Lincoln "got it into" his "head to try to be U.S. Senator," and maintaining he had run "only . . . because it was supposed" his "doing so would help Yates," Lincoln refused to serve in the legislature. A member of the legislature could not by law be elected to the Senate. The decision proved costly to the Whig party, as the Democrats picked up the seat Lincoln abandoned.

Lincoln was still a Whig, but the only cause he was currently championing was anti-Nebraska. Early in 1855 the legislature met to choose a senator, either the incumbent Democrat James Shields, Lincoln, or perhaps Lyman Trumbull, an anti-Nebraska Democrat. Lincoln began with 44 votes, Shields had 41, and Trumbull had 5. After several ballots a new candidate emerged, a Democrat named Joel Matteson. Eventually, to head off Matteson, Lincoln had to see his votes go to Trumbull; a Whig could not be elected.

Lincoln did not jump to the conclusion that he should abandon the Whigs and throw in his lot with the new Republican party. He had refused to join earlier because the party seemed dominated by abolitionists. Besides, there was a complicating factor. The immigrants from Ireland and the German states, who had thronged into America after 1848, were concluding their five-year naturalization periods and beginning to vote. Staggered by this new presence in politics, and especially by the prominence of Catholic voters in the Democratic party, some concerned voters formed the American (or Know Nothing) party to resist them. In the East it grew rapidly, and it gained a foothold even in states less affected by the recent immigration. Lincoln knew that no party could beat the Democrats without absorbing the anti-Catholic and anti-immigrant Know Nothings. He would wait, hoping their organization would disintegrate and leave its members to seek an alternative political home, before he had to face "the painful necessity of . . . taking an open stand against them." He despised their principles, but they were mostly his "old political and personal friends." Even Mrs. Lincoln hoped for their success. Her experience with "wild Irish" servants convinced her in the next presidential contest to support a candidate who "feels the *necessity* of keeping foreigners, within bounds." Lincoln could avoid the problem for a while, because there were no elections in Illinois in 1855, and besides he had to rededicate himself to his law practice to make up for the lost income while he had campaigned.

All was not political calculation, either. Lincoln never flirted with Know Nothing principles, and slavery sincerely bothered him. To his old personal friend Joshua Speed, now too much a Kentuckian to be a political friend also, Lincoln explained his views. Speed had asserted in a letter written in May 1855 that he would rather see the Union dissolved than surrender his legal right to slavery. Lincoln responded, "It is hardly fair for you to assume, that I have no interest in a thing which has, and continually exercises, the power of making me miserable. You ought rather to appreciate how much the great body of the Northern people do crucify their feelings, in order to maintain their loyalty to the constitution and the Union." Lincoln, of course, had never challenged the right of southerners to own slaves in the states where it was legal. Such insinuations as Speed's were symptomatic of the brewing sectional conflict. Lincoln had here listened to prosecession sentiments from a person he knew to be a moderate man and, at one time in the past at least, a like-minded man; yet Lincoln did not learn from this exchange that the life of the Union was seriously threatened. In this sad correspondence, a monument to an old and rare friendship dissolving because of geographical separation in regions with different institutions, one can see, writ small, the sectional misunderstandings of the 1850s.

When Speed asked Lincoln at the end of August in 1855 where he stood politically, Lincoln said he still was not sure—except of one thing:

I am not a Know-Nothing. That is certain. How could I be? How can any one who abhors the oppression of negroes, be in favor of degrading classes of white people? Our progress in degeneracy appears to me to be pretty rapid. As a nation, we began by declaring that "*all men are created equal.*" We now practically read it "all men are created equal, *except negroes*." When the Know-Nothings get control, it will read "all men are created equal, except negroes, *and foreigners, and catholics.*" When it comes to this I should prefer emigrating to some country where they make no pretence of loving liberty—to Russia, for instance, where despotism can be taken pure, and without the base alloy of hypocracy.

By February 1856 Lincoln was ready to cast his lot with the Republican party, and thus he became one of the founders of the party in Illinois. His embrace of the new organization was aided, no doubt, by the final split in the national Know Nothing party into northern antislavery and southern wings. That occurred in February at the same time that Lincoln was meeting with a group of Illinois newspaper editors to draft principles for the new political organization. At the Illinois Republican party's first convention in May, Lincoln delivered his customary message: "The *Union must be preserved in the purity of its principles as well as in the integrity of its territorial parts.*" In the following summer and early autumn he made numerous speeches in support of the first Republican candidate for president, John C. Frémont, who ran unsuccessfully against Democrat James Buchanan.

Lincoln shared with most Republicans a critical outlook on slavery as an economic system that made labor inefficient and forever doomed the South to poverty and backwardness. The southern defense of slavery in the 1850s as a superior arrangement of capital and labor elicited from Lincoln the theoretical assumptions that had long underlain his Whig views:

They insist that their slaves are far better off than Northern freemen. What a mistaken view do these men have of Northern laborers! They think that men are always to remain laborers here—but there is no such class. The man who labored for another last year, this year labors for himself, and next year he will hire others to labor for him . . . When these reasons can be introduced, tell me not that we have no interest in keeping the Territories free for the settlement of free laborers.

Such arguments added a dynamic appeal to Lincoln's reliance on the abstract political ideas of Thomas Jefferson and on the moral denunciation of slavery as a cruel denial of black humanity. An Illinois newspaper described the economic message stressed in Frémont's campaign: Lincoln, a "Kentuckian, as he is, familiar with Slavery and its evils . . . vindicated the cause of free labor, 'that national capital,' in the language of Col. FREMONT, 'which constitutes the real wealth of this great country, and creates that intelligent power in the masses alone to be relied on as the bulwark of free institutions.'"

Lincoln's economic ideas were to him secondary to the question of slavery. He hated slave expansion for what it would do to the American economy and, more particularly, to free white American laborers, degrading their efforts to rise in life. But mainly he hated the expansion of slavery because he deemed the institution itself immoral. That was the first and foremost problem to him. Abraham Lincoln was an arch-capitalist, but the theoretical statements of his economic views were elicited by the controversy over slavery. The capitalist theory came in the context of a critique of the claims made for slavery as a labor system by southern defenders of their peculiar institution. Lincoln did not make his statements as a defense of the practices of corporations or as a criticism of organized labor. After his death his words would sometimes be put to such uses.

Old Whig economic ideas were bound to appear in new Republican platforms because, as the ex-Whig Lincoln once pointed out to the ex-Democrat Lyman Trumbull, "Nine tenths of the Anti-Nebraska votes have to come from old whigs." Some conservative Republicans stressed economic development of the country much more than Lincoln, who kept the question of halting slavery's expansion central to his campaign appeals, old Whig though he was.

The Dred Scott decision, rendered early in 1857, provided additional ammunition for Lincoln's changing political appeal. His first response was a thoughtful critique respectful of the place of the Supreme Court in the American system yet pointing out damaging errors of historical fact in Roger B. Taney's lengthy decision ultimately denying that a Negro could sue in the U.S. courts and that Congress could forbid slavery in the territories. Lincoln argued that this was not a binding decision because in order to overturn a congressional act, unanimity of opinion and nonpartisan alignment among the justices would be needed. Lincoln denounced Taney's attempt to exclude the black man from the sweeping assertions of the equality of all men found in the Declaration of Independence. This was going back to the well-plowed ground of 1854.

Then a strange political development caused Lincoln to recast his argument. Stephen Douglas broke with the Buchanan administration over its acceptance of Kansas's 1857 "Lecompton constitution," a proslavery document. The Lecompton constitution had come about after antislavery voters, believing the election districts to have been gerrymandered, boycotted the election in which delegates to the Kansas constitutional convention were chosen. In the absence of the free-staters, the proslavery delegates drafted a document legalizing slavery, and then submitted to the vote of the people only one of its provisions: whether to allow *more* slaves into Kansas or not. Antislavery settlers did not think such a document offered a real choice for or against slavery and therefore boycotted the ratification vote, which consequently went in favor of the constitution. But in a second referendum, engineered this time by the free-staters, the proslavery constitution was rejected by a landslide.

Douglas rejected it, too, but the Democratic administration in Washington decided to accept the Lecompton constitution as a final settlement of the long and bloody Kansas controversy. Although Douglas had often avoided specifying the exact practices and timing that would constitute "popular sovereignty," the Lecompton exercise seemed a far cry from any genuinely "popular" decision. Douglas was an able politician, and when he suddenly began to cause President Buchanan and the southern wing of the Democratic party serious political trouble, many Republicans were heartened. Republicans in Illinois, however, were not. Douglas was the incumbent Senator and would be up for reelection the next year. Lincoln feared that perhaps the eastern Republicans had "concluded that the republican cause, generally, can be best promoted by sacraficing us here in Illinois." As usual, Lincoln's concern was not abstract. He was interested in Douglas's Senate seat himself, and his ambition would be completely undermined by any such Republican rapprochement with the Little Giant.

Now needing to make it clearer than ever that his brand of Republicanism differed in crucial ways from Douglas's popular sovereignty ideas, Lincoln was driven to the most radical utterances of his political career. The Republican convention met in Springfield, and delegates chose him as their candidate for Senator. At the conclusion of the meeting on June 16, 1858, he delivered a speech that took its theme from the biblical passage, "A house divided against itself cannot stand." The United States could not endure half slave and half free any longer, Lincoln said. The Union would not dissolve, but it would "become *all* one thing, or *all* the other." By saying this, Lincoln left himself more exposed than ever to the charge of fomenting sectional conflict. But his statements were not as politically dangerous as they may seem. Other prominent Republicans were expressing similar views, even those with definite presidential aspirations for 1860. William H. Seward of New York, for example, enunciated the same idea when he described the strife between North and South as an "irrepressible conflict" later the same year.

After his dramatic opening, Lincoln had to follow with bold assertions, and he did. He pointed to the course of the country from early 1854, a time when slavery was excluded from "more than half the States . . . and from most of the national territory." Then the Kansas-Nebraska Act "opened all the national territory to slavery." Then the President, Franklin Pierce, paved the way for endorsing an upcoming Supreme Court decision on the status of slavery in the territories. Then James Buchanan, the new President, in his inaugural address prepared the people to accept the decision of the Supreme Court on the question of slavery in the territories when it came. Then Roger B. Taney rendered his decision forbidding Congress to prevent the spread of slavery into the territories. Meanwhile, in a "squabble" between the President and Stephen Douglas "on the *mere* question of *fact*, whether the Lecompton constitution was . . . made by the people of Kansas," the Senator "declares that all he wants is a fair vote for the people, and that he *cares* not whether slavery be voted *down* or voted *up*." This statement of the "Nebraska doctrine" was "to *educate* and *mould* public opinion, at least *Northern* public opinion, to not *care* whether slavery is voted *down or voted up*." Finally Lincoln made his point with an elaborate metaphor:

> We can not absolutely *know* that all these exact adaptations are the result of preconcert. But when we see a lot of framed timbers, different portions of which we know have been gotten out at different times and places and by different workmen—Stephen, Franklin, Roger and James, for instance—and when we see these timbers joined together, and see they exactly make the frame of a house or a mill, all the tenons and mortices exactly fitting, and all the lengths and proportions of the different pieces exactly adapted to their respective places, and not a piece too many or too few—not omitting even scaffolding—or, if a single piece be lacking, we can see the place in the frame exactly fitted and prepared to yet bring such piece in—in *such* a case, we find it impossible to not *believe* that Stephen and Franklin and Roger and James all understood one another from the beginning, and all worked upon a common *plan* or *draft* drawn up before the first lick was struck.

Thus, in the House Divided Speech—among the most famous of his career, a speech that has been called the keynote for the Lincoln-Douglas debates to follow in the Senate campaign, themselves the most famous examples of political debate in American history—Lincoln created a conspiracy theory. He charged that Pierce, Buchanan, Taney, and Douglas—two Presidents, the Chief Justice of the U.S. Supreme Court, and the country's leading senator—conspired to spread slavery to the territories, and that their next move would likely spread it into the *states* where it was now illegal. "We shall *lie down*," he alleged, "pleasantly dreaming that the people of *Missouri* are on the verge of making their State *free;* and we shall *awake* to the *reality,* instead, that the *Supreme* Court has made *Illinois* a *slave* State. To meet and overthrow the power of that dynasty, is the work now before all those who would prevent that consummation."

Lincoln's conspiracy charge was baseless, as most such charges in the nation's history have been. Leaders of the South's slave interests loathed Douglas as an apostate. And Douglas and Buchanan, far from scheming together to spread slavery into the free states, were locked in one of the bitterest political battles in American history, with Buchanan ruthlessly removing from office any Democrats who supported Douglas's position on Kansas. Moreover, it seems likely that Lincoln knew the conspiracy charge could not be true; Lincoln's particular problem in the campaign was that Douglas was now so opposed to the Democratic administration that some Republicans regarded him as a fellow traveler.

In the Senate campaign that followed, Lincoln pressed his conspiracy charge and followed the likeliest strategy for an underdog candidate: he challenged Douglas to debate on the same platform. The favored candidate cannot refuse without looking as though he fears matching wits with his challenger, and if he consents, the incumbent must share the platform—and the limelight he has earned—with the newcomer. Douglas followed the likeliest strategy of the frontrunner: he strictly limited the number of debates and stipulated their conditions. Lincoln and Douglas met in seven Illinois towns, each in a different congressional district, and on alternating occasions followed this format: one spoke for an hour, the other answered for an hour and a half, and the first speaker then had one-half hour's rebuttal—three solid hours of political oratory in the open air. The main events were preceded by parades, and usually other speakers held forth at night following the afternoon debates. Tens of thousands heard Lincoln and Douglas debate, in hot weather and cold, in these all-day affairs.

The distinguishing characteristic of Lincoln's political age was the electoral system's domination by extremely vigorous political parties. All the system's virtues and vices were featured in this campaign. The parties made interest in politics so high that American citizens would stand out in the open to listen to three hours of intense discussion of the issues. Yet the issues could be grossly distorted—and usually were;

it proved easier to unite Americans *against* a perceived threat than to bring them together on a platform of policies they all wanted to see implemented. It was easier for Lincoln to unite the voters of Illinois against the slave power's aggressive assault on freedom than it was to unite them on a detailed positive program that explained the future of the black race on this continent. Spreading fear of the opposition actually made the politicians themselves fearful of the other party's unscrupulous methods of winning elections and led to equally unscrupulous attempts to counteract them.

We know about these in the Illinois campaign because of the limited technology of the day: without telephones, politicians were forced to discuss sensitive subjects in letters, and not all sensitive letters were destroyed. Thus near the end of the Senate campaign, Lincoln wrote to a Republican operative:

> I now have a high degree of confidence that we shall succeed, if we are not over-run with fraudulent votes to a greater extent than usual. On alighting from the cars and walking three squares at Naples on Monday, I met about fifteen Celtic gentlemen, with black carpet-sacks in their hands.
>
> I learned that they had crossed over from the Rail-road in Brown county, but where they were going no one could tell. They dropped in about the doggeries, and were still hanging about when I left. At Brown County yesterday I was told that about four hundred of the same sort were to be brought into Schuyler, before the election, to work on some new Railroad; but on reaching here I find Bagby thinks that is not so.
>
> What I most dread is that they will introduce into the doubtful districts numbers of men who are legal voters in all respects except *residence* and who will swear to residence and thus put it beyond our power to exclude them. They can & I fear will swear falsely on that point, because they know it is next to impossible to convict them of Perjury upon it.
>
> Now the great remaining part of the campaign, is finding a way to head this thing off. Can it be done at all?

I have a bare suggestion. When there is a known body of these voters, could not a true man, of the "*detective*" class, be introduced among them in disguise, who could, at the nick of time, control their votes? Think it over. It would be a great thing, when this trick is attempted upon us, to have the saddle come up on the other horse.

The roving gangs of Irish-American laborers who built the great works of the transportation era in American history were, in the eyes of old Whigs and Republicans, also roving bodies of Democratic voters who could show up in tight districts at election time. The fear of fraud was probably as much an index of Lincoln's ingrained suspicion of the Democratic party as it was of that party's actual election-day strategies; and Democrats had similar fears of Republican tricks.

Abraham Lincoln was thus a product of this party system and a master practitioner of politics under it. He knew its abuses, and he could be provoked to instigate some of them himself (suborning votes with private detectives was election fraud by any standard). He took the high road, but he could never ignore the low one. He recognized the power of empty display, of spectacle, of ritual, of sheer enthusiasm. But he also sought genuine debate on the merits of programs to shape the future of his country. Back in 1848 he had given advice to his disgruntled law partner, Herndon, who was infected with a growing fatalism about the Whig party's chances in the next election:

> You young men get together and form a . . . club, and have regular meetings and speeches. Take in every body that you can get . . . but as you go along, gather up all the shrewd wild boys about town, whether just of age, or little under age . . . Let every one play the part he can play best—some speak, some sing, and all hollow. Your meetings will be of evenings; the older men, and the women will go to hear you; so that it will not only contribute to the election . . . but will be an interesting pastime, and improving to the intellectual faculties of all engaged.

Such advice to make politics a matter of hollering and amusement to the entertainment-starved Americans of the nineteenth century could have come from any party wire-puller and organizer of the day. The semicomic tone of his "Celtic gentlemen" letter, despite its serious subject (the perversion of the people's will), likewise typified the fraternal and sporting atmosphere of the trade, sometimes best practiced by "wild boys." On the other hand, Lincoln appreciated the serious side of the political system as well. Shortly after the House Divided Speech, he wrote a Republican associate, "I think too much reliance is placed in noisy demonstrations—importing speakers from a distance and the like. They excite prejudice and close the avenues to sober reason." These were the poles of Lincoln's party-dominated political sphere. His life revolved around them.

In the summer of 1858 Lincoln's life revolved mostly around the small towns of Illinois, the seven where the formal debates took place (Ottawa, Freeport, Jonesboro, Charleston, Galesburg, Quincy, and Alton) and many others where he campaigned (like the places mentioned in the letter about the Celtic gentlemen). In the end Lincoln's campaign failed. Senators were not elected by popular vote but by the state representatives and senators, most of them recently chosen in local fall elections. The Republicans gained a majority in the popular vote, about 125,000 to 121,000 with 5,000 for the Democratic third ticket of Buchananites, but the Douglas Democratic margin in the legislature from holdover senators could not quite be overcome by Republican successes. Lincoln felt bad at first but quickly realized that his excellent showing against one of the most famous political figures in the country was going to help him in the future.

One of the beneficial results of two-party politics was that it occasionally forced politicians to articulate positions they would rather have left unsaid or made their silences conspicuous. Lincoln exposed Douglas's entirely mechanical political device for dealing with slavery in the territories as morally bankrupt. Douglas never once said in public in his entire life that slavery was a moral evil. But Douglas's constant harping on racial fears was equally awkward for Lincoln, who knew that this was a Douglas strategy and had said so in a speech a year before the Senate campaign: "There is a natural disgust in the minds of nearly all white people, to the idea of an indiscriminate

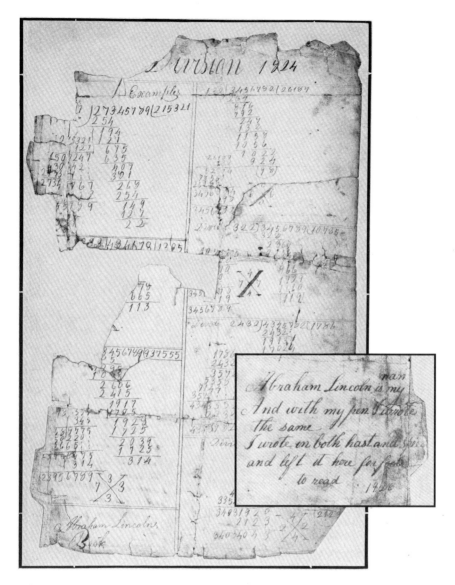

The earliest known surviving examples of Abraham Lincoln's hand-writing come from the pages of a crude sum book in which he practiced long division when he was in his late teens. Lincoln methodically solved the problems and then checked by multiplying the answer by the divisor and adding the remainder. He checked his multiplication, in turn, in the large "X" by the method of casting out nines. The youth practiced writing by including some saucy doggerel (inset) as well. [*Louise and Barry Taper Collection*]

I CERTIFY, That *David M. Pantier* volunteered and served *as a private* in the Company of Mounted Volunteers under my command, in the Regiment commanded by Col. SAMUEL M. THOMPSON, in the Brigade under the command of Generals S. WHITESIDE and H. ATKINSON, called into the service of the United States by the Commander-in-Chief of the Militia of the State, for the protection of the North Western Frontier against an Invasion of the British Band of Sac and other tribes of Indians,—that he was enrolled on the *21* day of *April* 1832, and was HONORABLY DISCHARGED on the *7* day of *June* thereafter, having served *48 days*.

Given under my hand, this *26* day of *September* 1832.

A Lincoln Capt.

One day after date we or either of us promise to pay Reuben Radford Three hundred and Seventy nine dollars and Eighty two cents for value received as witness our hands and seals this 19 of Oct 1833

W. F. Berry
A. Lincoln
William G. Green

(*Top*) In 1832 Captain Abraham Lincoln filled out and signed this document discharging a private from his militia company in the Black Hawk Indian War. The Pantier family was among the earliest settlers of New Salem, and like most of the members of this notoriously ill-disciplined unit of tough frontiersmen, David Pantier was a neighbor of Lincoln's. [*Huntington Library*]

(*Bottom*) In what passed for high finance in New Salem, Lincoln and his partner William Berry assumed two notes of indebtedness from William "Slicky Bill" Green to Reuben Radford, whose stock the partners had purchased to open their ill-fated store. On the day the notes fell due, October 19, 1833, Lincoln, Berry, and Green consolidated the debt and drafted this note. Such notes represented frontier speculative optimism more than the true worth of the debtors. Lincoln had been sued twice the preceding August and was in the process of accumulating a debt that took him years to pay off. [*Louise and Barry Taper Collection*]

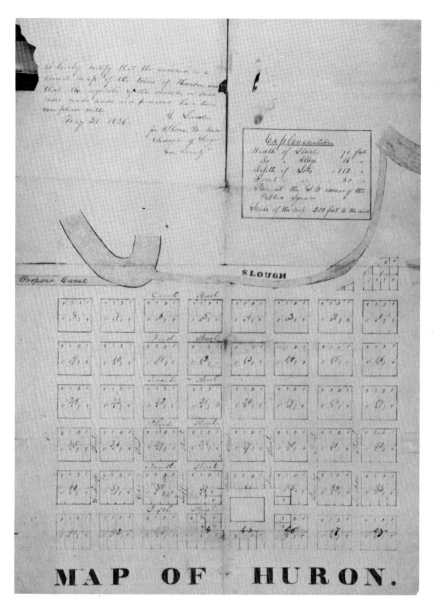

As deputy surveyor for Sangamon County, Lincoln literally charted on this map of Huron the sorts of dreams he abetted in the state legislature. Note the "Proposed Canal," which was never constructed. Lincoln himself speculated in property in the Huron area, but map, canal, property, and all amounted mostly to fantasy. Only one house was ever built here, despite the 385 neatly mapped town lots, the 70-foot wide streets (all named), and the town square designated at Fifth and Madison. [*Illinois State Historical Library*]

ATTENTION!
THE
PEOPLE!!

A. LINCOLN, ESQ'R.,
OF *Sangamon County*, one of the *Electoral Candidates*, will ADDRESS the PEOPLE

This Evening!!

At Early Candlelighting, at the ☞ *OLD COURT ROOM,* ☜ (Riley's Building.)
By request of
MANY CITIZENS.
Thursday, April 9th, 1840.

This rare broadside announces a speech by Lincoln to be given in Alton, Illinois, in April 1840. The Whig party had chosen him as a candidate for the electoral college, pledged to William Henry Harrison, because of his speaking abilities. In this famous "hurrah" campaign known as the "log cabin and hard cider campaign," Lincoln witnessed—and himself helped perfect—political techniques that would be put to use in his own presidential campaign twenty years later. [*Huntington Library*]

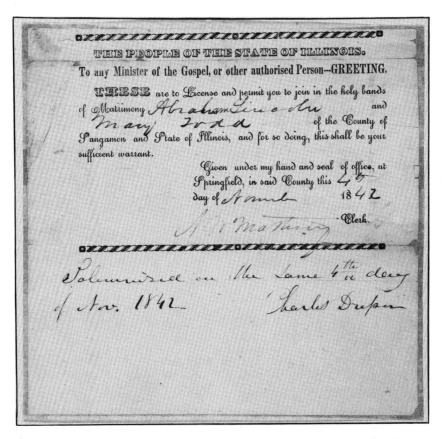

The Episcopal minister Charles Dresser filled out the marriage license of Abraham Lincoln and Mary Todd on November 4, 1842, the day of their exchange of vows. Lincoln regarded the event with sober good humor, writing a friend a week later, "Nothing new here, except my marrying, which to me, is matter of profound wonder." [*Illinois State Historical Library*]

THE

ANTI-SLAVERY

ALPHABET.

"IN THE MORNING SOW THY SEED."

PHILADELPHIA.
PRINTED FOR THE ANTI-SLAVERY FAIR.
1847.

Merrihew & Thompson, Printers.

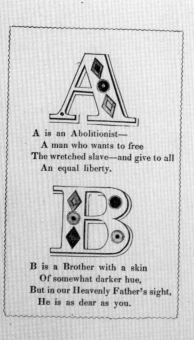

A is an Abolitionist—
  A man who wants to free
The wretched slave—and give to all
  An equal liberty.

B is a Brother with a skin
  Of somewhat darker hue,
But in our Heavenly Father's sight,
  He is as dear as you.

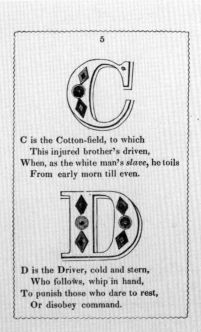

C is the Cotton-field, to which
  This injured brother's driven,
When, as the white man's *slave*, he toils
  From early morn till even.

D is the Driver, cold and stern,
  Who follows, whip in hand,
To punish those who dare to rest,
  Or disobey command.

The *Anti-Slavery Alphabet* provides a vivid example of the advanced propaganda methods of the antislavery movement, the first of many causes in American history to adopt mass-media techniques to spread a political message. By 1847, when this charming juvenile book was produced, the various antislavery societies were old hands at broadcasting their ideas for people of all ages and intellectual levels, using illustrations, bandannas, candy wrappers, and pamphlets galore. [*Huntington Library*]

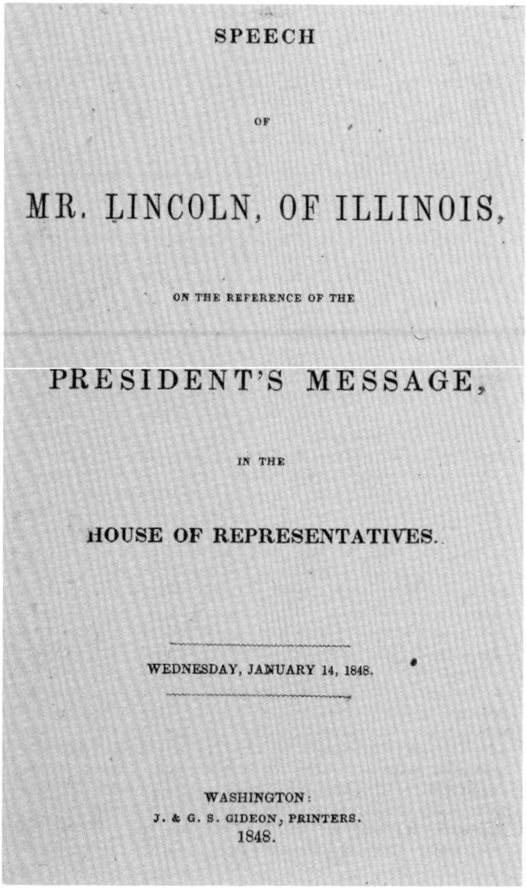

SPEECH

OF

MR. LINCOLN, OF ILLINOIS,

ON THE REFERENCE OF THE

PRESIDENT'S MESSAGE,

IN THE

HOUSE OF REPRESENTATIVES.

WEDNESDAY, JANUARY 14, 1848.

WASHINGTON:
J. & G. S. GIDEON, PRINTERS.
1848.

Lincoln's attempt to make his mark in the House of Representatives came in a speech opposing the Mexican War, delivered on January 12 and misdated in the pamphlet version shown here. Concerned to meet the one-hour time limit imposed by the House, Lincoln had shortened the speech; and then, excited in the delivery, he finished in forty-five minutes. A month later, Lincoln wrote to an old associate, "I wish you to know that I have made a speech in Congress, and that I want you to be *enlightened* by reading it; to further which object, I send a copy of the speech by this mail." [*Huntington Library*]

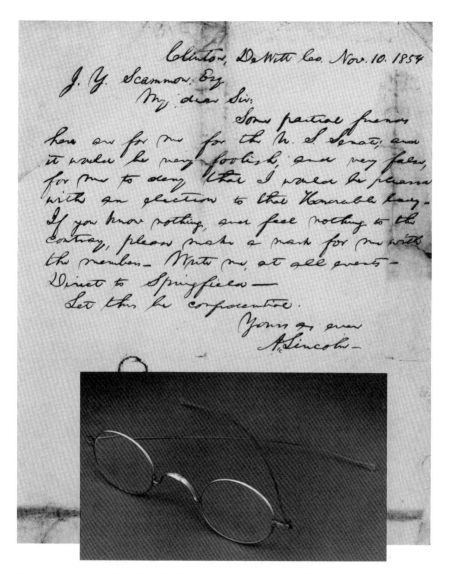

Clinton, DeWitt Co. Nov. 10. 1854

J. Y. Scammon, Esq

My dear Sir:

Some partial friends here are for me for the U. S. Senate, and it would be very foolish, and very false, for me to deny that I would be pleased with an election to that Honorable body — If you know nothing, and feel nothing to the contrary, please make a mark for me with the members — Write me, at all events — Direct to Springfield —

Let this be confidential.

Yours as ever
A. Lincoln —

Lincoln's letter to Jonathan Y. Scammon is remarkable for its tone of modesty even as he charts a course of ambition. Scammon, a free-soil Whig with whom Lincoln had worked since the mid-1840s, was a lawyer and businessman in Chicago. Lincoln obviously felt he could rely on him for support in 1854. [*Illinois State Historical Library*]

In Ottawa, Illinois, on August 21, 1858, on the occasion of the first of his famous debates with Senator Stephen A. Douglas, Lincoln began by reading part of his 1854 speech at Peoria from a printed copy. "Put on your specs," shouted a voice from the crowd. "Yes, sir," Lincoln replied, "I am obliged to do so. I am no longer a young man." He was 49 years old. [*Louise and Barry Taper Collection*]

The case to which these notes refer resulted in a decision exempting the Illinois Central Railroad from county and local taxation. Lincoln billed his client $5,000 and eventually had to sue for payment. Four years later Stephen A. Douglas charged Lincoln with being "on very cozy terms with the Railroad Company." Lincoln defended himself by noting that he and his partner split the big fee and that he was not a candidate for an office that could affect the tax arrangement, which was a state matter. [*Huntington Library*]

Preston Butler's photographs of the Springfield square on which the state capitol stood in 1860 are the best surviving representations of Abraham Lincoln's hometown as it looked when he lived in it. The photograph of the south side, reproduced here, shows Butler's own studio, advertised in the sign atop the second building from the viewer's right. [*Lincoln Museum*]

SLAVERY

ORDAINED OF GOD.

"The powers that be are ordained of God."
Romans xiii. 1.

BY

REV. FRED. A. ROSS, D.D.

PASTOR OF THE PRESBYTERIAN CHURCH, HUNTSVILLE, ALABAMA.

PHILADELPHIA:
J. B. LIPPINCOTT & CO.
1857.

In 1857 Frederick A. Ross, a Presbyterian minister from Huntsville, Alabama, published this little volume of speeches and articles answering antislavery churchmen. In public debate Ross liked nothing better than to quote passages from Exodus and Leviticus in which God instructed the Hebrews in buying, inheriting, and punishing bondmen. "*The second paragraph* of the Declaration of Independence," wrote Ross, "contains *five affirmations*, declared to be self-evident truths, which, if truths, do sustain . . . all abolitionists . . . as to the right of the negro to liberty . . . Each one is contrary to the Bible." [*Huntington Library*]

(*Right*) This undated fragment in Lincoln's hand presents his reply to the "Pro-slavery theology" of "the Rev. Dr. Ross." Lincoln did not tackle the Biblical argument, except to say that no text bearing on the subject could be applied without "a squabble, as to its meaning." Otherwise, he argued that it was in Ross's interest, as an Alabaman, to interpret the text in ways that endorsed slavery. But Lincoln ignored the Presbyterian minister's careful disclaimer, "I have no selfish motive in giving . . . the true Southern defence of slavery." Ross was not himself a slaveholder and had freed "slaves whose money-value would now be $40,000." [*Illinois State Historical Library*]

Suppose it is true, that the negro is inferior to the white, in the gifts of nature; is it not the exact reverse of justice that the white should, for that reason, take from the negro, any part of the little which has been given him? "Give to him that is needy" is the christian rule of charity; but "Take from him that is needy" is the rule of slavery—

Pro-slavery Theology.

The sum of pro-slavery theology seems to be this: "Slavery is not universally right, nor yet universally wrong; it is better for some people to be slaves; and, in such cases, it is the Will of God that they be such."

Certainly there is no contending against the Will of God; but still there is some difficulty in ascertaining it, and applying it, to particular cases— For instance we will suppose the Rev. Dr. Ross has a slave named Sambo, and the question is "Is it the Will of God that Sambo shall remain a slave, or be set free?" The Almighty gives no audible answer to the question, and his revelation—the Bible—gives none—or, at most, none but such as admits of a squabble, as to its meaning— No one thinks of asking Sambo's opinion on it— So, at last, it comes to this, that Dr. Ross is to decide the question— And while he considers it, he sits in the shade, with gloves on his hands, and subsists on the bread that Sambo is earning in the burning sun— If he decides that God Wills Sambo to continue a slave, he thereby retains his own comfortable position; but if he decides that God Wills Sambo to be free, he thereby has to walk out of the shade, throw off his gloves, and delve for his own bread— Will Dr. Ross be actuated by that perfect impartiality, which has ever been considered most favorable to correct decisions?

GRAND RALLY

OF THE

LINCOLN MEN

OF

OLD TAZEWELL.

WE      THE

HONOR   ABRAHAM   LINCOLN.   HONEST.

The opponents of those twin cherries on a split stem, BUCHANAN and DOUG-
LAS, in TAZEWELL and adjoining counties, are requested to assemble in

GRAND COUNCIL!

AT PEKIN, ON TUESDAY, OCTOBER 5TH, 1858.

ABRAHAM LINCOLN!

Will address the People at 2 o'clock, P. M. on the Political Topics of the day.   Let good men of every name and
tongue who love the patriotic principles of the Fathers of our Country, come together and sustain the man who represents those principles. When Presidents, Senators
and Supreme Courts decide to make the constitution carry slavery all over our free states and territories, it is time for the people to rise in their might and sustain our Glorious Union upon the cherished Republican Principles of Washington, Jefferson, Clay and Lincoln.

WM. KELLOGG.

candidate for re-election to Congress, will also address the meeting.

HON. LYMAN TRUMBULL

is expected to speak in the evening.

President of the day. DAVID MARK, Esq.

VICE PRESIDENTS.—Washington, JOHN L. MARSH; Groveland, JOHN HAMOCK; Marion, JOEL W. CLARK; Deer Creek, JOSEPH HIGGINS; Tremont, JOHN A. JONES; Elm Grove, JOHN BUCKLEY; Mackinaw, C. O. NEVILLE; Little Mackinaw, G. W. MINIER; Cincinnati, SAMUEL WOODROW; Springlake, TIMOTHY CLARK; Sand Prairie, W. S. RANKIN; Dillon, NATHAN DILLON, Hopedale, E. HODGESON; Boyington, P. BALDING; Fon du lac, JACOB WILSON;
Delavan, W. W. CROSSMAN; Hittle, DANIEL ALBRIGHT; Mabee, C. F. BUCKMAN—Chief Marshal, W. GAITHER.

 FARE ON STEAMERS NILE AND DELTA,
HALF PRICE.

T. J. PICKETT, T. KING, Jr., J. WAGENSELLER, D. A. CHEEVER, C. GRONDENBERG, I. A. HAWLEY, TEIS SMITH, Committee of Arrangements.

As I would not be a slave, so I would not be a master. This expresses my idea of democracy — Whatever differs from this, to the extent of the difference, is no democracy —

The extent of Lincoln's preoccupation with the slavery question after 1854 is evident in the unusual definition of democracy shown in this fragment. The exact date of composition is unknown, as are the circumstances surrounding the origin of this strange but widely quoted sentiment. [*Illinois State Historical Library*]

(*Left*) Several of the most fascinating qualities of the political system of Lincoln's era are embodied in this poster, perhaps the only one surviving from the famous Illinois campaign for the U.S. Senate of 1858. The small print contains the conspiracy charge that Lincoln and other Republicans used to rally the faithful: "When Presidents, Senator and Supreme Courts decide to make the constitution carry slavery all over our free states and territories, it is time for the people to rise." Even though only Lincoln "Men" were summoned in the broadside, women often attended these afternoon-through-evening events as well. Tazewell County is north of Springfield, and Pekin sits on the Illinois River near Peoria. [*Illinois State Historical Library*]

In this letter of September 1860 to a young lawyer, Lincoln characteristically emphasized hard work as the route to success. Inured to hardship early in life, he rarely complained; the revelation here that he had found the study of the classic works of English and American law "laborious, and tedious" is unusual. [*Illinois State Historical Library*]

Robert Todd Lincoln had this ambrotype photograph taken in 1859 or 1860, when he was a student at Exeter Academy preparing for the Harvard entrance exams. It was during this period that he lost his last chance to get to know his father well. "Henceforth," he recalled sadly, "any great intimacy between us became impossible." "I scarcely even had ten minutes quiet talk with him during his Presidency," Robert added, "on account of his constant devotion to business." [*Lincoln Museum*]

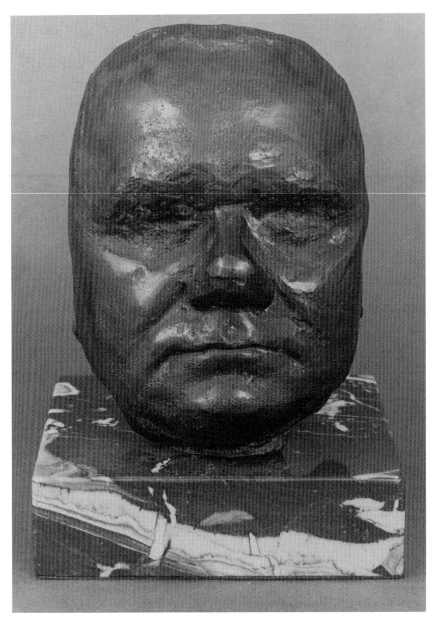

Stephen A. Douglas repeatedly crossed political swords with Lincoln in the period 1858-1860, when the original plaster impression for this bronze life mask
was made. The sculptor, Leonard W. Volk, who was a cousin of Douglas's
wife, Adele, probably thought he would one day sculpt a likeness of President
Douglas based on this mask. Little did he know that he would sculpt a monument for Senator Douglas's tomb instead. [*Louise and Barry Taper Collection*]

Springfield, April 16 1859.

T. J. Pickett, Esq
My dear Sir:

Yours of the 13th is just received
My engagements are such that I can not, at any
very early day, visit Rock-Island, to deliver a
lecture, or for any other object—
As to the other matter you kindly mention, I must,
in candor, say I do not think myself fit for the
Presidency— I certainly am flattered and gratified that some
partial friends think of me in that connection;
but I really think it best for our cause that no
concerted effort such as you suggest should be
made—
Let this be considered confidential—
Yours very truly
A. Lincoln—

Thomas J. Pickett, editor of the Rock Island *Register*, to whom this letter of
April 1859 is addressed, was among the earliest supporters of Lincoln for President. Declaring "I do not think myself fit" for the office, Lincoln declines Pickett's offer of some "concerted effort" to make him an active candidate. Like
most early supporters, Pickett got his reward when Lincoln won the presidency—in his case, appointment to a minor agency of the army's Quartermas-
ter Department on Rock Island in 1861. [*Illinois State Historical Library*]

Franklin H. Brown's crude woodcut likeness, based on an 1857 photograph famous for what Lincoln described as the "disordered condition of the hair," was the first mass-produced picture of Lincoln. The prints were "showered through the Wigwam immediately after . . . Lincoln's nomination." [*Lincoln Museum*]

THE REPUBLICAN WIGWAM.
Erected by the Republicans of Chicago for the use of the Republican Convention.
Dedicated May 12th 1860. — Capable of holding 10.000 Persons.
Published by JONES, PERDUE & SMALL, Stationers, N.º 122 Lake St. Chicago. Ill.ª

The "Wigwam" was specially constructed by Chicago Republicans for the presidential nominating convention of May 16, 1860. The wooden structure, long since destroyed, was jammed to capacity with roaring delegates, a disproportionate share of whom were Illinoisans committed to Lincoln's candidacy. This lithograph, the best-known view of the convention hall, suggests the high status of most political activists in the dress of the crowd and the number of carriages. Likewise, the presence of many women attests to the importance of politics in daily life even for a group legally disenfranchised. [*Illinois State Historical Library*]

Price] [25 cts.

THE

LIFE, SPEECHES, AND PUBLIC SERVICES

OF

ABRAM LINCOLN.

LINCOLN.

NEW YORK:

RUDD & CARLETON, 130 GRAND STREET.

M DCCC LX.

The presidential candidate posed with his sons (one of whom hid behind the corner fence post) in front of his home in Springfield for a Boston photographer in the summer of 1860. [*Lincoln Museum*]

(*Left*) Rudd & Carleton in New York, who produced this, the earliest campaign biography of Lincoln, misspelled his first name. Lincoln was the least known of the four presidential candidates. Calling the biography the "Wigwam edition" perhaps made it seem as though its production virtually coincided with Lincoln's nomination in that building. [*Huntington Library*]

Chicago's Alexander Hesler traveled to Springfield to photograph four different poses of Lincoln on June 3, 1860, shortly after his nomination for the Presidency. This oval photograph in an original Hesler mat was signed by Lincoln. [*Louise and Barry Taper Collection*]

The American flag shown here became a partisan banner for the 1860 Republican candidates. Before the 1920s, when the Red Scare led to the passage of rigidifying ultra-patriotic flag laws, the American flag often constituted a form of folk art. The unstandardized star field and the white stripes lent themselves to political adaptations. [*Louise and Barry Taper Collection*]

UNCLE ABE'S

REPUBLICAN

SONGSTER

For "Uncle Abe's Choir."

SAN FRANCISCO:
TOWNE & BACON, BOOK, CARD AND FANCY JOB PRINTERS,
Southwest corner Clay and Sansome Streets.
1860.

The campaign songs printed in this rare California songster, meant to be sung to widely known popular tunes, reveal the participatory quality of nineteenth-century politics in the heyday of the party system. [*Illinois State Historical Library*]

The principal rivals for northern votes in 1860 face each other from the covers of these pieces of sheet music printed for the presidential campaign. [*Lincoln Museum*]

This Wide-Awake torch in the shape of the patriotic symbol, the eagle, is hollow. Wicks were placed in the tubes projecting from the wings, and the body of the bird was filled with oil. The whole was attached to the top of a wooden pole and carried in nighttime parades for Lincoln. [*Illinois State Historical Library*]

(*Right*) Abraham Lincoln appears as a "Wide-Awake" in the woodcut illustration on the cover of this rare surviving copy of ephemeral campaign literature. The Wide-Awakes were marching clubs of young Republicans organized during the 1860 campaign for nighttime torchlit parades. Because the oil-burning lamps spewed hot sparks and oil, the uniforms consisted of oilcloth capes and glazed caps. [*Illinois State Historical Library*]

Wide-Awake Pictorial.

FOR NOVEMBER, 1860.

HONEST OLD ABE MARCHING FORTH TO THE WHITE HOUSE.

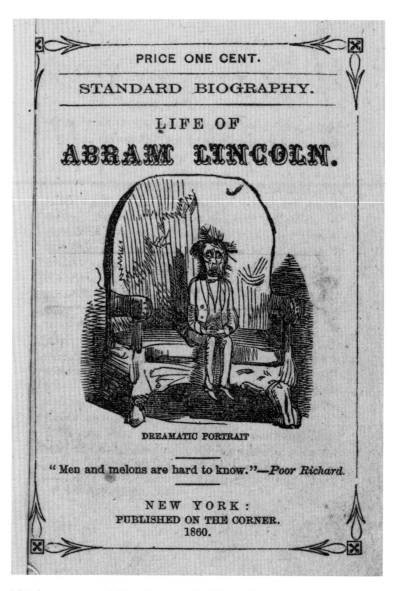

PRICE ONE CENT.

STANDARD BIOGRAPHY.

LIFE OF
ABRAM LINCOLN.

DREAMATIC PORTRAIT

"Men and melons are hard to know."—*Poor Richard.*

NEW YORK:
PUBLISHED ON THE CORNER.
1860.

This humorous anti-Lincoln campaign biography, now rare, was replete with factual errors and with the usual Democratic malice. The little book characterized "Abram" as "partial to the Ethiopian" but willing to see "the white man . . . entitled to the same regard if he behaved himself." [*Huntington Library*]

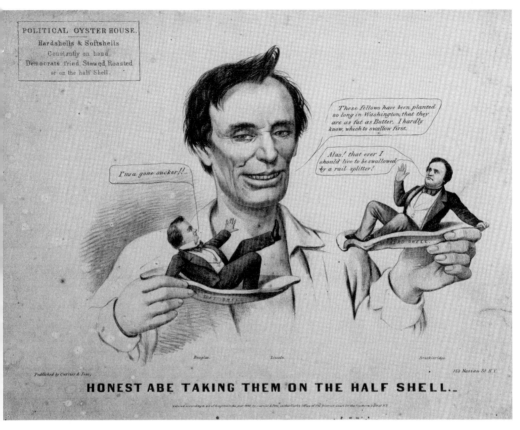

In this 1860 cartoon drawn by Currier & Ives's Louis Maurer, anti-incumbent sentiment is combined with the expectation that the split in the Democratic party will hand victory to the Republicans. "Soft" and "hard" shell referred to the candidates' attitudes toward the rights of slaveowners in the territories. Stephen Douglas refers to himself as a "sucker," the nickname of Illinoisans. [*Huntington Library*]

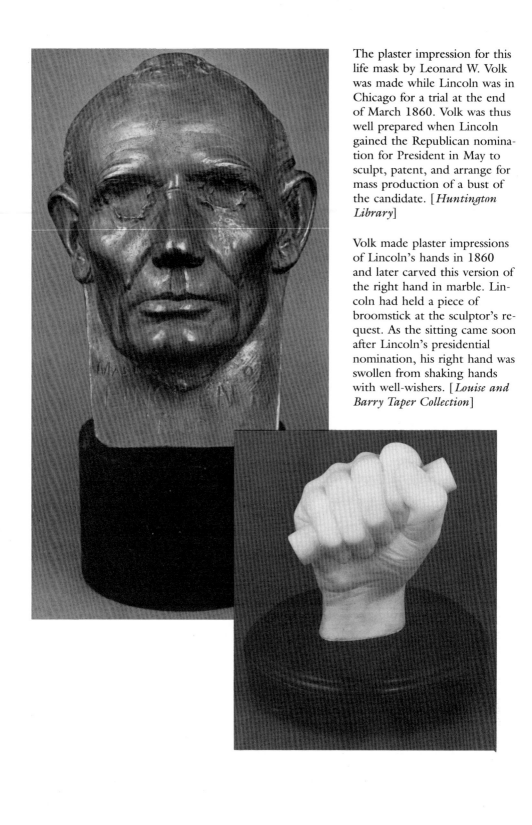

The plaster impression for this life mask by Leonard W. Volk was made while Lincoln was in Chicago for a trial at the end of March 1860. Volk was thus well prepared when Lincoln gained the Republican nomination for President in May to sculpt, patent, and arrange for mass production of a bust of the candidate. [*Huntington Library*]

Volk made plaster impressions of Lincoln's hands in 1860 and later carved this version of the right hand in marble. Lincoln had held a piece of broomstick at the sculptor's request. As the sitting came soon after Lincoln's presidential nomination, his right hand was swollen from shaking hands with well-wishers. [*Louise and Barry Taper Collection*] amalgamation of the white and black races; and Judge Douglas evidently is basing his chief hope, upon the chances of being able to appropriate the benefit of this disgust to himself." In 1858 Lincoln had to deal with the tactic before live audiences of voters, and at Charleston, Illinois, on September 18, he went as far as he was going to go in denying racial equality:

> I will say . . . that I am not, nor ever have been in favor of bringing about in any way the social and political equality of the white and black races,—that I am not nor ever have been in favor of making voters or jurors of negroes, nor of qualifying them to hold office, nor to intermarry with white people; and I will say in addition to this that there is a physical difference between the white and black races which I believe will for ever forbid the two races living together on terms of social and political equality. And inasmuch as they cannot so live, while they do remain together there must be the position of superior and inferior, and I as much as any other man am in favor of having the superior position assigned to the white race.

In 1859 Lincoln tried to recuperate financially from the campaign of the previous year, but his political skills were much in demand now. Requests for his speeches and opinions multiplied and caused him to think deeply about political issues. He grew even more devoted to the political ideas of Thomas Jefferson as enunciated in the Declaration of Independence. On April 6, 1859, he wrote:

> One would start with great confidence that he could convince any sane child that the simpler propositions of Euclid are true; but, nevertheless, he could fail, utterly, with one who should deny the definitions and axioms. The principles of Jefferson are the definitions and axioms of free society. And yet they are denied, and evaded, with no small show of success. One dashingly calls them "glittering generalities"; another bluntly calls them "self evident lies"; and still others insidiously argue that they apply only to "superior races."
> These expressions, differing in form, are identical in object and

effect—the supplanting the principles of free government, and restoring those of classification, caste, and legitimacy.

In the fall Lincoln campaigned in Ohio for Republican candidates.
Gradually, he became a hopeful—a minor one—for the Republican
presidential nomination in 1860. Seward seemed the most likely candidate, and his rivals helped Lincoln a good deal when they invited
him to New York to speak. Lincoln's appearance at Cooper Institute,
on February 27, 1860, constituted a sort of introduction to eastern
Republicans. He prepared the speech carefully, researching the records
of the constitutional convention in Philadelphia in 1787, early printings of U.S. statutes, and the journals of early Congresses, and sought
to prove that the founders of the government initiated the policy to
restrict slavery's growth. The first part of the address thus resembled
a history lecture more than a stump speech, Illinois style, but Lincoln
may have been thinking of his new eastern audience and thinking as
well that Horace Greeley, editor of the New York *Tribune* and enemy
of Seward, would find it easy to use his giant steam presses to publish
the speech. Even so, the rest of the Cooper Institute address reiterated
the conspiracy charge that Lincoln had added to his original 1854
arguments from the intentions of the founders.

Presidential nominations do not "come" to anyone; they have to
be gone after. Lincoln and his political friends and managers pursued
an astute strategy to gain the nomination. Yet circumstance more than
effort ultimately made him the Republican candidate. Republican
managers could look at the results of the 1856 election and know
what had to be done. They needed to retain the states they carried in
1856, essentially the upper tier of northern states, and gain Pennsylvania along with Indiana or Illinois. To do so they decided to broaden
the economic appeal of the party's platform—keeping Pennsylvania's
insatiable desire for tariffs in mind—and, following a strategy similar
to Lincoln's in 1855, to avoid giving offense to anti-Catholic voters
moving over from the Know Nothing party. A candidate with appeal
in conservative Indiana and Illinois would be especially attractive. At
the Republican convention in Chicago, where Lincoln began largely
as a political unknown, the various delegations only gradually became

aware of his assets and saw that he had no liabilities from the standpoint of 1860 party strategy. He had lived in Indiana and Illinois. His old Whig economic ideas would look fine to Pennsylvanians. And though he had always personally despised Know Nothing principles, he had avoided denouncing the party publicly or offending its members openly.

Lincoln was little known and rarely thought of as a genuine rival to Seward or to the other Republican hopefuls, Salmon P. Chase of Ohio, Edward Bates of Missouri, or Simon Cameron of Pennsylvania. As late as March 17, 1860, Lincoln could write, "I could not raise ten thousand dollars if it would save me from the fate of John Brown. Nor have my friends, so far as I know, yet reached the point of staking any money on my chances of success." The Republicans met on May 16. Lincoln remained home in Springfield, but he had managers on the scene, led by the 300-pound Judge David Davis. Lincoln was already Illinois' choice, of course. Seward's reputation as an antislavery radical hurt him in Indiana, and his previous cooperation in New York politics with Archbishop John Hughes, America's highest-ranking Catholic prelate, made him anathema to old Know Nothings (or to state party leaders worried about attracting the Know Nothing vote in their states). Chase also seemed too radical on the slavery question and could not unite behind him the delegates of his home state, Ohio. Bates was too conservative, having declared for the central and defining plank of the Republican platform, opposition to the expansion of slavery into the territories, only on the eve of the convention. Cameron was a former Democrat (in a party made up mostly of old Whigs) and had a reputation for corruption.

"I suppose I am not the *first* choice of a very great many," Lincoln wrote on March 24, 1860. "Our policy, then, is to give no offence to others—leave them in a mood to come to us, if they shall be compelled to give up their first love." The strategy, recognizing Lincoln's essentially negative virtues (he had offended the fewest), succeeded, and on the third ballot he won the nomination. An ex-Democrat from Maine, Hannibal Hamlin, was nominated as his vice-presidential running-mate.

The Democratic party split, with northern Democrats nominating

Douglas and southern ones nominating John C. Breckinridge, Buchanan's Vice President. A fourth party, remnants of the old Whig and Know Nothing parties, now called the Constitutional Union party, nominated John Bell of Tennessee. Many considered the election a foregone conclusion after the Democratic party split, but the parties campaigned as though it would be a cliffhanger.

Because of the customs of presidential electioneering and the structure of political parties in the middle of the nineteenth century, the presidential election canvass did not involve Lincoln in a relentless schedule of grueling campaigning. Presidential candidates were not supposed to campaign (the office was to seek the man and not the man the office). Lincoln did not give a single speech or leave Springfield until 1861. Likewise, it is not clear that he necessarily set the tone of the campaign. The parties were really a loose amalgam of state organizations that banded together every four years to choose a president. Much of the campaigning and the strategy for it was devised at the state level. The Republicans ran a "hurrah" campaign that stressed hollering, parades, songs, barbecues, fireworks, spectacle, and marching by groups of young men called "Wide Awakes." They did not emphasize issues. The Democrats followed suit.

The image of Lincoln forged in this campaign endured, partly because it was by no means entirely false to the real man and partly because it so neatly personified the Republican message. At the Illinois nominating convention before the national convention, an old settler came forward with logs from a rail fence Lincoln had split years before when he first entered Illinois; the candidate was thus christened the "Railsplitter." He really had split rails (though not necessarily the ones paraded at the enthusiastic convention), and he really had been born in a log cabin (as the first object of a log-cabin "hurrah" campaign, William Henry Harrison back in 1840, had *not*). The idea that Lincoln had risen from such rustic poverty to the presidential nomination captured the American imagination, always lured by the myth of social mobility, and it fit the Republican message well. Economically backward slave societies offered no opportunities for poor boys to become grand planters, Republicans argued; the Republicans championed "free soil," which would provide economic opportunity for free labor in the new territories by forbidding the introduction of slavery into them. Lincoln's reputation for honesty, embodied in the nickname "Honest Abe," also was true to the man and useful as a contrast to the incumbent Democratic administration, which was tainted by scandals and corruption.

Adherence to political custom and the "hurrah" campaign, probably a frontrunner's strategies, offered the voters little opportunity to learn more about the candidate from Illinois. In the South, of course, that had tragic consequences. Lincoln and the Republicans were generally depicted as extreme abolitionists bent on destroying southern institutions.

November 6 was election day. Lincoln received about 39 percent of the popular vote, but it was concentrated in states with many electoral votes, and he would have won even if the popular vote of all three of his rivals had been concentrated on one candidate. He took every free northern state except New Jersey, which split its electoral vote. He failed to get a single vote in any future Confederate state except Virginia.

CHAPTER THREE

Commander in Chief

Lincoln entered the presidency with virtually no background in military affairs. The experience he had gained as a volunteer in Illinois' Black Hawk Indian War in 1832 seemed so trifling that he had made fun of it in a speech in the United States Congress in 1848. Lincoln made "charges upon the wild onions" and "had a good many bloody struggles with the musquetoes" but did not see "any live, fighting indians." A different kind of man would have gone by "Captain" for the rest of his days. Making light of one's own military service record has not been common practice among aspiring politicians in America. The country's first President was a military hero, and Lincoln had come to political maturity while Andrew Jackson and William Henry Harrison showed the continuing political appeal of men on horseback. Even the speech in which Lincoln belittled his own military experience was meant to boost the presidential candidacy of Mexican War hero Zachary Taylor. Perhaps the speech showed that Lincoln's ambitions were not yet soaring to the heights they would reach in the 1850s. In any event, it was proof of genuine humility on the topic of military affairs.

Lincoln had followed the Mexican War closely, and from it he learned an important lesson. Disgusted by President Polk's "rascality" in attempting to create a post for a supreme Democratic commander over the high-ranking Whig generals Zachary Taylor and Winfield Scott, Lincoln would go to extremes as President to avoid partisanship in selecting battlefield commanders. Otherwise during the Mexican War he was absorbed in the boundary issue between Mexico and the United States and apparently picked up little about strategy or tactics.

If it worried Lincoln, when war broke out in 1861, that the President of the Confederacy could legitimately boast of much greater military experience, he never said so. In fact, he almost never said anything about Jefferson Davis, and historians have no idea what measure Lincoln took of the rival commander in chief. Like Ulysses S. Grant, the general in whom Lincoln would place his greatest confidence, Lincoln thought more about what he would do to the enemy than what the enemy *might* do to him.

The time from Lincoln's election on November 6, 1860, through his inauguration on March 4, 1861, and the weeks immediately following were a nerve-racking period for the nation as well as for the President. It is difficult to imagine how war could have been avoided after Lincoln's election if he adhered to the Republican platform—and he did.

The initial wave of secession, commencing on December 20, 1860, and ending February 1, 1861, took South Carolina, Mississippi, Florida, Alabama, Georgia, Louisiana, and Texas out of the Union. The impulse to secession was the obverse of the political forces that had led to Republican success. The leaders of the southern secession movement had less difficulty than the Republican leaders in describing a pattern of conspiracy against their citizens' liberties. The John Brown raid at Harpers Ferry, Virginia, in 1859 constituted prime evidence of violent designs against the southern way of life, and talk of the "ultimate extinction" of slavery seemed nothing more than thinly veiled abolitionism. The wonder is that a majority of slave states—eight—still remained in the Union after the initial wave of secession ended in February. The population and resources of the eight reluctant slave states were great enough to determine the outcome of a sectional war. If all eight went, the Confederacy could not be conquered. If none went, the Confederacy would be beaten in a hurry. The politicians jockeyed for advantage in the undecided states between November and March, but there was little that Lincoln could do. In the first place, he was not President yet, and as a common citizen until his inauguration he had less formal legal power than any constable. In the second place, the informal power Lincoln in fact held as President-elect he regarded as inseparable from the Republican platform pledge not to allow the creation of new slave states. Unless he surrendered on that issue, he had nothing to offer that the slave states really wanted.

Before South Carolina's secession Lincoln told Senator Lyman Trumbull privately: "Let there be no compromise on the question of *extending* slavery. If there be, all our labor is lost, and, ere long, must be done again. The dangerous ground—that into which some of our friends have a hankering to run—is Pop. Sov. Have none of it. Stand firm. The tug has to come, & better now, than any time hereafter." Lincoln's response here was characteristic: he thought challenges should be met and not avoided. Avoidance to him was mere procrastination. Lincoln did not change his tune after secession, and his leadership on this issue meant that Republicans in Congress would not cooperate with any compromise measures involving slavery extension. No "transition team" was in contact with the Buchanan administration (the era was too partisan for that) to orchestrate administrative measures and military policies to prevent confrontation. Buchanan allowed most federal installations to fall into secessionist hands, and only Fort Pickens and Fort Sumter, offshore bases in Florida and South Carolina, respectively, remained as prominent symbols of national authority in the deep South.

Lincoln seemed tired of southern blackmail and took an intransigent position at first. When he circulated his proposed inaugural address, Seward and Orville H. Browning took exception to the President-elect's avowal that "all the power at my disposal will be used to reclaim the public property and places which have fallen," and in the end Lincoln adopted a more passive policy, saying in his inaugural address only that "the power confided to me, will be used to hold, occupy, and possess the property, and places belonging to the government, and to collect the duties and imposts." He was willing to leave federal

offices vacant where the local populace would oppose outside appointees, and he expressed willingness to support a constitutional amendment explicitly forbidding the interference of the federal government
with slavery in the states forever. Such concessions failed to improve
the deteriorating political relations with the slave states.

Shortly after his inauguration, Lincoln learned that Fort Sumter
would run out of food and have to be evacuated within about a month.
This forced his hand. At first only one member of his cabinet,
Montgomery Blair, urged reinforcing the fort. The situation worsened
daily, until Secretary of State Seward, inclined to compromise by
evacuating the fort and thinking Lincoln really had no policy, drafted
a memorandum on April 1 proposing to abandon Sumter and provoke
a foreign crisis that might reunite the two sections against a common
outside threat. He also suggested that it might fall to a cabinet member
to instrument the plan. Lincoln was not passive with his own advisers,
however, and quickly asserted his authority, maintaining that he did
have a policy and that if a new one were needed the President would
devise it.

Lincoln had put his own house in order, but the national house
continued to divide. He decided to send provisions to Sumter—food
only, no arms or soldiers—and to notify the governor of South Carolina of his intentions. The governor informed Jefferson Davis, and the
President of the Confederate States of America, after consultation with
his cabinet, decided to resist the attempt. On April 12 the southerners
fired the first shot of the Civil War.

Jefferson Davis held all the cards. Any appearance of aggression on
Lincoln's part would have pushed the rest of the slave states out.
Merely supplying the beleaguered fort with food risked war—a risk
Lincoln proved willing to take. When Lincoln called out the militia to
put down the rebellion, four of the holdout states quickly joined the
departed states: Tennessee, Arkansas, North Carolina, and Virginia.
One, Missouri, was kept in the Union by a military coup d'état and
two others, Kentucky and Maryland, remained precarious for some
months.

Once war began, Lincoln had many things to learn. After an initial disastrous Union defeat at the First Battle of Bull Run, fought July 21, 1861, he issued a call for 500,000 volunteers and brought General George B. McClellan to Washington to command the confused and demoralized eastern armies. The President now knew, although not all the public or all the eager politicians did, that it would require time to reorganize the troops and train new ones so that their performance would improve. Most of the soldiers who had marched to Bull Run, fought reasonably well, and then fled in abject and disorderly retreat had enlisted for a term of only three months. McClellan needed more time than that to make real soldiers out of volunteers, and Lincoln allowed him to organize and train. On November 1 he replaced the aged, wheezing, and bulbous Winfield Scott as general-in-chief with the 34-year-old McClellan, making the "young Napoleon" the head of all the armies in the country, east and west.

Lincoln's dealings with McClellan illustrate the command problems he faced. By December President Lincoln began to wonder how much longer he would have to wait for action. Many Republicans in Congress had already lost their patience, and on January 15, 1862, McClellan was required to testify before Congress's Joint Committee on the Conduct of the War. Pressure for attack was mounting steadily and uneasiness between the two men was growing. In late autumn, McClellan, in intimate letters to his wife, regularly referred to the President as "the gorilla" and made fun of his western manners and of his penchant for telling anecdotes.

By late January relations between McClellan and Congress as well as between McClellan and the President had grown quite strained. On the 27th Lincoln issued "General War Order No. 1," designating George Washington's birthday as the "day for a general movement of the Land and Naval forces of the United States against the insurgent forces." On the 31st, he issued another order, directing the Army of the Potomac, "after providing safely for the defense of Washington," to make a point on the railroad southwest of Manassas Junction its military objective.

McClellan, fearing leaks and having little respect for the military judgment of his civilian superiors, had not yet informed the President of his own plans. Nothing in Lincoln's foolish and unrealistic orders, which ignored the intentions of the enemy, the weather, and myriad factors any conscientious general would have to consider before advancing, was calculated to increase McClellan's confidence in the commander in chief. But now the general had to act. Writing to the newly appointed Secretary of War, Edwin M. Stanton, McClellan explained that it had required time to reinvigorate the army and fortify Washington. The army had been ready for defense weeks or months ago, but making ready for attack was another matter. More of his time was absorbed when appointment to overall command had brought McClellan the problems of the western armies as well.

Finally, McClellan revealed his plan to attack Richmond not by marching an army overland directly from Washington against Manassas but rather by approaching from Chesapeake Bay. He sought "decisive" results and "destruction" of the enemy's main army, not mere possession of a field of battle after a victory. There was nothing wrong with McClellan's plan except that he had not bothered to tell the commander in chief about it earlier. After close cross-examination by the President, McClellan got his way. Nevertheless, Lincoln issued two more peremptory orders on matters of detailed military organization, troop dispositions, and times of movement. He required commencement of the Chesapeake Bay initiative by the 18th of the month, and the President ordered McClellan to leave in and about Washington a force large enough to keep the city secure. Because McClellan would soon be on active campaign with the Army of the Potomac in Virginia, Lincoln removed him as general-in-chief, relieving him of his responsibility for the western armies. The President did not then immediately appoint another general-in-chief, thus leaving the civilian authorities in Washington with too many departmental commanders reporting directly to them.

As soon as McClellan embarked for the Virginia Peninsula, disagreements erupted over the adequacy of the troops left for Washington's defense. Then McClellan—and Lincoln—fell victim to what is widely regarded as one of the most brilliant campaigns in military history: Thomas Jonathan "Stonewall" Jackson's Shenandoah Valley campaign. To appreciate it, one must understand two things. First, the geography of Virginia is such that the Shenandoah Valley, protected on either side by mountain ranges, runs from southwest to northeast along what is now Virginia's western border. An army could march safely up and down the Valley because its flanks were protected by the mountains. If the Federals marched an army down the Valley, however, they ended up in the underdeveloped area of southwest Virginia, farther from Richmond, the capital of the Confederacy, than if they had remained in Washington. But if the Confederates marched an army *up* the Valley, they emerged in a position to attack Harrisburg, Baltimore, or Washington, D.C. The Valley was a gun aimed at the North's head.

The second point is that Jackson, who demonstrated genius for leading small armies, and his superiors fully understood the strategic importance of the Valley. When McClellan, who self-consciously believed in the Napoleonic principle of concentration rather than dispersion of forces, began to draw Union forces from the Valley for the big assault on Richmond via the Chesapeake route, Jackson attacked. Lincoln behaved exactly as the Confederates had hoped he would. He began detaching troops to the Shenandoah Valley that McClellan had assumed he would have available for his offensive.

Relations between General McClellan, a Democrat, and the commander in chief, a Republican, were much worsened by political suspicion. When, for example, Lincoln first detached a division to western Virginia, they in fact went to the Mountain Department. The commander of the Mountain Department was John C. Frémont, a great explorer, an incompetent general, and the first Republican nominee for President. To McClellan, Lincoln's move looked suspiciously like an attempt to build up a vain Republican's army at the expense of a hard-working Democrat's army poised for the decisive military campaign of the war. Nearly every event in the dialogue between Lincoln and McClellan was similarly darkened by the shade of political suspicion.

The ensuing Peninsula campaign and Seven Days' Battles took place amidst the continuing disagreements between Lincoln and the commander of the Army of the Potomac. By July 1862 McClellan had failed to take Richmond or to destroy the Confederate army before him. Lincoln realized the necessity of having a general-in-chief and called in Henry W. Halleck from the West, where Union forces had been faring better. With McClellan now stymied before Richmond, Lincoln also summoned from the West General John Pope to assume command of the forces in Virginia defending the Potomac. As the President had desired in the first place, overland attack via Manassas again became the Union strategy.

Even now, in the war's second summer, Lincoln felt himself an amateur, and on this subject he retained his refreshing humility and candor. For example, Agénor-Etienne de Gasparin, a rare French sup-porter of the Union cause, wrote Lincoln an encouraging letter on July 18, 1862, that nevertheless inquired about the reasons for Union military failure. The President replied, "You ask 'why is it that the North with her great armies, so often is found, with inferiority of numbers, face to face with the armies of the South?' While I painfully know the fact, a military man, which I am not, would better answer the question." Lincoln by this time knew quite a lot, including the diplomatic wisdom that he should not appear to lecture an ally. He now proceeded to explain, "The fact I know, has not been overlooked; and I suppose the cause of its continuance lies mainly in the other facts that the enemy holds the interior, and we the exterior lines; and that we operate where the people convey information to the enemy, while he operates where they convey none to us."

The idea of interior and exterior lines was embraced by the military experts of the day to explain the Confederacy's ability to counteract superior Union numbers and resources, and a discussion of it inevitably appears in any work on Civil War strategy. It is commonsensical enough: if one thinks of the northern border of the Confederacy as a semicircular arc or perimeter, then the Union forces were obliged to travel by the circumference while the Confederate forces could move on shorter straight lines within the arc to reinforce threatened spots.

Lincoln paid close attention to military developments. The daily tension of these events for Lincoln was often all but unbearable. When Lee invaded Maryland in 1862, for instance, the President sent telegrams to General McClellan at 10:15 A.M. on September 10, asking for news; at 6:00 P.M. on September 11, explaining available reinforcements; and at 4:00 A.M. on September 12, asking, "How does it look now?"

By the late summer of 1862 Lincoln had also learned to state his military objectives simply. When General McClellan, whom Lincoln restored to command in Virginia after General Pope's stunning defeat at the Second Battle of Bull Run in August 1862, telegraphed the news of victories over Robert E. Lee's armies at South Mountain and Crampton's Gap, Maryland, Lincoln replied, "God bless you, and all with you. Destroy the rebel army, if possible."

McClellan did not do it, and Lincoln's letter irritated him. He complained to his wife that he had heard "nothing in regard to South Mountain except from the Pres[i]d[en]t in the following *beautiful* language. ' . . . God bless you & all with you. Can't you beat them some more before they get off?'!!! I don't look for any thanks at their hands & believe that they scarcely pretend to conceal their malevolence." By "their" McClellan referred to Lincoln, Halleck, and the Secretary of War perhaps, but the implication was surely that he could not hope for praise or fair-dealing from the Republican administration. The subsequent Battle of Antietam, fought in Maryland September 17, forced Lee to retreat to Virginia. A week later, the President still did "not know the particulars," but he was apparently growing distressed that McClellan was not pursuing Lee and traveled to Antietam on October 1 for a three-day visit with the victorious general and the Army of the Potomac. A famous series of photographs resulted, but no meeting of the minds.

McClellan had been apprehensive, suspecting "that the real purpose of his visit is to push me into a premature advance into Virginia." The general considered his army "not fit to advance—the old r[e]g[imen]ts are reduced to mere skeletons & are completely tired out—they need rest and filling up. The new rgts are not fit for the field . . . Cavalry & artillery horses are broken down—so it goes." The scene seemed set for a decisive confrontation, but the President was a gifted politician and displayed his disarming charm. Even though he apparently told McClellan to his face that he was "over-cautious," the general reported to his wife after Lincoln left, "The Pres[i]d[en]t was very kind personally—told me he was convinced I was the best general in the country . . . He was very affable & I really think he does feel very kindly towards me personally." McClellan decided to do his best "to hit upon some plan of campaign . . . to drive the rebels entirely away from this part of the country forever."

The commander in chief returned to Washington and grew irritable and sarcastic—a rare mood and unusual tone for this man who generally held tight rein on his temper. On October 6 General Halleck telegraphed McClellan at Lincoln's direction to order him to "cross the Potomac and give battle to the enemy or drive him south." "The President advises the interior line between Washington and the enemy, but does not order it," Halleck added, using Lincoln's newly learned military vocabulary. Lincoln grew testy with everyone, rebuking Henry Clay's son Thomas when he requested as a favor the reassignment of a division to Kentucky on the grounds that the men deserved it for recent hard-marching. "You *can not* have reflected seriously," Lincoln chided with unusual pique; others marched hard, too, and "the precedent . . . would instantly break up the whole army . . . I sincerely wish war was an easier and pleasanter business than it is; but it does not admit of holy-days."

Meanwhile, McClellan had decided not to take the interior line, and on the seventh he explained that to Halleck. He also explained why pursuit of Lee at this point seemed impossible. He lacked wagons and horses enough to supply his army over more than twenty or twenty-five miles and would be forced to abandon the campaign to link up with a rail or sea supply source. If this was true on the seventh of the month, it had probably been true on the fourth, when he saw the President. McClellan should have told Lincoln then, or, if he had not yet figured it out, he should have been thinking about it earlier rather than spending his time preparing his official report of the Battle of Antietam. He spent one day working on a preliminary report and another riding over the ground again for the final report. Stonewall Jackson turned his reports in late.

On the 13th McClellan had to inform his superiors that Confederate cavalry under J. E. B. Stuart had completed a full circuit around the Army of the Potomac (Stuart had done this to McClellan once before, in June). "The President has read your telegram," replied Halleck, "and directs me to suggest that, if the enemy had more occupation south of the river, his cavalry would not be so likely to make raids north of it." Lincoln had clearly decided that charm and flattery would not work. But withering scorn surely offered no long-range solution to the problem of communication, either. "Are you not over-cautious," Lincoln now asked tellingly in a very long letter written that same day, "when you assume that you can not do what the enemy is constantly doing? Should you not claim to be at least his equal in prowess, and act upon that claim?" Lincoln had been studying maps closely and knew that McClellan was now effectively closer to Richmond than the enemy was. "It is all easy," Lincoln insisted, "if our troops march as well as the enemy; and it is unmanly to say they can not do it." In an era of rigid gender roles, "unmanly," now an almost antique term, constituted strong language.

McClellan promised to give the President's "views the fullest & most unprejudiced consideration . . . it is my intention to advance the moment my men are shod & my cavalry are sufficiently remounted to be serviceable." To the layman such a response may seem insubordinate. But relations between statesmen and soldiers are different from those between statesmen and other members of the government, as General Frederick Maurice observed in 1926: "The civil servant can be trusted to carry out the plans of the Government, even when he does not agree with them, and after he has expressed that disagreement to his political chief. But a soldier in war cannot do the same . . . It is not in human nature for a man to prosecute wholeheartedly a plan which involves great risks and the lives of others, if he does not believe in it absolutely."

Lincoln wrote one of the few ill-tempered and mean-spirited letters of his life on October 25 after reading a dispatch from McClellan showing that pursuit still remained impossible because his cavalry was overworked. The general had forwarded as evidence a report from a Massachusetts cavalry colonel saying that almost half of his regiment's horses were "positively and absolutely unable to leave the camp, from the following causes, viz, sore-tongue . . . lameness, and sore backs." "I have just read your despatch about sore tongued and fatiegued horses," Lincoln responded. "Will you pardon me for asking what the horses of your army have done since the battle of Antietam that fatigue anything?" McClellan explained calmly that the cavalry had been "constantly employed in making reconnaissances, scouting, picketing." Eventually, Lincoln appeared to insult the U.S. cavalry by saying that Stuart's had "outmarched" it, and McClellan begged to differ. The President apologized and admitted "something of impatience" had crept into his dispatches. But he still referred bitterly to the "more than five weeks total inaction of the Army." McClellan's army at last crossed the Potomac on November 1, but Lincoln had had enough. In a politically timed move, he relieved the general on November 5 (after election day so as not to upset Democrats) and replaced him with Ambrose Burnside, who, in McClellan's estimation, was not competent to command anything larger than a regiment (1,000 men).

In dealing with General McClellan, Lincoln learned that certain factors in war affected friend and foe alike and that it was wrong to dwell exclusively on their effects on one's own forces. Lincoln told McClellan on October 13, 1862, "One of the standard maxims of war, as you know, is 'to operate upon the enemy's communications as much as possible without exposing your own.' You seem to act as if this applies *against* you, but can not apply in your *favor*." Where McClellan's attitude proved most exasperating was in the question of pursuit of defeated enemies. Lincoln's disagreement with McClellan on this score after the Battle of Antietam is now legendary—hence the fame of the "sore-tongued horses" letter. Lincoln was little impressed by protestations about tired horses when he knew that the defeated enemy's horses had to be at least as tired and its armies demoralized in the bargain.

For his part, the commander in chief had made his fair share of mistakes in the first year and a half of war, as he was always willing to admit. Ulysses S. Grant, who first met the President in March 1864, recalled that Lincoln

> stated to me that he had never professed to be a military man or to know how campaigns should be conducted, and never wanted to interfere in them; but that procrastination on the part of commanders, and the pressure from the people at the North and Congress, *which was always with him,* forced him into issuing his series of 'Military Orders' . . . He did not know but they were all wrong, and did know that some of them were. All he wanted or had ever wanted was some one who would take the responsibility and act, and call on him for all the assistance needed, pledging himself to use all the power of the government in rendering such assistance.

Grant's recollection has an authentic ring to it, echoing the language Lincoln had used while McClellan was moving slowly up the Peninsula:

> It is indispensable to *you* that you strike a blow. *I* am powerless to help this. You will do me the justice to remember I always insisted, that going down the Bay in search of a field, instead of fighting at or near Manassas, was only shifting, and not surmounting, a difficulty—that we would find the same enemy, and the same, or equal, intrenchments, at either place. The country will not fail to note—is now noting—that the present hesitation to move upon an intrenched enemy, is but the story of Manassas repeated. I beg to assure you that I have never written you, or spoken to you, in greater kindness of feeling than now, nor with a fuller purpose to sustain you, so far as in my most anxious judgment, I consistently can. *But you must act.*

Lincoln despised avoiding rather than surmounting difficulties—it was the same offense he had accused his shiftless stepbrother of committing. It constituted, as Grant remembered Lincoln's phrase, "procrastination." This was a characteristic way for Lincoln to think. But the analogy between enterprise in private life and in war was perhaps imperfect. Such an outlook underestimated the value of maneuver and risked headlong attack of the foolish sort indulged in by Burnside, McClellan's successor, at Fredericksburg in December 1862, when against the advice of junior officers on the ground he ordered frontal assaults uphill across open ground against well-protected Confederate infantry and artillery.

Whatever Lincoln's mistakes, he had gained a profound grasp of war by the time of the Battle of Fredericksburg. Put simply, Lincoln understood the essential nature of war as it had to be fought before the germ theory of disease. Of course, he could not have phrased his understanding in this anachronistic manner, but he did know that losses to disease in camp and on campaign exceeded those incurred on the battlefield. He revealed his outlook in a statement made to his office secretaries during the gloomy aftermath of the Battle of Fredericksburg. As one of his secretaries, William O. Stoddard, recalled the scene,

> We lost fifty per cent more men than did the enemy, and yet there is sense in the awful arithmetic propounded by Mr. Lincoln. He says that if the same battle were to be fought over again, every day, through a week of days, with the same relative results, the army under Lee would be wiped out to its last man, the Army of the Potomac would still be a mighty host, the war would be over, the Confederacy gone, and peace would be won at a smaller cost of life than it will be if the week of lost battles must be dragged out through yet another year of camps and marches, and of deaths in hospitals rather than upon the field. No general yet found can face the arithmetic, but the end of the war will be at hand when he shall be discovered.

Nevertheless, Fredericksburg left even Lincoln a little gun-shy. "Be cautious," he told Burnside in January. And when he continued his search for a pugnacious general who would bring the nation victories, replacing Burnside with Joseph Hooker later that month, he cautioned the new commander to "avoid rashness."

This was but a temporary condition with the President. Lincoln had demonstrated from the start a quality that is not easily squared with his kind and forgiving nature—he possessed an instinct for the jugular. He found it easier than other statesmen to sort out the essential and the unessential in war aims. Unlike Jefferson Davis, Lincoln did not fret about all the property and territory the President was ideally supposed to protect. When a naval blockade required most of the navy's ships and thus meant that the U.S. merchant marine was un-protected on the high seas and at the mercy of a handful of Confed-erate commerce raiders like the *Alabama* and the *Florida,* Lincoln did not lose sleep over the plight of his country's helpless carrying trade. He felt the blockade was essential to defeat the Confederacy (and as a result the American merchant marine was essentially driven from the seas and replaced by neutral British ships).

Likewise, he could leave substantial land areas to their fate—Mis-souri, for example. Early in 1861 Francis P. Blair, Jr., and General Nathaniel Lyon accomplished a coup d'état in Missouri by driving the pro-Confederate government out of Jefferson City despite their being the duly elected representatives of the Missouri people. That bold move helped secure the upper Mississippi River. In deference to border state public opinion, President Lincoln revoked John C. Frémont's premature emancipation proclamation for Missouri on September 11, 1861. A foolish Confederate invasion of Kentucky on September 3, 1861, which drove that wavering slave state into the arms of the Union, further insured the upper Mississippi. Once those objectives were attained, Missouri became unimportant to Union strategy, but the state still held many citizens of southern leanings under an illegal pro-Union government. Lincoln left pacification and defense to in-competent local militias and other nearby forces, including some from neighboring rival Kansas, that often nursed grudges against southern sympathizers. The result was the worst daily guerrilla excesses of the whole Civil War: terrorism, robbery, extortion, murder of civilians, arson, and mutilation of corpses.

Because of what Lincoln called, in resignation, "Missouri troubles," he came to endorse the single most controversial order of the war, General Orders No. 11. General Thomas Ewing issued the order on August 25, 1863, in retaliation for a raid on Lawrence, Kansas, led by the Confederate guerrilla William C. Quantrill. Quantrill's attack resulted in the slaughter of over 180 civilian men and boys. In response Ewing essentially decreed the evacuation of four Missouri counties on the Kansas border where Quantrill usually recruited his men, creating perhaps 20,000 refugees. It embittered even moderate men in Missouri, like the great American painter George Caleb Bingham, a pro-Union Missourian, who later painted a large, melodramatic canvas depicting a scene of murder and dislocation under the orders. On October 1, 1863, less than six weeks after Ewing's order, the President had written: "With the matters of removing the inhabitants of certain counties *en masse;* and of removing certain individuals from time to time, who are supposed to be mischievous, I am not now interfering, but am leaving to your own discretion." Lincoln left too much to unwise local discretion in Missouri and focused his attention farther south because after 1861 Missouri was largely irrelevant to the fate of the Union.

As he grew more experienced, Lincoln successfully created a command structure, developed a grasp of military theory, as embodied in ideas like "interior lines" and "concentration of force," and made increasingly accurate judgments of the fighting qualities of the available generals. Equally important, he did not neglect the western theater of war. Personal experience as a flatboatman and the initial strategic plan drawn up by General Winfield Scott conspired to make Lincoln aware of the importance of the Mississippi Valley. Scott had proposed the "Anaconda Plan" to seize the Mississippi River, blockade the southern ports, and strangle the Confederacy. It was too passive to accomplish the necessary goals of a war against secession, but Lincoln learned from it that the commander in chief must look to all fronts.

And Lincoln did. His decision to bring Henry W. Halleck to Washington as general-in-chief in 1862, though not particularly successful in gaining strategic direction for military campaigns, did have the effect of putting in place someone who felt the importance of the western theater and had the President's ear. Halleck did not believe that the United States could take Richmond without so concentrating forces as to leave Washington defenseless. The resulting "swapping of queens," to use Robert E. Lee's chess analogy, would not accomplish anything decisive, but Halleck did think that conquering vast areas of the western Confederacy would deprive the South of its essential breadbasket. Given his prominent place in the command hierarchy, Halleck helped keep the administration from too great a preoccupation with the East.

Well before Henry Halleck was summoned to Washington, the President had shown his concern with the western theater. Indeed, Lincoln's first known statement of the strategic view that would prevail in the overall northern war effort came in a letter to a general in the West, Don Carlos Buell:

> I state my general idea of this war to be that we have the *greater* numbers, and the enemy has the *greater* facility of concentrating forces upon points of collision; that we must fail, unless we can find some way of making *our* advantage an over-match for his; and that this can only be done by menacing him with superior forces at *different* points, at the *same* time; so that we can safely attack, one, or both, if he makes no change; and if he *weakens* one to *strengthen* the other, forbear to attack the strengthened one, but seize, and hold the weakened one, gaining so much.

The President realized the possible practical shortcomings of so highly theoretical a formulation. "In application of the general rule I am suggesting," Lincoln added, "every particular case will have its modifying circumstances, among which the most constantly present, and most difficult to meet, will be the want of perfect knowledge of the enemies' movements." Yet, Lincoln never visited the western front, though he visited the armies in the East several times.

General Halleck's presence in Washington meant not only that the West gained full representation in strategic councils but also that General Ulysses S. Grant did not have to share whatever military glory he won with a superior. If he could gain control of the Mississippi River by capturing Vicksburg, there would be much glory indeed. His campaign, beginning as early as the winter of 1862–1863 and continuing into spring and summer, was impeded by the impossibly swampy terrain to the north of Vicksburg. That was the direction from which he must approach as he advanced from Tennessee—and from which the Confederates expected attack—unless he could somehow get his army south of the city. After several schemes failed, Grant relied on the Navy to run its ships past the Vicksburg forts. Then he marched his army down the *west* side of the river, met the Navy vessels which in turn carried his army back to the Vicksburg side of the great river, and marched northeast across dry terrain. He laid siege from reasonably dry approaches to the fortress city. On July 4, 1863, the Confederate army in Vicksburg surrendered.

Nine days later Lincoln wrote Grant:

> When you first reached the vicinity of Vicksburg, I thought you should do, what you finally did—march the troops across the neck, run the batteries with the transports, and thus go below; and I never had any faith, except a general hope that you knew better than I, that the Yazoo Pass expedition, and the like, could succeed. When you got below, and took Port-Gibson, Grand Gulf, and vicinity, I thought you should go down the river and join Gen. Banks; and when you turned Northward East of the Big Black, I feared it was a mistake. I now wish to make the personal acknowledgment that you were right, and I was wrong.

Such letters from Presidents to subordinates are rare, and there is no counterpart in Jefferson Davis's correspondence. Yet for all the letter's many commendable qualities, it does reveal perhaps a little more tendency to passiveness on Lincoln's part in dealing with the West than with the East.

There were many important differences between the western and eastern theaters but none more important than the presence of Robert E. Lee in the East. Lincoln stood in awe of no man—no political rival and no military opponent, with the possible exception of "Stonewall" Jackson, whose unchivalric Cromwellian fanaticism fascinated even northern abolitionists like the Quaker poet John Greenleaf Whittier. But for Lincoln the great Robert E. Lee remained only "Bobby Lee."

Many Union generals saw the enemy differently. Up close, Lee looked frightening. He was unpredictable and fearless. Lee made most of them worry, as Ulysses Grant learned in 1864 when he came east to take command. When a Union general, familiar with Lee's bold methods, warned the newly arrived Grant at the Battle of the Wilderness in May 1864 that the Confederate leader might "throw his whole army between us and the Rapidan, and cut us off completely from our communications," Grant showed rare animation. "Oh," he said, "I am heartily tired of hearing what Lee is going to do. Some of you always seem to think he is suddenly going to turn a double somersault, and land in our rear and on both of our flanks at the same time. Go back to your command, and try to think what we are going to do ourselves, instead of what Lee is going to do."

Before Grant's arrival, battlefield victories against Robert E. Lee's Army of Northern Virginia had been rare enough to bring any Union general fame, whatever happened on the morrow. George B. McClellan managed to ride his reputation, gained mainly by turning Lee back once, at Antietam in 1862, to the Democratic nomination for President two years later. General George Gordon Meade could hardly believe his good fortune in besting Lee at Gettysburg in 1863, and the Army of the Potomac's long record of previous failures left in Meade a disposition to "sit on his lead," so to speak. He did not really want to tangle with Lee again, despite the Confederate general's situation, defeated and with his back to a river, which appeared quite precarious to Lincoln.

Lincoln exploded in exasperation when he read Meade's July 4th order congratulating the army on its victory at Gettysburg of the previous day. "Our task is not yet accomplished," Meade had written, "and the commanding general looks to the army for greater efforts to drive from our soil every vestige of the presence of the invader." To Lincoln, Meade's routine exhortation accidentally revealed a shocking gap between the general's goals and the President's. Lincoln wrote General Halleck, "You know I did not like the phrase . . . 'Drive the invaders from our soil' . . . These things all appear to me to be connected with a purpose to cover Baltimore and Washington, and to get the enemy across the river again without a further collision, and they do not appear connected with a purpose to prevent his crossing and to destroy him." "Please look to it," Lincoln implored. The next day, he found an excuse to say the same thing again. He told General Halleck, "We have certain information that Vicksburg surrendered to General Grant on the 4th of July. Now, if General Meade can complete his work, so gloriously prosecuted thus far, by the literal or substantial destruction of Lee's army, the rebellion will be over." Lee's army crossed the river, and the Battle of Gettysburg, instead of being a decisive battle to end the war, was to be rated a mere turning point of the war. In an angry letter to Meade (he chose in the end not to send it) the President said, "You fought and beat the enemy at Get-tysburg; and, of course, to say the least, his loss was as great as yours. He retreated; and you did not, as it seemed to me, pressingly pursue him." To this day military historians share Lincoln's puzzlement at the nearly chronic inability of Civil War armies effectively to pursue defeated enemies.

Many of the important duties of the commander in chief cannot be described in discussions of strategy alone. Where military and political matters intersected, the President, naturally, caught on quickly. Thus Lincoln understood perfectly the large manpower demands of armies in the Civil War. As he explained to the Frenchman Gasparin after McClellan's failures before Richmond in the summer of 1862, "With us every soldier is a man of character and must be treated with more consideration than is customary in Europe. Hence our great army for slighter causes than could have prevailed there has dwindled rapidly, bringing the necessity for a new call, earlier than was anticipated." Lincoln's philosophical acceptance of lack of discipline differed sharply from the stern reaction of professional soldiers. General-in-Chief Halleck, in a dyspeptic report on army operations in the fall of 1862, noted that "absenteeism" in the Union army was high. Straggling and desertion could be remedied best, he said, by "severe and summary punishment inflicted on the spot." "In this and many other important particulars," Halleck went on, "our military laws require revision and amendment. They were mostly enacted for a small army and for times of peace, and are unsuited to the government of the army we now have and the war in which we are now engaged."

Despite his initial insecurity about military matters, Lincoln never sought advice about war from his cabinet or other politicians. *He* was the commander in chief, and Lincoln seemed to interpret that title as meaning that war, even in a republic, required unitary control, and in this republic it was the President's duty to exercise it. His approach differed markedly from that of President Polk, who had held cabinet meetings where proposed strategies for the Mexican War were gone over paragraph by paragraph and who sometimes sought decisions on the best plan by majority vote of his cabinet.

When it came to war, the duties of a head of a republic resembled those of most heads of state in the middle of the nineteenth century, and like them, Lincoln held some rather antique notions of his duty. He came close as well to the ideas of the founders of the republic, who seem to have conceived of the commander in chief as an actual battlefield commander, like George Washington. On occasion President Lincoln almost saw his task as literally taking command in the field. He did directly oversee a small campaign in Norfolk, Virginia, in the spring of 1862. Other leaders of the era exhibited similar behavior in war. Jefferson Davis impetuously rushed to the Bull Run battlefield on horseback in 1861, but arrived too late to play any role in the battle. In the previous decade Napoleon III had led French armies in the wars of Italian unification, but he had a special need to live up to his notorious name. In the decade following the Civil War, Bismarck and Wilhelm I both accompanied German troops on their campaigns in France in the Franco-Prussian War, and Napoleon III was taken as a prisoner of war in that conflict.

As for the acknowledged powers of the commander in chief to choose the highest-ranking generals, Lincoln exercised them without hesitation or political advice. On August 31, 1862, while Washington, D.C., remained unsure of the fate of Union General John Pope's army at the Second Battle of Bull Run, Secretary of War Stanton and Secretary of the Treasury Chase began circulating a protest among the

cabinet demanding the dismissal of General McClellan, still commanding another Union force in Virginia. The next day was Tuesday, and
at the regular cabinet meeting Lincoln announced that McClellan had
been appointed to replace Pope and control all Union forces in Virginia. The President had consulted with General-in-Chief Halleck but
not with any member of his cabinet, including the Secretary of War.
Chase grumbled to Secretary of the Navy Welles, "Conversations
amounted to but little with the President on subjects of this importance . . . It was like throwing water on a duck's back." On this score
Lincoln never changed. By the end of the year Lincoln had lost
confidence in Halleck too and made decisions without any advice at
all. On January 1, 1863, having asked for his views on a strategic
question, Lincoln wrote Halleck bluntly, "If in such a difficulty as this
you do not help, you fail me precisely in the point for which I sought
your assistance . . . Your military skill is useless to me, if you will not
do this." Halleck tended to supply information rather than advice and
often evaded responsibility. When Lincoln selected Joseph Hooker to
replace General Burnside on January 26, 1863, he made the decision
alone and in a matter of hours. "The removal of General Burnside and
appointment of General Hooker was the sole act of the President,"
Halleck said later. "My advice was not asked at all in the matter and
I gave no opinion whatever."

Willing assumption of vast responsibility was a trait Lincoln had long
admired. He could not help respecting it even in political adversaries,
like Andrew Jackson. As early as 1849 Lincoln understood that a
President "must occasionally say, or seem to say, 'By the Eternal,' 'I
take the responsibility.' Those phrases were the 'Samson's locks' of
Gen. Jackson, and we dare not disregard the lessons of experience."
Such assertions of authority at least guaranteed popularity, if not
wisdom. "It is said Gen. [Zachary] Taylor and his officers held a
council of war, at Palo Alto . . . and that he then fought the battle
against unanimous opinion of those officers. This fact (no matter
whether rightfully or wrongfully) gives him more popularity than ten
thousand submissions, however really wise and magnanimous those

submissions may be." Lincoln shared this trait with Grant. The general once told his staff:

> I never held what might be called formal councils of war, and I do not believe in them. They create a divided responsibility, and at times prevent that unity of action so necessary in the field . . . I believe it is better for a commander charged with the responsibility of all the operations of his army to consult his generals freely but informally, get their views and opinions, and then make up his mind what action to take, and act accordingly. There is too much truth in the old adage, "Councils of war do not fight."

War seemed a simple enterprise with clear measures of success and failure. Lincoln usually discounted its moral dimension, especially because superior materiel resources and population were the North's undeniable advantage. Besides, Lincoln knew that both sides prayed to the same God, and he was never prone to the radical Republican or partisan fallacy of believing that superior generalship—a sincere zeal to beat the enemy—came from moral conviction that one's cause was superior. Thus in commenting to Gasparin about McClellan's failure in the Seven Days' Battles before Richmond back in the summer of 1862, Lincoln had said, "The moral effect was the worst of the affair before Richmond; and that has run its course downward; we are now at a stand, and shall soon be rising again, as we hope. I believe it is true that in men and material, the enemy suffered more than we, in that series of conflicts; while it is certain he is less able to bear it." It seemed "unreasonable," Lincoln complained, that this "single half-defeat should hurt us so much."

Lincoln did not otherwise see war as a complex cultural phenomenon with a historical dimension. One cannot imagine Lincoln's matching Jefferson Davis's speech, delivered after the fall of Atlanta, in which the Confederate President declared that Sherman's army would have to retreat or starve and that if he retreated, it would prove more disastrous than Napoleon's retreat from Moscow. Grant, who, like Lincoln, was interested only in the practical side of war, said, after reading about Davis's speech in southern newspapers, "Mr. Davis has not made it quite plain who is to furnish the snow for this Moscow retreat through Georgia and Tennessee." Lincoln knew the details of the Battle of Waterloo too and, to make a political point before the war, once referred to an anecdote about the French cavalry charging the British infantry squares, but he never mentioned the battle during the war. More typical of the era was Confederate General P. G. T. Beauregard's remark to a council of officers on the eve of the First Battle of Bull Run, "Now, gentlemen, let to-morrow be their Waterloo." Lincoln did not make historical allusions, and the metaphors he lent to descriptions of war came from the barnyard.

By the summer of 1864 the congruence of the President's thinking with the strategy of his general-in-chief is striking. Having engaged Robert E. Lee for the better part of the month of May in the campaigns of the Wilderness and Spotsylvania, Grant was contemplating his next move in early June. The initiative remained his, and Grant could choose attack or maneuver. The strategy of attack might force Lee back into Richmond and cause the Confederate capital and the Confederate government to fall without a lengthy siege. The strategy of maneuver would mean crossing the James River and capturing Petersburg, which lies well south of Richmond, in order to close off the principal rail supply route to the capital. As Horace Porter, who served on Grant's staff at the time, recalled:

> The general considered the question not only from a military standpoint, but he took a still broader view of the situation. The expenses of the war had reached nearly four million dollars a day. Many of the people in the North were becoming discouraged at the prolongation of the contest. If the army were transferred south of the James without fighting a battle on the north side, people would be impatient at the prospect of an apparently indefinite continuation of operations; and as the sickly season of summer was approaching, the deaths from disease among the troops meanwhile would be greater than any possible loss encountered in the contemplated attack.

This assault, a shockingly bloody one on Cold Harbor on June 3, 1864, failed, and Grant lost 7,000 men before lunchtime, to the Confederates' 1,500. But Lincoln and Grant were bound to continue the offensive; even bloody assaults might be more economical of lives than long campaigns with their deaths from camp diseases. Grant felt this imperative especially because he believed the southerners, who were acclimated to the warmer regions, were more resistant to the diseases of the "sickly season" and delay therefore played to their relative advantage.

Lincoln and Grant agreed not only on the importance of attack but also on the practical outlines of a grand strategy that would finally counter the Confederacy's advantage of interior lines. As General Porter explained it,

> General Grant felt, as he afterward expressed it in his official report, that our armies had acted heretofore too independently of one an-other—"without concert, like a balky team, no two ever pulling together." To obviate this, he had made up his mind to launch all his armies against the Confederacy at the same time, to give the enemy no rest, and to allow him no opportunity to reinforce any of his armies by troops which were not themselves confronted by Union forces.

Grant liked the homely way Lincoln had expressed the idea (making it seem as though his untutored frontier mind had perceived the essentials of the military expert's wisdom). John Hay recalled the scene in a diary entry for April 30, 1864:

> The President has been powerfully reminded, by General Grant's present movements and plans, of his . . . old suggestion so constantly made and as constantly neglected, to Buell & Halleck, et al., to move at once upon the enemy's whole line so as to bring into action to our advantage our great superiority in numbers. Otherwise by inte-rior lines & control of the interior railroad system the enemy can shift their men rapidly from one point to another as they may be

required. In this concerted movement, however, great superiority of numbers must tell: as the enemy, however successful where he concentrates, must necessarily weaken other portions of his line and lose important positions. This idea of his own, the Pres[iden]t recognized with especial pleasure when Grant said it was his intention to make all the line useful—those not fighting could help the fighting. "Those not skinning can hold a leg," added his distinguished interlocutor.

If such ideas revealed a mastery of the strategic principles of nineteenth-century warfare, neither Grant nor Lincoln, it must be said, initially grasped the military genius of William T. Sherman's famous March to the Sea. Grant quizzed Sherman on the scheme mercilessly while the Georgia campaign was in the planning stage, and Lincoln withheld judgment (and faith in its success) until the end. The President did have the humility and candor to admit to Sherman, after the general succeeded, that he had been wrong. After Sherman had captured Savannah in December 1864, Lincoln wrote:

> Many, many, thanks for your Christmas gift—the capture of Savannah. When you were about leaving Atlanta for the Atlantic coast, I was *anxious*, if not fearful; but feeling that you were the better judge, and remembering that "nothing risked, nothing gained" I did not interfere. Now, the undertaking being a success, the honor is all yours; for I believe none of us went farther than to acquiesce. And, taking the work of Gen. [George H.] Thomas [victor at the recent Battle of Nashville] into the count, as it should be taken, it is indeed a great success. Not only does it afford the obvious and immediate military advantages; but, in showing to the world that your army could be divided, putting the stronger part to an important new service, and yet leaving enough to vanquish the old opposing force of the whole—[John Bell] Hood's army—it brings those who sat in darkness, to see a great light. But what next?

Sherman already had the next step in mind, a similar march through the symbolic capital of secession, South Carolina, and then across North Carolina to join Grant in Virginia. Grant could not understand the point of this plan either at first and wanted to bring Sherman's army by ship from Savannah, until he learned that not enough naval transports were immediately available.

Thus Lincoln grasped only after the campaign was over what many regard as the most important military innovation of the Civil War, and Grant had not understood it even then, or he would surely not have opposed the subsequent Carolinas campaign. The idea that marching an army unopposed through the enemy's heartland would undermine Confederate morale and demonstrate to the world at large that the South could not fulfill the most elementary requirement of nationhood, defending its people from invasion, apparently had too much of a psychological element to be readily understood in its time.

Even Sherman himself did not fully comprehend it. When he wrote his memoirs after the war, he laid no claim to having devised new forms of warfare, and he particularly denied the novelty of the March to the Sea. He maintained that all he had done was to change his base of supply from Atlanta, with its perilous single rail line prone to disruption by the Confederacy's skilled cavalry, to Savannah, where Union naval superiority guaranteed supplies from the sea routes. Although the march had been destructive, neither Sherman nor Lincoln laid emphasis on that aspect of the campaign. Lincoln was not squeamish, and kidded with Sherman about the inglorious exploits of his "bummers" who confiscated supplies from southern civilians on the march route, but destructiveness simply was not the point of the campaign. "Mere" destruction of Georgia, as Sherman on September 20, 1864, put it, without an ultimate military goal such as establishing a secure base of supply, would not be "productive of much good. I can start east and make a circuit south and back, doing vast damage to the State, but resulting in no permanent good." On November 6, 1864, he explained to Grant:

> If we can march a well-appointed army right through his territory, it is a demonstration to the world, foreign and domestic, that we have a power which Davis cannot resist. This may not be war, but rather statesmanship . . . If the North can march an army right through the

south, it is proof positive that the North can prevail in this contest, leaving only open the question of its willingness to use that power . . . Now Mr. Lincoln's election, which is assured . . . makes a complete logical whole.

Sherman may have sensed that mere destructiveness would likely have proved counterproductive, stiffening instead of destroying civilian morale (as strategic bombing apparently did in World War II). In any event, the American Civil War was fought throughout the four years with the restraints traditional to mid-nineteenth-century warfare. As late as August 14, 1864, President Lincoln instructed General Grant to "confer with Gen. Lee and stipulate for a mutual discontinuance of house-burning and other destruction of private property."

Lincoln tried to question his generals rather than to nag them, but abstaining from letting his views be known, as in the case of Meade after Gettysburg, had often brought poor results. Toward the end of the war he had developed considerable finesse and acute judgment as to what approach to use with individual commanders and particular situations. He allowed Grant to pursue his improbable plan of campaign for Vicksburg. He permitted Sherman to march to the sea despite his personal doubts about the likelihood of success.

He also adopted subtlety in the case of Grant after the Battle of Cold Harbor, June 3, 1864. Lincoln came to Virginia to visit the armies on June 21. Two weeks earlier he had been renominated for the presidency, but he shrugged off questions from the generals about the election with a joke. "Among all our colleges," the President said, "the Electoral College is the only one where they choose their own masters." He seemed to the generals absorbed in the military rather than the political campaign, but on more than one occasion, when future battles were mentioned, Lincoln said, "I cannot pretend to advise, but I do sincerely hope that all may be accomplished with as little bloodshed as possible." Such a statement was more than an innocuous truism when pronounced *after* Cold Harbor *by* the commander in chief *to* his subordinate military officers. Lincoln must have sensed that Grant would be touchy on the subject of the disastrous Cold Harbor assault.

On less sensitive points Lincoln did not hesitate to put in his oar. When he saw Grant's orders sending General Philip H. Sheridan to the Shenandoah Valley to dispose of the Confederate army that had recently menaced Washington, D.C., the President sent Grant a letter (dated August 3, 1864):

I have seen your despatch in which you say, "I want Sheridan put in command of all the troops in the field, with instructions to put himself South of the enemy, and follow him to the death. Wherever the enemy goes, let our troops go also." This, I think, is exactly right, as to how our forces should move. But please look over the despatches you may have received from here, even since you made that order, and discover, if you can, that there is any idea in the head of any one here, of "putting our army *South* of the enemy," or of "following him to the *death*" in any direction. I repeat to you it will neither be done nor attempted unless you watch it every day, and hour, and force it.

Grant left immediately for the Valley and started asking questions.

A characteristic instance in which Lincoln asserted his views occurred in the fateful summer of 1864. Though it was a presidential election year and ominously close to the first anniversary of terrible riots in New York City against the draft, the President found it necessary to issue a new call for 500,000 men for the army. The proclamation was issued July 18 and stipulated that a draft would ensue on September 5 for those districts failing to reach their quotas in fifty days.

General Halleck was soon beset with fear. On August 11 he sent Grant a confidential letter, saying, "Pretty strong evidence is accumulating that there is a combination formed, or forming, to make a forcible resistance to the draft . . . To enforce it may require the withdrawal of a very considerable number of troops from the field . . . The evidence of this has increased very much within the last few days . . . Are not the appearances such that we ought to take in sail and prepare the ship for a storm?" Grant suggested other ways of meeting the emergency and would not budge from his siege in Virginia. Lincoln saw Grant's reply to Halleck and immediately scrawled a message himself: "I have seen your despatch expressing your unwillingness to break your hold where you are. Neither am I willing. Hold on with a bull-dog gripe, and chew & choke as much as possible." The telegram brought smiles to Grant's face. "The President has more nerve than any of his advisers," Grant commented. Lincoln once told John Hay, "I who am not a specially brave man have had to sustain the sinking courage of these professional fighters in critical times."

Generals like thus to be sheltered from what are essentially political questions, and Lincoln's clear-sighted unwillingness to allow partisan concerns to interfere with decisions critical to the army was an admirable trait crucial to winning a major war in a democracy. The politically unpopular draft was essential to the success of the army itself, and it was difficult to draw the line between politics and mobilization. The President had never been above seizing every available partisan advantage, and the war did not change him. On September 19, 1864, Lincoln wrote General Sherman the following letter:

> The State election of Indiana occurs on the 11th of October, and the loss of it to the friends of the Government would go far towards losing the whole Union cause. The bad effect upon the November election, and especially the giving the State Government to those who will oppose the war in every possible way, are too much to risk, if it can possibly be avoided. The draft proceeds, notwithstanding its strong tendency to lose us the State. Indiana is the only important State, voting in October whose soldiers cannot vote in the field. Any thing you can safely do to let her soldiers, or any part of them, go home and vote at the State election, will be greatly in point. They need not remain for the Presidential election, but may return to you at once. This is, in no sense, an order, but is merely intended to impress you with the importance, to the army itself, of your doing all you safely can, yourself being the judge of what you can safely do.

The President's language suggests that he knew of Sherman's diabolical hatred of politicians and politics.

William T. Sherman believed in a hard war and a soft peace. In later years, the general maintained that he took his cue on that point from Lincoln. In a conference with Sherman, General Grant, and Admiral David Dixon Porter held near the end of the war, Lincoln showed a characteristic lack of vengeful feelings. Sherman recalled:

> As to Jeff. Davis, he was hardly at liberty to speak his mind fully, but intimated that he ought to clear out, "escape the country," only it would not do for him to say so openly. As usual, he illustrated his meaning by a story: "A man once had taken the total-abstinence pledge. When visiting a friend, he was invited to take a drink, but declined, on the score of his pledge; when his friend suggested lemonade, which was accepted. In preparing the lemonade, the friend pointed to the brandy-bottle, and said the lemonade would be more palatable if he were to pour in a little brandy; when his guest said, if he could do so 'unbeknown' to him, he would not object." From which illustration I inferred that Mr. Lincoln wanted Davis to escape, "unbeknown" to him.

From such kernels of truth, and from deep political and cultural needs later in the century, arose the powerful southern myth that at the Hampton Roads peace conference of February 3, 1865, President Lincoln had told Confederate peace commissioners, "Let me write 'Union' at the top of that page, and you may write below it whatever else you please."

It was satisfying to southerners, dismayed by the new racial order in the postwar South but faced with Lincoln's towering reputation, to think that Lincoln, had he lived, would never have pursued emancipation so thoroughly and reconstructed the old states of the Confederacy. But the idea bore little relation to the realities of Lincoln's late life, and there is no proof that Lincoln said any such thing at Hampton Roads. He did apparently attempt to resurrect his old scheme for compensated emancipation, promising to draft a bill for compensation to any state that ratified the Thirteenth Amendment to the Constitution, abolishing slavery forever in the United States.

A countervailing myth now holds sway that argues the opposite point: that Lincoln insisted on "unconditional surrender" of the South. It was boosted by events in World War II and especially by President Franklin Delano Roosevelt, who like many twentieth-century Presidents, found that his own policies, if passed off as policies that Lincoln had pursued, became all the more palatable to American voters.

Though also bolstered by some facts—the Republican platform in 1864 called for unconditional surrender, for example—this myth is as false as the old southern one. As the war neared its end, Lincoln on several occasions wrote his peace terms down on paper. On July 9, 1864, he told Horace Greeley, who was on his way to Canada to meet Confederate commissioners, that he had two conditions for surrender: "If you can find, any person anywhere professing to have any proposition of Jefferson Davis in writing, for peace, embracing the restoration of the Union and abandonment of slavery, whatever else it embraces . . . he may come to me with you." As Union military fortunes sank later that summer, Lincoln drafted a letter for *New York Times* editor Henry J. Raymond, saying, "You will propose, on behalf [of] this government, that upon the restoration of the Union and the national authority, the war shall cease at once, all remaining questions to be left for adjustment by peaceful modes." Lincoln never completed this letter, and Raymond never used it; to give up on emancipation at that moment, of course, was to give up on something Lincoln thought lost anyway, if the Democrats won the election.

In his annual message to Congress of December 6, 1864, Lincoln stated "a single condition of peace," by which he meant "that the war will cease on the part of the government, whenever it shall have ceased on the part of those who began it." He explained that "if questions should remain, we would adjust them by the peaceful means of legislation, conference, courts, and votes, operating only in constitutional and lawful channels." He hastened to add that he retracted "nothing heretofore said as to slavery. I repeat the declaration made a year ago, that 'while I remain in my present position I shall not attempt to retract or modify the emancipation proclamation, nor shall I return to slavery any person who is free by the terms of that proclamation, or by any Act of Congress.'" Finally, on January 31, 1865, Lincoln's instructions to Seward for the Hampton Roads meeting insisted on emancipation and Union but added a new condition: "No cessation of hostilities short of an end of the war, and the disbanding of all forces hostile to the government." But he still said "that all propositions . . . not inconsistent with the above, will be considered and passed upon in a spirit of liberality."

The real focus on problems of peace should be on Jefferson Davis, not Abraham Lincoln. At the end, as at the beginning, the decision for peace or war lay in the Confederate President's hands. By the summer of 1864 if not earlier, any realistic Confederate strategy for victory required the Democrats to win the presidential election in the North. In his memoirs, Davis recalled, "Political developments at the North [in 1864] . . . favored the adoption of some action that might influence popular sentiment in the hostile section. The aspect of the peace party was quite encouraging, and it seemed that the real issue to be decided in the Presidential election of that year was the continuance or cessation of the war." Confederate agents operating from Canada, however, were never able to organize any significant peace movement in the North, and the election went to Lincoln.

At that point Jefferson Davis should have sued for peace. The Confederacy's last chance, if any, to win the war had passed on election day. The Confederate peace movement was large enough by then that the President would have encountered little political resistance from civilian leaders in the South. And the army was probably amenable, too. Robert E. Lee had long since premised any hope of Confederate victory on military successes in the field *and* the elimination of the Republicans in the northern election of 1864. Back in the spring of 1863, at the height of Confederate optimism, Lee had written his wife to say that the Confederacy must "establish" their "supplies on a firm basis" in 1863 and then, "if successful this year, next fall there will be a great change in public opinion at the North. The Republicans will be destroyed & I think the friends of peace will become so strong that the next administration will go in on that basis." That chance gone, Lee was probably ready to obey an order to lay down his arms.

But Jefferson Davis never gave such an order. Instead, after Sherman's capture of Atlanta and with Lincoln's reelection growing daily more certain, he continued to exhort the Confederacy to further efforts and pledged, "Every faculty of my head and my heart is devoted to your cause, and to that I shall, if necessary, give my life." No doubt he would have, but the Confederate people did not have to, and he should have taken them more into consideration. Not surrendering in 1864 was the Confederate President's worst decision as commander in chief.

Abraham Lincoln made no such mistakes. He may not have been, as one of his earliest admirers among British military historians put it, a "military genius." That term may best be reserved for General Sherman or some other Civil War military figure who still looms large in strategic discussions at West Point. But as commander in chief, who must combine military perception with political vision and the skillful handling of personalities, Lincoln had no superior in American history.

CHAPTER FOUR

Emancipation

The duties of commander in chief proved the most absorbing of the roles Abraham Lincoln assumed as President. A war threatening the existence of the United States and the survival of the republican example in the world dictated that importance, of course, but so did Lincoln's expansive interpretation of the powers that the commander in chief enjoyed. Under these, he greatly increased freedom for black Americans.

The framers of the Constitution meant the commander in chief's powers to be essentially "ministerial" in nature, having to do with the command and direction of the armed forces once war had begun. Declaring war (as Lincoln had asserted in the controversies surrounding the Mexican War), raising armies, and establishing the rules that governed the armed forces were regarded as congressional functions. Lincoln's problems tested the assumed boundaries of these powers.

President Lincoln's first message to Congress, a special session of which convened on July 4, 1861, expressed his dilemma:

This issue embraces more than the fate of these United States. It presents to the whole family of man, the question, whether a constitutional republic, or a democracy—a government of the people, by the same people—can, or cannot, maintain its territorial integrity, against its own domestic foes. It presents the question, whether discontented individuals, too few in numbers to control administration, according to organic law, in any case, can always . . . without any pretence, break up their Government, and thus practically put an end to free government upon the earth. It forces us to ask: "Is there, in all republics, this inherent, and fatal weakness?" "Must a government, of necessity, be too *strong* for the liberties of its own people, or too *weak* to maintain its own existence?"

Cheek by jowl with this ably rendered expression of the problem presented by secession lay the threatening term "war power": "So viewing the issue, no choice was left but to call out the war power of the Government; and so to resist force, employed for its destruction, by force, for its preservation."

Lincoln had written "military power" instead of "war power" in the original draft of this message, but he changed it, surely with an eye to broader powers than directing the operations of the soldiers. He had long since suspended the writ of habeas corpus, and he admitted in the message that

> other calls were made for . . . large additions to the regular Army and Navy. These measures, whether strictly legal or not, were ven-tured upon, under what appeared to be a popular demand, and a public necessity; trusting, then as now, that Congress would readily ratify them. It is believed that nothing has been done beyond the constitutional competency of Congress.

Whether the President could assume congressional powers if faced with an emergency when Congress was not in session was a contro-versial question. It would have stirred more controversy had the Democrats controlled Congress. In 1864 a humorous Democratic pamphlet called *The Lincoln Catechism* asked:

> Who invented the war power?
> Abraham Lincoln.
> . . . For what purpose did he invent the war power?
> That he might not have to return to the business of splitting rails.

In fact, Lincoln used the powers he found or "invented" exclusively at first to preserve the Union, to raise armies, and to combat traitors. Lincoln was not by nature either dictator or visionary reformer. He did not initially embrace the powers to maintain his own position in government or to attack slavery. He had long ago warned of the dangers of tyranny that lay in attempts to free the slaves. The black leader Frederick Douglass and other abolitionists during the Civil War grew painfully aware of his conservatism and thought they understood its source. Douglass reflected in 1876,

> He was pre-eminently the white man's President, entirely devoted to the welfare of white men. He was ready and willing at any time during the first years of his administration to deny, postpone, and sacrifice the rights of humanity in the colored people to promote the welfare of the white people of this country. In all his education and feeling he was an American of the Americans . . . We are at best only his step-children . . . the Union was to him more than our freedom or our future.

Douglass added, "Viewed from the genuine abolition ground, Mr. Lincoln seemed tardy, cold, dull, and indifferent; but measuring him by the sentiment of his country, a sentiment he was bound as a statesman to consult, he was swift, zealous, radical, and determined." Here in one speech by someone who knew Lincoln personally were presented both sides of the great man.

Abraham Lincoln was not a reformer by nature. He consistently minimized his role in bringing about great social change, laying responsibility for the rise of the slavery question on the Democratic party. He said that he had been more controlled by events than controlling them himself. And there was a sense in which this was true. Lincoln repeatedly vowed that he would not free slaves in any state. More important than words when dealing with politicians are actions, and President Lincoln's actions spoke eloquently: in 1861 he more than once actually forced others who were trying to free slaves to cease doing so. He could not stop Congress, but he regarded their tentative efforts as unenforceable and thought long and hard about vetoing one law that contained a provision to free the slaves of rebels.

Only dramatic changes in events beyond Lincoln's control altered his outlook. But once Lincoln changed his mind, he did everything himself. He resolved to issue the proclamation entirely on his own, and he wrote the first draft of the document by himself and in secret. Nobody forced him to do it. Nobody persuaded him. Lincoln did it.

In the late summer of 1861, however, Lincoln was as far from deciding to free the slaves as he had been back in 1838, when he had equated such an action with tyrannical impulses. When General John C. Frémont, on August 30, 1861, issued a proclamation freeing the slaves of rebels in Missouri, Lincoln intervened immediately, saying, "I think there is great danger that . . . liberating slaves of traiterous owners, will alarm our Southern Union friends, and turn them against us—perhaps ruin our rather fair prospect for Kentucky." Less than two weeks earlier, the President had been reminded of the fragility of loyalty in the Blue Grass State. Governor Beriah Magoffin had addressed him a short and peremptory note protesting the presence of Union troops in Kentucky "without the advice or consent of the Authorities of the State." The troops were all Kentuckians, Lincoln pointed out, and he had consulted many leaders from the state, including most of its congressional delegation, on the matter, and they had not protested.

More important, a policy of "neutrality" still prevailed in Kentucky, uneasily and unofficially observed by the Lincoln administration. The two antagonists, Lincoln and Jefferson Davis, were dancing gingerly around the state, trying not to scare it off to the other side. But the very day Lincoln wrote Frémont, Confederates invaded Kentucky, upsetting the balance and tipping it in the direction of the Union. Meanwhile, on September 8, Frémont refused to modify his proclamation without a direct order, and Lincoln gave that order on the 11th. On the same day the Kentucky legislature instructed Magoffin to order the Confederate forces to leave the state.

Lincoln had made clear the paramount reason for rescinding Frémont's proclamation—public opinion in Kentucky—but when an old friend from Illinois, Republican Senator Orville Hickman Browning, wrote to protest Lincoln's act, the President felt compelled to respond, in much the same way as he had lectured Herndon on the Mexican War years ago. "You must not understand I took my course on the proclamation *because* of Kentucky. I took the same ground in a private letter to General Frémont before I heard from Kentucky." But what the President meant by the phrase "because of Kentucky" in this instance was precise and a little misleading. He meant "because Kentuckians had protested to him." He had acted before any Kentuckians protested, but the reason he acted was Kentucky.

In the letter to Senator Browning, Lincoln adopted the for him unusual tack of addressing the constitutional question before the practical one:

Genl. Fremont's proclamation . . . is *purely political,* and not within the range of *military* law, or necessity. If a commanding General finds a necessity to seize the farm of a private owner, for a pasture, an encampment, or a fortification, he has the right to do so, and to so hold it, as long as the necessity lasts; and this is within military law, because within military necessity. But to say the farm shall no longer belong to the owner, or his heirs forever; and this as well when the farm is not needed for military purposes as when it is, is purely political, without the savor of military law about it. And the same is true of slaves. If the General needs them, he can seize them, and use them; but when the need is past, it is not for him to fix their permanent future condition. That must be settled according to laws made by law-makers, and not by military proclamations. The proclamation in the point in question, is simply "dictatorship" . . . I cannot assume this reckless position; nor allow others to assume it on my responsibility. You speak of it as being the only means of *saving* the government. On the contrary it is itself the surrender of the government. Can it be pretended that it is any longer the government of the U.S.—any government of Constitution and laws,—wherein a General, or a President, may make permanent rules of property by proclamation?

Here Lincoln showed that he still viewed the powers of the commander in chief substantially as the founders of the republic had. Generals and the commander in chief might impress property for temporary military purposes; but the permanent laws of property were matters for lawmakers.

If nothing else did, Lincoln's letter to Browning would forbid any easy characterization of Abraham Lincoln as a consistent and crusading emancipationist. When someone actually attempted to abolish slavery in the United States, for the first time in a generation, the man who would come to be called "the Great Emancipator" stopped him. It brought despair to antislavery partisans, like James Russell Lowell, who remarked wearily, "How many times are we to save Kentucky and lose our self respect?" Surprisingly, it also angered many moderate Republicans, like Browning, who shared the party's common antisouthern animus and loved emancipation for the enemies it made—the slavocracy.

The letter to Browning also greatly complicates any straightforward characterization of Lincoln as a careful steward of the Constitution. If Lincoln himself could construe issuing an emancipation proclamation as "dictatorship" in 1861, then little wonder the Democrats leveled the same charge at him when he issued such a proclamation himself one year later.

The letter, far from showing that Lincoln's ideas were fixed on a conservative policy, reveals that they were in flux. Lincoln had no firm constitutional ideas on the question, though he appeared at first to think emancipation was a legislative matter, if legal at all. To Browning he wrote:

I do not say Congress might not with propriety pass a law, on the point, just such as General Frémont proclaimed. I do not say I might not, as a member of Congress, vote for it. What I object to is, that I as President, shall expressly or impliedly seize and exercise the permanent legislative functions of the government.

Before the war no prominent Republican, least of all Lincoln, believed that Congress could pass a law emancipating slaves in any state. Lincoln had already come a long way.

Though his constitutional ideas may have been changing, Lincoln's actions continued to chart a conservative course on slavery. On May 9, 1862, General David Hunter issued a proclamation for the military department he commanded, including South Carolina, Georgia, and Florida (actually he controlled only tiny parcels of those states, of course), freeing the slaves there on the nonsensical grounds that "slavery and martial law in a free country are altogether incompatible." (Many American jurists regarded martial law itself as incompatible with a free country.) True to form, Lincoln revoked it by public proclamation. But the President took the occasion to urge his own plan for gradual abolition, with compensation, to be adopted by the slave states that were not "blind to the signs of the times."

Lincoln did not allow General Hunter to free any slaves, but he did proclaim some new and strange ideas. Lincoln no longer characterized emancipation as dictatorship. Instead, he said that he reserved the decision on slavery to himself because he could "not feel justified in leaving [it] to the decision of commanders in the field. These are totally different questions from those of police regulations in armies and camps." He completely abandoned any constitutional objections. Lincoln did not mention Congress, either (except to say that it endorsed his voluntary, compensated, and gradual emancipation scheme).

In fact, this proclamation, rescinding one emancipation proclamation, announced legal justification for another: "Whether it be competent for me, as Commander-in-Chief of the Army and Navy, to declare the Slaves of any state or states, free, and whether at any time, in any case, it shall have become a necessity indispensable to the maintenance of the government, to exercise such supposed power, are questions which, under my responsibility, I reserve to myself." Here was the first indication, public or private, that Lincoln thought slavery could be abolished under the powers of the commander in chief.

It may seem strange to modern readers that the army should play such a prominent role on the "cutting edge" of emancipation, ahead of the President and Congress. There were many reasons for this. Even the professional officer corps in the United States was imbued with republican values. Hunter himself was a West Point graduate. There were a few extreme reactionaries, like William T. Sherman, who despised politicians and the free press and equated democracy almost with anarchy, but most seem to have held ordinary political opinions without great intensity. Ulysses S. Grant, for example, had held Whiggishly antiwar views during his service in Mexico but proved to be a good soldier in that war anyway. His views on blacks and slavery were not strongly held, though he, like others in the officer class in the Western world, was tainted with anti-Semitism. George B. McClellan, who held more systematic and intense political opinions and was readily identifiable as a Democrat, nevertheless loyally issued an order for support of the Emancipation Proclamation after it was issued. And when he later lost the presidential election to Lincoln, he simply resigned his commission and returned to civilian life, accepting the people's verdict lawfully registered.

Moreover, the swollen volunteer armies of the Civil War embraced numerous officers who had previously been civilians all or most of their lives. Such men carried with them the customary range of political opinions found in the civilian populace—indeed many were called "political generals." In their ranks could be found old revolutionaries like the German-American Carl Schurz; abolitionists like James Wadsworth and Thomas Wentworth Higginson; temperance crusaders like Neal Dow; prominent politicians like Frémont and Nathaniel Banks; and clever political scamps like Benjamin F. Butler. Naturally, innovations in social policy were more likely to come from such men than from officers like Sherman and Grant.

Most important, however, were the physical location of the military men and the practical problems they faced. The army, unlike the

President and Congress, came into daily contact with slavery and had
to do something about it. Butler, a political general (but not a Republican), made the first attempt to deal with the presence of slaves in
Union lines. While commanding at Fortress Monroe in Virginia, three
escaped slaves came into Butler's camp. When their owner, a Confederate colonel, approached under a flag of truce to demand the return
of his property, Butler declared the slaves "contraband of war," retained them, and put them to work in his own camp. The joke lay in
the idea that "contraband" dealt with property useful to an enemy
belligerent, not with persons, and thus Butler was turning the southerners' definition of slaves as property against them. This occurred in
May 1861, at a time when the Lincoln administration had no defined
policy on the question of slaves encountered by Union forces. Butler's
action was not disallowed and thus, to some, became policy. Escaped
slaves became "contrabands" in slang for the rest of the Civil War.
Perhaps the generals like Frémont and Hunter, who later also took the
question into their own hands, had General Butler's popular success
in the backs of their minds.

When President Lincoln had pointed out to Gasparin that local
informants on enemy movements were a strategic strength of the
Confederacy, he ignored a compensating factor, "the reliable contrabands." The Confederacy was no monolith, and black people were the
members of that society most likely to collaborate with the enemy.
Blacks so frequently provided information that military men dubbed
them "reliable contrabands," a name applied in derision, because the
slaves, who were hardly privy to the secrets of Confederate strategy,
on occasion gave erroneous information. The racial attitudes of the
white Union soldiers made them quick to attribute mistaken information to stereotypical stupidity. Still, blacks remained a crucial source
of information about Confederate troop movements, fortifications,
and geography.

Some slaves not only helped the Union army but also helped themselves, seizing the initiative to realize their own freedom. Attempting
escape was always dangerous. If the absence of most young white males
away in military service offered opportunities for escape from planta-

tions, running away now carried with it the taint of treason, and punishment was likely to be severe. C. C. Jones, a Princeton-educated Presbyterian minister in Georgia, warned of the runaways, "They are traitors who may pilot an enemy into your *bedchamber!* They know every road and swamp and creek and plantation in the county, and are the worst of spies." They were not actually treated as traitors in law.

Only a courageous minority risked escape, and no one, then or since, has enumerated them. Lincoln estimated their number at 200,000 near the end of the war. Whatever the number, it was never high enough to suit the President, once the decision for emancipation was made.

Despite appearances fostered by the noisy Frémont and Hunter episodes, Lincoln in fact did not have as consistently conservative an early policy on slavery as it seemed. He did not rebuke Butler's "contraband" policy and attempted some innovative thinking of his own. In his annual message to Congress of December 3, 1861, Lincoln had sent the American public mixed signals. On the one hand, he warned against haste in deciding to resort to "radical and extreme measures, which may reach the loyal as well as the disloyal." On the other, he concluded the message with a reiteration of his argument for the superiority of free to slave labor, his capitalist assumptions once again put at the service of the antislavery movement. Labor, the President wrote, "is prior to, and independent of, capital. Capital is only the fruit of labor . . . Labor is the superior of capital, and deserves much the higher consideration." The hired laborer was not "fixed in that condition for life." Instead, free labor provided the dynamic of a progressive society:

> Many independent men everywhere in these States, a few years back in their lives, were hired laborers. The prudent, penniless beginner in the world, labors for wages awhile, saves a surplus with which to buy tools or land for himself; then labors on his own account another while, and at length hires another new beginner to help him. This is the just, and generous, and prosperous system, which opens the way to all—gives hope to all, and consequent energy, and progress, and

improvement of condition to all. No men living are more worthy to
be trusted than those who toil up from poverty—none less inclined
to take, or touch, aught which they have not honestly earned.

Of the free white men of the South, Lincoln warned, "Let them
beware of surrendering a political power which they already possess,
and which, if surrendered, will surely be used to close the door of
advancement against such as they, and to fix new disabilities and
burdens upon them, till all of liberty shall be lost." The President even
brought forth a novel antislavery suggestion: a proposal that slaves
from states that initiated voluntary emancipation schemes be accepted
in lieu of taxes.

He was careful to soothe any racial fears aroused by such antislavery
talk. Any freed slaves should be colonized "in a climate congenial to
them." "It might be well," Lincoln added ominously, "to consider,
too,—whether the free colored people already in the United States
could not, so far as individuals may desire, be included in such colonization."

Nothing came of any of this. Nor did the situation in the war change
dramatically. But in the ensuing period it could not be said that Lincoln
was guided entirely by events. For while events changed little, he
continued, if not to agitate the slave question, at least to experiment
with proposals that would alter the status quo.

With loyal border states now "unchangeably . . . ranged on the side
of the Union," Lincoln on March 6, 1862, addressed a special message
to Congress, urging pecuniary aid to any state that adopted gradual
abolishment of slavery. He suggested that the hope of gaining the loyal
border areas was all that sustained the rebellion, and that abolition in
Maryland, Kentucky, Delaware, and Missouri would "substantially"
snuff out that hope. Without going into details, Lincoln's message
stated that "any member of Congress, with the census-tables and
Treasury-reports before him, can readily see for himself how very soon
the current expenditures of this war would purchase, at fair valuation,
all the slaves in any named State." The *New York Times* nevertheless
criticized the message as well-intentioned but certain to fail because

of the expense. The President immediately wrote the editor, Henry J. Raymond, and said, "I do hope you will reconsider this. Have you noticed the facts that less than one half-day's cost of this war would pay for all the slaves in Delaware, at four hundred dollars per head?— that eighty-seven days cost of this war would pay for all in Delaware, Maryland, District of Columbia, Kentucky, and Missouri at the same price? Were those states to take the step, do you doubt that it would shorten the war more than eighty seven days, and thus be an actual saving of expense?" Raymond quickly explained that he had been away from the office when the article in question was written and said that he had telegraphed the office since, urging support of Lincoln's message without qualification. (Lincoln gave the government a bargain: the price of a prime field hand in the New Orleans market in 1860 was $1500!)

Lincoln realized fully the potential risks, "a total disruption of society in the South," that lay in interference with the institution of slavery, but he continued to tinker. Then despair accomplished what hope might never have achieved. By July 1862 Union fortunes had turned quite sour. McClellan's campaign in Virginia had failed, and the President was required to make a call on the first of the month for another 300,000 volunteers. With Confederate armies apparently concentrated for the defense of Richmond, Lincoln felt that with another 50,000 men he might "substantially close the war in two weeks," but they were not immediately available.

On July 12 Lincoln read an appeal to the representatives of the border states summoned to the White House for a meeting. He repeated to their faces his belief that "the war would now be substantially ended" had they voted four months earlier for his resolution proposing emancipation for the border states. He appealed to them earnestly with dire predictions that were perhaps as candid as they were threatening:

> Discarding punctillio, and maxims adapted to more manageable times, and looking only to the unprecedentedly stern facts of our case, can you do better in any possible event? . . . The incidents of

the war can not be avoided. If the war continue long, as it must, if the object be not sooner attained, the institution in your states will be extinguished by mere friction and abrasion—by the mere incidents of the war. It will be gone, and you will have nothing valuable in lieu of it. Much of it's value is gone already. How much better for you, and for your people, to take the step which, at once, shortens the war, and secures substantial compensation for that which is sure to be wholly lost in any other event.

He continued to offer the assurance of an all-white society to come: "Room in South America for colonization can be obtained cheaply, and in abundance; and when numbers shall be large enough to be company and encouragement for one another, the freed people will not be so reluctant to go." Black people were in fact more American than white people—only one percent of black people by the time of the Civil War had been born abroad. Little wonder they expressed scant willingness to expatriate, despite the inhospitable circumstances in their native land. Lincoln also threatened the border state representatives. His revocation of General Hunter's proclamation had dissatisfied or insulted "many whose support the country can not afford to lose." Antislavery forces pressured him too.

The border state men responded to Lincoln's appeal on July 14, and by a margin of 20 to 8 rejected his plans. They argued that emancipation in the border states would spur the Confederacy to keep fighting rather than to return to the Union and that it would lead to unconstitutional emancipation by presidential order. Several dissenters came from upcountry West Virginia and East Tennessee, traditional areas of opposition to the slave interest in the South.

Lincoln had already made up his mind, and the appeal was the last chance for the border state slaveowners before he made public a policy that would likely ruin them. On July 13, Lincoln revealed to Welles and Seward, during a carriage ride to the funeral of Edwin Stanton's infant child, his resolve to free the slaves if the war did not end. "It was a new departure for the President," recalled Welles, "for until this time, in all our previous interviews, whenever the question of emancipation or the mitigation of slavery had been in any way alluded to, he had been prompt and emphatic in denouncing any interference by the General Government with the subject. This was . . . the sentiment of every member of the Cabinet, all of whom, including the President, considered it a local, domestic question appertaining to the States respectively." From first mention to last, the President emphasized military necessity. "The reverses before Richmond," Welles recollected, "and the formidable power and dimensions of the insurrection . . . impelled the Administration to adopt extraordinary measures to pre-serve the national existence. The slaves, if not armed and disciplined, were in the service of those who were, not only as field laborers and producers, but thousands of them were in attendance upon the armies in the field, employed as waiters and teamsters, and the fortifications and intrenchments were constructed by them."

Within less than a week, Lincoln bore out Welles's description of his views. Congress passed the Second Confiscation Act, which among other provisions, authorized the confiscation of the property, including slaves, of persons in the Confederacy who supported the rebellion. It was submitted for his signature, he did not veto it, but he did send along a veto message he had prepared anyway, for the edification of Congress. It included some niggling and obscure objections on the grounds that some of its provisions amounted to unconstitutional "attainder for treason," and it also included the remark, "It is startling to say that congress can free a slave within a state."

Many years later when an air of solemn majesty surrounded Lin-coln's legendary actions, it was said that he drafted the Emancipation Proclamation over a period of weeks after the Seven Days' Battles, a sentence or two a day amidst much silent contemplation, at the War Department telegraph office. Lincoln's own office in his determinedly open presidency was so often interrupted by visitors that the telegraph office, where he walked every day to read the dispatches from the front offered quiet refuge. In fact the anecdote seems dubious. For one thing, Lincoln had no time for contemplation in or out of the White House. When a delegation of veterans of the War of 1812 visited him on the Fourth of July, for example, the President confessed that he had not had a minute to ready himself for the occasion, admitted that he did not have "a pretty speech, or any other sort of speech, prepared," and complained of "the continual and intense engrossment" of his attention "by very trying circumstances." For another, the first paragraph was in fact an order to implement the Confiscation Act, passed only on July 17, five days before Lincoln showed the document to the cabinet. The rest of the document consisted of only two sentences.

It does not much matter whether the story is false, but the generally unquestioned anecdote does serve to suggest the way that myths about Lincoln grow. The person who told the story did so in a book about his contacts with Lincoln, and as he was only a clerk in the telegraph office, they were not many or important. But to have witnessed the gestation of the Emancipation Proclamation would have been something of which to boast.

Whatever the precise origins of the document, on July 22, the third day in a row of meeting with the cabinet, the President read them what he had been composing. He did not offer it for approval or disapproval—his mind was made up to issue it—but he did want advice on timing and composition. He received two important pieces of advice. Postmaster General Montgomery Blair objected to issuing the document on the grounds that it would damage Republican chances in the fall's off-year elections. The President ignored this—a decision that should forever silence those who criticize the proclamation for being somehow "politically" inspired.

Secretary of State Seward's rambling response included an observation of which the President took notice: that Lincoln should wait for a military victory before issuing the proclamation; otherwise, it would look like a desperate measure, a plea for help from the "Ethiopian" population.

Seward's idea was grounded in two assumptions that may seem strange today. First, Seward believed that the outbreak of war had sealed slavery's doom, and he ceased worrying about the question—it would be taken care of as long as the really important matter of saving the Union was successfully concluded. John Hay heard in the summer of 1864 that Seward had said, "Slavery was destroyed years ago: the formation of the Republican Party destroyed slavery; the anti-slavery acts of this administration are merely incidental. Their great work is the preservation of the Union, and in that, the saving of popular government for the world." Second, a little over a year's experience in foreign policy had apparently imbued the Secretary of State with the notion that the European powers cared nothing about moral questions and scrutinized the news from America only to discover whether the Confederacy was powerful enough to maintain independence. "Proclamations are *paper*, without the support of armies," Seward wrote his wife after the cabinet meeting. "It is mournful to see that a great nation shrinks from a war it has accepted, and insists on adopting proclamations, when it is asked for force." Seward even raised at the meeting the specific foreign-policy objection that the proclamation might at last ensure the success of the Confederacy's "King Cotton" diplomacy. The war caused only temporary interruption of the cotton supply to Great Britain, but the proclamation threatened to disturb cotton production for sixty years, in Seward's estimation, and that might force British intervention.

The President shared none of the assumptions underlying Seward's advice and was not thinking about foreign policy, but he could appreciate the effect on public opinion of a proclamation that seemed prompted by national weakness. He would wait for a battlefield victory.

While he waited, Lincoln chose, without actually lying, to give the American public the impression that he was not likely to free the slaves. The most famous instance came in August when the mercurial Horace Greeley, editor of the widely read *New York Tribune*, published an editorial called "The Prayer of Twenty Millions," saying that the influence of "fossil" politicians from the border states was keeping Lincoln from attacking the "inciting cause" of the rebellion, slavery. Lincoln responded in a public letter:

I would save the Union . . . If there be those who would not save the Union, unless they could at the same time *save* slavery, I do not agree with them. If there be those who would not save the Union unless they could at the same time *destroy* slavery, I do not agree with them. My paramount object in this struggle *is* to save the Union, and is *not* either to save or to destroy slavery. If I could save the Union without freeing *any* slave I would do it, and if I could save it by freeing *all* the slaves I would do it; and if I could save it by freeing some and leaving others alone I would also do that. What I do about slavery, and the colored race, I do because I believe it helps to save the Union; and what I forbear, I forbear because I do *not* believe it would help to save the Union . . . I have here stated my purpose according to my view of *official* duty; and I intend no modification of my oft-expressed *personal* wish that all men every where could be free.

Eight days earlier Lincoln had addressed a group of black men led by the president of the Anglo-African Institute for the Encouragement of Industry and brought to the President by an Interior Department official in charge of colonization. To them he spoke this way:

You and we are different races. We have between us a broader difference than exists between almost any other two races. Whether it is right or wrong I need not discuss, but this physical difference is a great disadvantage to us both, as I think your race suffer very greatly, many of them by living among us, while ours suffer from your presence . . . If this is admitted, it affords a reason at least why we should be separated.

On another occasion Lincoln received a petition from a mass meeting of Chicago Christians, urging emancipation. He used the technique of the misleading question again. (This political tactic was so much a habit of Lincoln's that he had used it on the eleven-year-old girl who had recommended that he grow a beard back in 1860. "Do you not think people would call it a piece of silly affec[ta]tion if I were to begin it now?" Lincoln asked, and started growing it within weeks.) His reply of September 13 asked, "What *good* would a proclamation of emancipation from me do, especially as we are now situated? I do not want to issue a document that the whole world will see must necessarily be inoperative, like the Pope's bull against the comet! Would *my word* free the slaves, when I cannot even enforce the Constitution in the rebel States?" Close readers of the report of the meeting might have noted once more Lincoln's new-found constitutional justification for such action *and* an altogether new consideration of the social consequences of such a proclamation: "Understand, I raise no objections against it on legal or constitutional grounds; for, as commander-in-chief of the army and navy, in time of war, I suppose I have a right to take any measure which may best subdue the enemy. Nor do I urge objections of a moral nature, in view of possible consequences of insurrection and massacre at the South. I view the matter as a practical war measure, to be decided upon according to the advantages or disadvantages it may offer to the suppression of the rebellion." The Chicago ministers argued with the President, and he replied:

> I admit that slavery is the root of the rebellion, or at least the *sine qua non* . . . I will also concede that emancipation would help us in Europe, and convince them that we are incited by something more than ambition. I grant further that it would help *somewhat* at the North, though not so much, I fear, as you and those you represent imagine . . . And then unquestionably it would weaken the rebels by drawing off their laborers, which is of great importance. But I am not so sure we could do much with the blacks. If we were to arm them, I fear that in a few weeks the arms would be in the hands of the rebels . . . I will mention another thing, though it meet only your scorn and contempt: There are fifty thousand bayonets in the Union armies from the Border Slave States. It would be a serious matter if, in consequence of a proclamation such as you desire, they should go over to the rebels. I do not think they all would—not so many indeed as a year ago, or as six months ago—not so many to-day as yesterday . . . Let me say one thing more: I think you should admit that we already have an important principle to rally and unite the people in the fact that constitutional government is at stake. This is a fundamental idea, going down about as deep as anything.

Four days later McClellan turned Lee back at Antietam, and five days after that Lincoln announced the Emancipation Proclamation.

The document, which has come to be called the Preliminary Emancipation Proclamation, was much longer than the brief paper Lincoln had read to his cabinet in July. It did not begin with reference to an act of Congress, either. Instead the first words were, "I, Abraham Lincoln, President of the United States of America, and Commander-in-chief of the Army and Navy thereof." In fact the actual words Lincoln employed must not have mattered much, for the document is written in a leaden legalese that reminded Karl Marx, who covered events in Civil War America for a Viennese newspaper, of the "mean pettifogging conditions which one lawyer puts to his opposing lawyer."

The Preliminary Emancipation Proclamation declared that the slaves in areas still in rebellion against the United States on January 1 would be free. Lincoln promised to recommend to Congress once again a program of voluntary, gradual, and compensated emancipation for any state that would adopt it, and he vowed to continue efforts at colonization. Otherwise, more than half the document enjoined the military not to enforce the fugitive slave laws. They were to "recognize and maintain the freedom" of the former slaves and "do no act or acts to repress such persons, or any of them, in any efforts they may make for their actual freedom." In that phrase lay a foreign policy gaffe.

Seward was correct about Europe: the important leaders were unmoved by the proclamation and generally eager to find fault with it. It was not difficult to do, and cynics, not disposed to cheer the social results of the proclamation, have been pointing to apparent flaws ever since. Popular opinion in Europe is not easy to gauge and did not really matter anyway. Even the freest of the old monarchies, Great Britain, allowed only fourteen percent of the adult males the vote. The opinion that did count—the most important in the world on this question—was that of the British Prime Minister, Lord Palmerston. He was unimpressed, terming the proclamation "a singular manifesto that could scarcely be treated seriously. It is not easy to estimate how utterly powerless and contemptible a government must have become which could sanction such . . . trash."

Those looking for flaws to exploit found a big one in the statement that the American military was not to suppress "any" effort for "actual freedom." The British Foreign Secretary, Lord John Russell, expressed shock at the "premium . . . given to acts of plunder, of incendiarism, and of revenge" in the document. The conservative London *Times* was more journalistically graphic. The American President had appealed "to the black blood of the African; he will whisper of the pleasures of spoil and of the gratification of yet fiercer instincts; and when the blood begins to flow and shrieks come piercing through the darkness, Mr. Lincoln will wait till the rising flames tell that all is consummated, and then he will rub his hands and think that revenge is sweet." One of Napoleon III's ministers, writing a recommendation for intervention, mentioned as pretext the possibility of "a servile war."

Both Palmerston and Russell held antislavery opinions, as did most enlightened Britons, but their official positions apparently allowed no room for indulging personal sentiment. Ironically, the proclamation put them in precisely the position President Lincoln occupied before its issuance: the nineteenth century's liberal statesmen could not necessarily indulge their personal preference that all men everywhere ought to be free and at the same time properly look after the national interests. Even so, it remains one of the great unsolved mysteries of nineteenth-century history that the most antislavery nation on earth, Great Britain, harbored so much sentimental identification with the cause of the Confederacy.

The most astonishing manifestation of that retrograde sentiment came in a speech delivered by the great British liberal leader William E. Gladstone, in Newcastle, on the same day that the London *Times* was denouncing the proclamation's incendiarism. "Jefferson Davis and other leaders of the South have made an army; they are making, it appears, a navy; and they have made what is more than either—they have made a nation . . . We may anticipate with certainty the success of the Southern States so far as regards their separation from the North."

That Lincoln could have misfired so illustrates the difficulties of drafting public papers, but it also reveals his preoccupation with the possible domestic consequences of the proclamation. He knew the hazards of the document's being seen as an invitation to insurrection and was apparently willing to brave them, for he had mentioned the idea to the Chicago Christians. He would apparently even risk its being so interpreted by the slaves themselves, but there was no need to advertise that risk to a hostile world, and Lincoln would not have if he had been thinking about it as a piece of foreign policy. That hardly crossed his mind.

Instead, he remained preoccupied with the military justification of the act and likely domestic criticism of it on constitutional grounds. Only that can explain the actions that followed the issuance of the proclamation and only that can explain the turbid legalistic language in which it was carefully drafted. To read the proclamation, the very first sentence of which contains a veritable lexicon of pettifogging ("thereof," "hereby," "hereafter," "heretofore"), and to contrast it with other explanations of the war's purpose from the President's pen is to understand that style with Lincoln was not a matter of ungovernable genius. He could craft his language carefully to any occasion. For example, less than three weeks after signing the final proclamation in January, a document as dismally written as the preliminary one, Lincoln sent a letter acknowledging resolutions of support adopted at a rally of Manchester workingmen in Great Britain. Many of these cotton operatives were unemployed because of the interruption of the cotton trade caused by Lincoln's blockade of the Confederate coast. The letter showed the President at his best:

> I know and deeply deplore the sufferings which the workingmen at Manchester and in all Europe are called to endure in this crisis. It has been often and studiously represented that the attempt to overthrow this government, which was built upon the foundation of human rights, and to substitute for it one which should rest exclusively on the basis of human slavery, was likely to obtain the favor of Europe . . . Under these circumstances, I cannot but regard your decisive utterance upon the question as an instance of sublime Christian heroism which has not been surpassed in any age or in any country. It is, indeed, an energetic and reinspiring assurance of the inherent power of truth and of the ultimate and universal triumph of justice, humanity, and freedom.

In the Emancipation Proclamation, Lincoln had been too worried about his potential domestic critics to unleash the full powers of his language. His purpose in that document was to calm fears, anticipate critics, and frustrate those who might doubt its constitutionality.

Lincoln's focus was narrowly and sincerely on military survival. It was not a matter of finding a way to free the slaves constitutionally through his new-found powers as commander in chief. Lincoln was seeking tangible advantages over the enemy, and he was rather impatient in his quest.

When the Vice President wrote Lincoln to congratulate him on issuing the proclamation, the President replied gloomily in a letter marked "strictly private":

> It is known to some that while I hope something from the proclamation, my expectations are not as sanguine as are those of some friends. The time for its effect southward has not come; but northward the effect should be instantaneous. It is six days old, and while commendation in newspapers and by distinguished individuals is all that a vain man could wish, the stocks have declined, and troops come forward more slowly than ever. This, looked soberly in the face, is not very satisfactory. We have fewer troops in the field at the end of six days than we had at the beginning—the attrition among the old outnumbering the addition by the new. The North responds to the proclamation sufficiently in breath; but breath alone kills no rebels.

So earnest was the President's military justification for the proclamation that he was already annoyed at the antislavery zealots who had promised so much in the way of renewed enthusiasm for the contest but who delivered so little. That was not the main reason he issued it: the time for its real effect had "not come" yet, but it would, he felt, when word spread via the grapevine telegraph on the plantations, and the secure labor base of the Confederacy began to crumble.

As promised, the President also gave the border states one last chance. In his annual message to Congress, of December 1, 1862,

Lincoln proposed a series of constitutional amendments for voluntary and compensated emancipation to be completed by 1900. It included a provision for voluntary colonization as well. No one took him up on the proposition.

Meanwhile, antislavery advocates worked hard to make the best of the coming proclamation. Massachusetts Senator Charles Sumner gave Lincoln a copy of George Livermore's little monograph entitled *An Historical Research: Opinions of the Founders of the Republic on Negroes as Slaves, as Citizens, and as Soldiers,* which argued that free black men had served in the armies of the American Revolution and that George Washington had valued their services. Whether it was because of this piece of historical research or the logic of the war, by January Lincoln was ready to authorize the acceptance of freedmen in the armed forces of the United States. The statement of that purpose was the most important change in the final document from the text of the preliminary proclamation. He had evidently been convinced that their arms would not wind up in the hands of the enemy, but as yet he thought them suitable only "to garrison and defend forts, positions, stations, and other places, and to man vessels of all sorts." This momentous decision guaranteed a multiracial future for the United States. Eager radicals and grumbling conservatives alike realized that the President could not ask a man to fight for his country and then tell him it was not his country after all.

Acting on advice from the cabinet concerning the reception of the preliminary document abroad, Lincoln now added this soothing advice to the freedmen: "And I hereby enjoin upon the people . . . declared to be free to abstain from all violence, unless in necessary self-defence; and I recommend to them that, in all cases when allowed, they labor faithfully for reasonable wages." Lincoln also listed the specific states and parts of states exempted from the proclamation because the military justification did not apply if they were already occupied by forces of the United States.

After the traditional New Year's Day open house in the Executive Mansion, his hand so sore from handshaking that he could hardly pen a steady signature, Lincoln signed the epochal document in the presence of the assembled cabinet. The night before, he had signed an agreement with a slippery character to attempt an experiment in colonization of free blacks on Cow Island, near Haiti. That expedition proved a tragic failure. The Emancipation Proclamation did not.

It succeeded in large measure because Lincoln worked at making it a success and because of the courage of many slaves who attempted to take advantage of the now explicit promise of freedom. The President did what he could to hasten "its effect southward." In March, having heard that Tennessee's Andrew Johnson was considering raising black troops in the state, Lincoln wrote him an eager letter, saying:

> In my opinion the country now needs no specific thing so much as some man of your ability, and position, to go to this work. When I speak of your position, I mean that of an eminent citizen of a slave-state, and himself a slave-holder. The colored population is the great *available* and yet *unavailed* of, force for restoring the Union. The bare sight of fifty thousand armed, and drilled black soldiers on the banks of the Mississippi, would end the rebellion at once.

Lincoln seems never to have shed his belief that the war would end with a decisive battle—with 50,000 more men before Richmond in the summer of 1862, for example. This same optimism was attached to the mobilization of black troops. In this perhaps overly enthusiastic letter, Lincoln allowed himself to contemplate a mere "demonstration" that would be decisive rather than a bloody battle.

Such an outlook was consistent with his initial justification for the Emancipation Proclamation, though it required a more aggressive image of the black soldiers than the one offered in the proclamation itself. Answering the arguments of his Democratic critics in a public letter on August 26, 1863, Lincoln asserted,

> I know as fully as one can know the opinions of others, that some of the commanders of our armies in the field who have given us our most important successes, believe the emancipation policy, and the use of colored troops, constitute the heaviest blow yet dealt to the rebellion; and that, at least one of those important successes, could

Private, & confidential

Springfield, Ills. Dec. 10. 1860

Hon. L. Trumbull.

My dear Sir,

Let there be no compromise on the question of *extending* slavery — If there be, all our labor is lost, and, ere long, must be done again — The dangerous ground — that into which some of our friends have a hankering to run — is Pop. Sov. Have none of it — Stand firm. The tug has to come, & better now, than any time hereafter —

Yours as ever

A. Lincoln.

Immediately following Lincoln's election to the Presidency but before the inauguration in March 1861, the U.S. House of Representatives established a committee to consider compromise measures in light of the forming of secession conventions in several southern states. Senator Lyman Trumbull did not think Republicans should compromise, and wrote Lincoln to make certain that he agreed. Lincoln's reply of December 10, 1860, reproduced here, not only confirmed Trumbull's position but also warned against any dalliance with popular sovereignty as a compromise solution. [*Huntington Library*]

For your own eye only.

Springfield, Ill. Dec. 22. 1860

Hon. A. H. Stephens—

My dear Sir

Your obliging ans=
wer to my short note is just received,
and for which please accept my
thanks— I fully appreciate the
present peril the country is in, and
the weight of responsibility on me—

Do the people of the South really
entertain fears that a Republican
administration would, directly, or
indirectly, interfere with their slaves,
or with them, about their slaves?
If they do, I wish to assure you, as
once a friend, and still, I hope,
not an enemy, that there
is no cause for such fears—

The South would be in no more
danger in this respect, than it
was in the days of Washington—

In this skillfully written letter of December 22, 1860, to the future vice president of the Confederacy, Alexander Stephens, Lincoln attempted to state the differences between North and South as moral ones. Stephens's reply attributed sectional difficulties to "fanaticism" only. [*Huntington Library*]

This rare first printing of Lincoln's preliminary version of his First Inaugural Address is one of several copies he had set in type for others to read and criticize. The second and third paragraphs of the version reproduced here were deleted from the address he delivered on March 4, 1861. [*Huntington Library*]

Escaping office-seekers and others pressing to see the President-elect, Abraham Lincoln hid himself in a dingy office above his brother-in-law's store in Springfield to write the first draft of his First Inaugural Address—hence the ordinary nature of the old wooden inkwell he used. Later, after Lincoln became president, he used the ornate pen pictured here. [*Illinois State Historical Library*]

1

In compliance with a custom as old as the government itself, I appear before you to address you briefly, and to take, in your presence, the oath prescribed by the Constitution of the United States, to be taken by the President "before he enters on the execution of his office."

The more modern custom of electing a Chief Magistrate upon a previously declared platform of principles, supercedes, in a great measure, the necessity of re-stating those principles in an address of this sort. Upon the plainest grounds of good faith, one so elected is not at liberty to shift his position. It is necessarily implied, if not expressed, that, in his judgment, the platform which he thus accepts, binds him to nothing either unconstitutional or inexpedient.

Having been so elected upon the Chicago Platform, and while I would repeat nothing in it, of aspersion or epithet or question of motive against any man or party, I hold myself bound by duty, as well as impelled by inclination to follow, within the executive sphere, the principles therein declared. By no other course could I meet the reasonable expectations of the country.

I do not consider it necessary at present for me to say more than I have, in relation to those matters of administration, about which there is no special excitement.

☞ Apprehension seems to exist among the people of the Southern States, that by the accession of a Republican Administration, their property, and their peace, and personal security, are to be endangered. There has never been any reasonable cause for such apprehension. Indeed, the most ample evidence to the contrary has all the while existed, and been open to their inspection. It is found in nearly all the published speeches of him who now addresses you. I do but quote from one of those speeches when I declare that "I have no purpose, directly or indirectly, to interfere with the institution of slavery in the States where it exists. I believe I have no lawful right to do so, and I have no inclination to do so." Those who nominated and elected me did so with full knowledge that I had made this, and many similar declarations, and had never recanted them. And more than this, they placed in the platform, for my acceptance, and as a law to themselves, and to me, the clear and emphatic resolution which I now read :

"*Resolved*, That the maintenance inviolate of the rights of the States, and especially the right of each State to order and control its own domestic institutions according to its own judgment exclusively, is essential to that balance of power on which the perfection and endurance of our political fabric depend ; and we denounce the lawless invasion by armed force of the soil of any State or Territory, no matter under what pretext, as among the gravest of crimes."

Basing their likeness on a photograph of Lincoln shot in 1860 in New York, the American Bank Note Company engraved this small portrait. The President-elect signed several copies in pencil while en route to Washington for his inauguration. It was a piece of ill fortune for the engravers that Lincoln began growing a beard shortly after his election and thus made their candidate for a presidential portrait immediately obsolete. [*Louise and Barry Taper Collection*]

"I am ashamed of not sooner answering your letter," Lincoln wrote an associate in 1850. "When I received the letter I put it in my old hat, and buying a new one the next day, the old one was set aside, and so, the letter lost sight of for a time." Such folksy anecdotes about Lincoln's top hats serve to cloud the image of the hat as a symbol of bourgeois social status. [*Louise and Barry Taper Collection*]

Mary Todd Lincoln ordered over 600 pieces of presidential china for the White House. The pattern shown here, called "royal purple," was Haviland porcelain manufactured in Limoges, France. Perhaps hoping that a little of Lincoln's luster might rub off on them, most if not all of the Presidents since the Civil War have dined off the Lincoln china at one time or another. [*Louise and Barry Taper Collection*]

This presidential invitation was addressed to Benjamin Brown French, the commissioner of public buildings, with whom Mrs. Lincoln worked closely early in the administration to refurbish the somewhat shabby Executive Mansion. The dinner was for Thomas Clay, Henry Clay's son, and other Kentuckians. [*Louise and Barry Taper Collection*]

Not as often photographed as her husband, Mrs. Lincoln disliked the majority of the few poses that were made. This one, taken in November 1861 at Mathew Brady's gallery in Washington, she deemed not "at all passable"; yet she signed this copy for someone in 1865. [*Illinois State Historical Library*]

The rare photograph and lock of hair of William Wallace "Willie" Lincoln, who died in 1862, less than two years after this photograph was taken in Springfield, was likely a keepsake of a relative. [*Louise and Barry Taper Collection*]

Dressed in a junior version of the uniform of a Union officer, complete with gauntlets, kepi, and a sword in a highly decorated scabbard, Thomas "Tad" Lincoln posed at Mathew Brady's gallery. Work for the father and play for the children focused on the war. [*Lincoln Museum*]

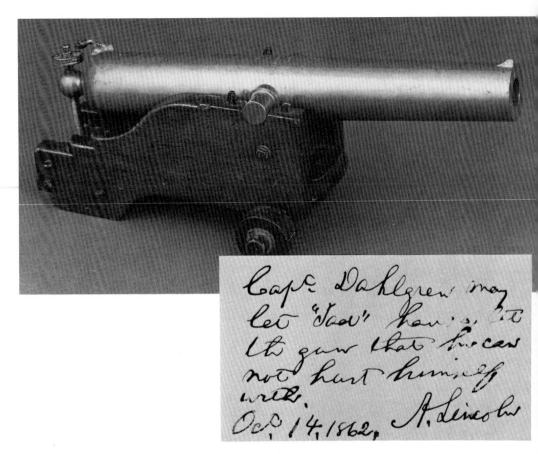

Capt Dahlgren may
let "Tad" have; it
the gun that he can
not hurt himself
with.
Oc^t 14, 1862, A. Lincoln

With the permission granted in this note from Lincoln, John A. Dahlgren—the U.S. Navy's chief ordnance officer and inventor of the Dahlgren cannon, standard armament on American naval vessels—gave Tad Lincoln this working model of a small howitzer (with the firing pin disabled), a weapon he had also invented. It is mounted on a model wooden naval truck wheeled in front but not in back, where the carriage's drag on the deck helped absorb the gun's kick. [*Illinois State Historical Library*]

(*Right*) The U.S. Constitution does not mention naval blockades, but the power to impose them was widely conceded to be among the powers of the commander in chief. Within a week of the fall of Fort Sumter, Lincoln, in the document shown here, proclaimed a blockade of the South. His own Secretary of the Navy regarded it of dubious legality, however, and the question later arose in the U.S. Supreme Court, which decided in the administration's favor. [*Louise and Barry Taper Collection*]

By the President of the United States of America.

A Proclamation.

Whereas an insurrection against the Government of the United States has broken out in the States of South Carolina, Georgia, Alabama, Florida, Mississippi, Louisiana and Texas, and the laws of the United States for the collection of the revenue cannot be effectually executed therein conformably to that provision of the Constitution which requires duties to be uniform throughout the United States:

And whereas a combination of persons, engaged in such insurrection, have threatened to grant pretended letters of marque to authorize the bearers thereof to commit assaults on the lives, vessels, and property of good citizens of the country lawfully engaged in commerce on the high seas, and in the waters of the United States:

And whereas an Executive Proclamation has been already issued, requiring the persons engaged in these disorderly proceedings to desist therefrom, calling out a militia force for the purpose of repressing the same, and convening Congress in extraordinary session to deliberate and determine thereon:

Now, therefore, I, Abraham Lincoln, President of the United States, with a view to the same purposes before mentioned, and to the protection of the public peace, and the lives and property of quiet and orderly citizens pursuing their

Washington, D. C. Sep. 15. 2⁴⁵ 1862.

Major General McClellan.

Your despatches of to-day received— God bless you, and all with you. Destroy the rebel army, if possible.

A. Lincoln

Washington City. D.C.
Oct. 24.   1862

Maj^r. Genl. McClellan

I have just read your despatch about sore tongued and fatigued horses— Will you pardon me for asking what the horses of your army have done since the battle of Antietam that fatigue anything?

A. Lincoln

President Lincoln's eagerness for a decisive battle of the sort familiar in the Napoleonic Wars was misinterpreted as ingratitude by General McClellan when he received this message of September 15, 1862. Lincoln meant to compliment the general for his victory at South Mountain. [*Illinois State Historical Library*]

Lincoln held tight rein on his temper, but the frustration of not being able to force his generals to act even in their own best interest could cause him to lose control. In this instance the President was so angry that he misdated the message, which was actually sent on the 25th of October. [*Illinois State Historical Library*]

Lincoln owned this copy of a photograph made by Alexander Gardner at McClellan's headquarters on the Antietam battlefield in October 1862. The sunburned face of the general contrasts with Lincoln's civilian pallor (only McClellan's brow, usually protected by a kepi, matches Lincoln's skin color). Although some of the artifacts in the tent may have been arranged for the photograph, the captured Confederate flags piled at left were not: McClellan had commented on them in letters home. [*Lincoln Museum*]

> Let this boy be pardoned for any supposed desertion, and discharged from the service,
>
> May. 28. 1864.   A. Lincoln

The President evidently wrote this pardon on a bandage during a hospital visit. Such charitable impulses increased Lincoln's popularity with the masses but, according to some army officers, contributed to the indiscipline of American armies. [*Louise and Barry Taper Collection*]

John Sartain's engraving of George Caleb Bingham's painting called *Martial Law* spread the infamy of the General Order that depopulated four counties in Missouri and made refugees of some 20,000 citizens of this ostensibly loyal state. Bingham had lost his own house in the border strife around Independence, Missouri. After the war was over he painted this scene of desolation (engraved in 1872). [*Lincoln Museum*]

General Ulysses S. Grant, in his own words, usually wore "rough garb . . .
when on horseback on the field." Then he wore only "a soldier's blouse for a
coat, with the shoulder straps of my rank to indicate to the army who I was."
He typically carried no sword. Though without saber in this 1865 photograph
by Wenderoth & Taylor of Philadelphia, the general wears a velvet-trimmed
jacket and a vest with brass buttons. [*Lincoln Museum*]

General William Tecumseh Sherman, who shares with Lincoln and Grant perhaps the highest reputation as an American military innovator in the Civil War, proved less eager than either Grant or Lincoln to pose for the camera. No hero of the war owed his reputation less to publicity or more to sheer merit than Sherman. He detested the press and did almost nothing to cultivate the good opinion of reporters. [*Lincoln Museum*]

Executive Mansion
Washington, April 30. 1864

Lieutenant General Grant.

Not expecting to see you again before the Spring campaign opens, I wish to express, in this way, my entire satisfaction with what you have done up to this time, so far as I understand it, The particulars of your plans I neither know, or seek to know. You are vigilant and self-reliant; and, pleased with this, I wish not to obtrude any constraints or restraints upon you. While I am very anxious that any great disaster, or the capture of our men in great numbers, shall be avoided, I know these points are less likely to escape your attention than they would be mine— If there is anything wanting which is within my power to give, do not fail to let me know it. And now with a brave Army, and a just cause, may God sustain you.

Yours very truly
A. Lincoln

In the last meeting with Grant preceding this letter of April 30, 1864, President Lincoln expressed his understanding of the general's proposed strategy for the spring campaign by saying "those not skinning can hold a leg." [*Huntington Library*]

THE OLD BULL DOG ON THE RIGHT TRACK.

There was something about General Grant that suggested the bulldog to the anonymous cartoonist who drew this for Currier & Ives in 1864 as well as to Lincoln, who that very summer encouraged the general to hold on "with a bulldog grip." In the cartoon, Lincoln identifies the rebel "pack of curs" for McClellan as the group that "chased you aboard of the Gunboat two years ago." [*Lincoln Museum*]

As to peace I have said before, and now repeat, that three things are indispensable.
1 The restoration of the national authority throughout all the States.
2. No receding by the Executive of the United States on the slavery question from the position assumed thereon in the late Annual Message to Congress, and in preceding documents.
3. No cessation of hostilities short of an end of the war, and the disbanding of all forces hostile to the government.
That all propositions coming from those now in hostility to the government, and not inconsistent with the foregoing, will be respectfully considered, and passed upon in a spirit of sincere liberality;
I now add that it seems useless for me to be more specific with those who will not say they are ready for the indispensable terms, even on conditions to be named by themselves. If there be any who are ready for those indispensable

President Lincoln met on April 4 and 5, 1865, in the former Confederate capital of Richmond with John A. Campbell, a U.S. Supreme Court Justice before the war and lately the Assistant Secretary of War of the Confederacy. There Lincoln repeated the peace terms he had written out for William H. Seward prior to the Hampton Roads Peace Conference in February, at which Campbell had been a participant. But now—as the document reproduced here shows—he added a new threat: payment of the additional cost of the war, if it continued, by confiscation of rebel estates. [*Illinois State Historical Library*]

John Rogers's parlor statuette, called *The Council of War*, was conceived in 1867 and patented in 1868. It depicted a meeting between President Lincoln, Secretary of War Edwin M. Stanton, and Ulysses S. Grant at the time of Grant's return to Washington after his first visit to the Army of the Potomac in Virginia early in March 1864. The statuette was expensive—$25—but sold well. Stanton pronounced the Lincoln likeness a good one, and so did Robert Lincoln, who owned this copy. [*Louise and Barry Taper Collection*]

Be it enacted by the State of Delaware that on condition the United States of America will, at the present
session of Congress, engage by law to pay, and thereafter
faithfully pay to the said State of Delaware, in the
six per cent bonds of said United States, the sum
of seven hundred and nineteen thousand, and two
hundred dollars, in thirty one equal annual instal-
ments, there shall be neither slavery nor involuntary servitude, at any time after the first day of January in the year of our Lord one thousand eight
hundred and ninety three, within the said State
of Delaware, except in the punishment of crime, whereof the party shall have been duly convicted; nor, except in the punishment of crime as aforesaid, shall
any person who shall be born after the passage of
this act, nor any person above the age of thirty five
years, be held in slavery, or to involuntary servitude, within said State of Delaware, at any time
after the passage of this act.

And be it further enacted that said State shall,
in good faith prevent, so far as possible, the carrying
of any person out of said state, into involuntary servitude,
beyond the limits of said State, at any time after
the passage of this act.

And be it further enacted that said State may
make provision of apprenticeship, not to extend beyond the age of twentyone years for males, nor eighteen
for females, for all minors whose mothers were not free
at the respective births of such minors—

Late in 1861 President Lincoln had drafted two plans for voluntary compensated emancipation for the state of Delaware. This is
the second version and the one Lincoln preferred. The President
calculated the value of a slave at $400 and thus came up with the
$719,200 figure for compensation. Even in a state where slavery
had such small presence (there were fewer than 2,000 there), Lincoln's proposal failed to convert the local legislators to emancipation. [*Huntington Library*]

Having flung over a patriotic wall statuette his Scottish cap with its diced bor-
der—a symbol of his allegedly cowardly entry into Washington—President
Lincoln drafts the Emancipation Proclamation amidst sulphurously satanic images and objects, in Adalbert Volck's cartoon. "St. Ossawotamie" [sic] is John
Brown, the abolitionist fanatic who led a raid in Kansas in 1856 in which
Brown's men hacked five prosouthern settlers to death with broadswords
(Osawatomie was a town in Kansas). The pike Brown carries was the kind he
carried on his raid into Virginia in 1859, with which he proposed to arm rebel-
lious slaves. The bloody slave uprising in Santo Domingo in the 1790s provides the subject of the painting at upper right. [*Huntington Library*]

> I never knew a man who wished to be himself a slave. Consider if you know any good thing, that no man desires for himself—
>
> March 22. 1864
>
> A. Lincoln

In the nineteenth century, autograph seekers often asked celebrities to write out and sign brief sentiments. Lincoln has done so here on what was probably a page in an autograph album. The page was auctioned for the United States Sanitary Commission during the war. [*Huntington Library*]

(*Right*) Frederick Douglass appraised Lincoln's accomplishments as emancipator in part from the perspective of a disappointed black abolitionist, eager for "the white man's President" to move more quickly for freedom. Few, if any, sized Lincoln up as fairly; none described him with more eloquence. [*Lincoln Museum*]

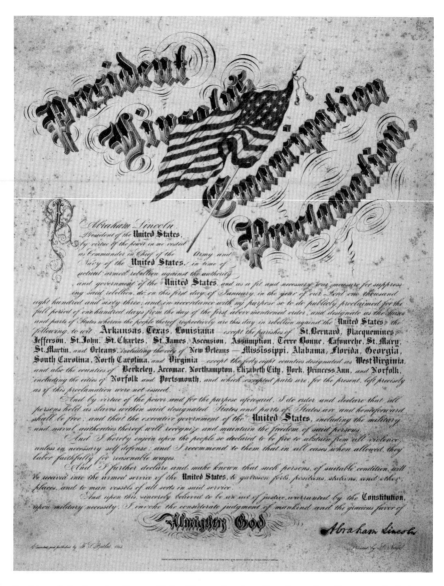

In Lincoln's day the fame of the Emancipation Proclamation far exceeded that of the Gettysburg Address and resulted in the production of numerous souvenir printings. This version, lithographed in California in 1864, likely did service in the presidential campaign. Visual interest is added by printing the names of the areas *excepted* from the proclamation in a bolder script, calling attention to a rather embarrassing aspect of the document. The emphasis on "Almighty God" at the end focused on a phrase that was an afterthought suggested by Salmon P. Chase and not originally in Lincoln's draft. The copy reproduced here was signed by Abraham Lincoln. [*Louise and Barry Taper Collection*]

Francis Bicknell Carpenter's 1864 painting depicting the first reading of the
Emancipation Proclamation before the cabinet is beautifully rendered here in
Alexander Hay Ritchie's immensely popular steel engraving of 1866. It exhib-
its a republican simplicity of setting and a lack of symbolic excess. Though Carpenter called this a "realistic" painting, to modern eyes it is stiffly posed, so
that none of the principals turns his back to the viewer. Carpenter set up his
easel in Lincoln's White House for months while painting the picture. [*Illinois
State Historical Library*]

This Currier & Ives cartoon celebrated the role of the black soldier and sympathized with his plight in the event of a triumph of Peace Democrats in the election, something Lincoln worried about as well. The figure of Jefferson Davis was drawn with the standard devices of northern caricature: the ragged pants legs of southern economic backwardness and the Bowie knives of planter violence. [*Lincoln Museum*]

ABRAHAM

AFRICANUS I.

His Secret Life,

AS REVEALED UNDER THE

MESMERIC INFLUENCE.

Mysteries of the White House.

J. F. FEEKS, PUBLISHER.
No. 26 ANN STREET, N. Y.

Abraham Africanus I, a substantial political satirical pamphlet of over fifty pages published in New York in 1864, brought together many of the themes stressed by Democrats in the presidential canvass of 1864. The cover illustration and title alone united the traditional republican fear of tyranny (in Lincoln's crown and regal title) and the accelerating Democratic attempt to become the party of the white man. [*Huntington Library*]

Private

Executive Mansion,

Washington. March 29, 1863.

Major General Banks

My dear Sir:

How. Daniel Ullmann, with a commission of Brigadier General, and two or three hundred other gentlemen as officers, goes to your department, and reports to you, for the purpose of raising a colored brigade. To now avail ourselves of this element of force, is very important, if not indispensable. I therefore will thank you to help Gen. Ullmann forward with his undertaking, as much, and as rapidly, as you can; and also, to carry the general object beyond his particular organization if you find it practicable. The necessity of this is palpable if, as I understand, you are now unable to effect anything with your present force; and which force is soon to be greatly diminished by the expiration of terms of service, as well as by ordinary causes.— I shall be very glad if you will take hold of the matter in earnest. You will receive from the Department a regular order upon this subject.

Yours truly,

A. Lincoln.

Lincoln's eagerness to see freedmen recruited is apparent in this letter of March 29, 1863, urging General Nathaniel P. Banks to help raise a brigade of black troops. The President pointed to black soldiers as "very important, if not indispensable" to the Union cause. [*Huntington Library*]

The "gallant rush" of the 54th Massachusetts Volunteer Infantry, a black regiment under white officers, at Battery Wagner in July 1863 failed to achieve the immediate military objective but did much to encourage those, like President Lincoln, who looked for great achievements from the newly enlisted black soldiers. [*Lincoln Museum*]

This is one of several souvenir engrossed copies (meaning the handwriting has been made larger) of the congressional resolution submitting to the states for ratification the Thirteenth Amendment to the Constitution. The original resolution was in fact a printed form. Lincoln "approved" and signed it too, but within the week the U.S. Senate passed a resolution declaring the President's signature unnecessary, citing a Supreme Court decision stating that the chief executive had "nothing to do with the proposition or adoption of amendments to the Constitution." [*Huntington Library*] not have been achieved when it was, but for the aid of black soldiers. Among the commanders holding these views are some who have never had any affinity with what is called abolitionism, or with republican party politics; but who hold them as purely military opinions. I submit these opinions as being entitled to some weight against the objections, often urged, that emancipation, and arming the blacks, are unwise as military measures, and were not adopted, as such, in good faith.

Lincoln exaggerated. At this early date (it required months to recruit, organize, and train Civil War troops for offensive action) black soldiers had played prominent roles only at the Battles of Port Hudson, Milliken's Bend, and Fort Wagner—all of them impressive baptisms of fire but none of them marked military successes or "important" actions. His idea of black soldiery seemed in flux. "I thought," he said, "that whatever negroes can be got to do as soldiers, leaves just so much less for white soldiers to do, in saving the Union." But he concluded the letter with a much more favorable image of the time when peace would return to the Union:

> Then, there will be some black men who can remember that, with silent tongue, and clenched teeth, and steady eye, and well-poised bayonet, they have helped mankind on to this great consummation; while, I fear, there will be some white ones, unable to forget that, with malignant heart, and deceitful speech, they have strove to hinder it.

By the summer of 1864 Lincoln's arguments had hardened. His thinking is known from the draft of a letter he wrote but never sent, answering criticisms from a Wisconsin War Democrat who maintained that Lincoln had made abolition an official goal of the war. Lincoln explained, "The way these measures were to help the cause, was not to be by magic, or miracles, but by inducing the colored people to come bodily over from the rebel side to ours." Without the motive of freedom to risk their lives for the Union, they would not come; "negroes, like other people, act upon motives." He asserted the moral argument, that, having made the promise, he could not now break it. "As a matter of morals," Lincoln asked, "could such treachery by any possibility, escape the curses of Heaven, or of any good man?" But quickly he moved from moral ground to physical, reiterating the military argument, now more strongly than ever:

> As a matter of policy, to *announce* such a purpose, would ruin the Union cause itself. All recruiting of colored men would instantly cease, and all colored men now in our service, would instantly desert us. And rightfully too. Why should they give their lives for us, with full notice of our purpose to betray them? Drive back to the support of the rebellion the physical force which the colored people now give, and promise us, and neither the present, nor any coming administration, *can* save the Union. Take from us, and give to the enemy, the hundred and thirty, forty, or fifty thousand colored persons now serving us as soldiers, seamen, and laborers, and we can not longer maintain the contest . . . It is not a question of sentiment or taste, but one of physical force, which may be measured, and estimated as horse-power, and steam power, are measured and estimated. And by measurement, it is more than we can lose, and live.

In an interview on the same subject on August 19, Lincoln is reported to have said,

> Abandon all the posts now possessed by black men, surrender all these advantages to the enemy, & we would be compelled to abandon the war in 3 weeks. We have to hold territory . . . There have been men who have proposed to me to return to slavery the black warriors of Port Hudson & Olustee to their masters to conciliate the South. I should be damned in time & in eternity for so doing . . . no human power can subdue this rebellion without using the Emancipation lever as I have done. Freedom has given us the control of 200,000 able bodied men, born & raised on southern soil. It will give us more yet.

To embrace the practical argument of force for Lincoln was not to deny the moral argument, and the sincerity of his antislavery feeling was never better revealed than in the trying August of 1864. On the same day that Lincoln met with his Wisconsin critic to convince him of the military necessity of emancipation to the Union cause, he met with Frederick Douglass. Lincoln had summoned him to the White House, and while the governor of Connecticut paced outside the office door, waiting to see the President, Lincoln told the black leader why he had asked him to come. "The slaves are not coming so rapidly and so numerously to us as I had hoped," Lincoln said, contradicting the rather rosier picture he had drawn for the disgruntled Wisconsin War Democrat previously occupying his office. Douglass replied "that the slave holders knew how to keep such things from their slaves, and probably very few knew of his Proclamation." Douglass was right, of course. Most slaves were illiterate, and as one slave who had not heard of the proclamation as late as 1864 explained, "De white folks nebber talk 'fore black men, dey mighty free from dat."

To remedy the problem, Lincoln proposed in August a daring, even revolutionary, secret plan for Douglass to organize a band of black "scouts" to pass through Union lines into the plantation South "and carry the news of Emancipation, and urge the slaves to come within our boundaries." Douglass thought of it as a scheme "somewhat after the original plan of John Brown." Ten days later Douglass responded with a plan to employ agents to infiltrate the South "to warn [the slaves] as to what will be their probable condition should peace be concluded while they remain within the Rebel lines: and more especially to urge upon them the necessity of making their escape." Naturally, those slaves who had already ventured toward the Union armies had come mostly from areas near the front lines and not from the interior. The chief job of each of Douglass's scouts would be "to conduct such squads of Slaves as he may be able to collect, safely within the Loyal lines."

The need for troops always seemed pressing, but Lincoln's conference with Frederick Douglass also came in the context of the election year and the gloomy prospects of the Republicans for reelecting the President. Lincoln figured he was going to lose, and he was initiating a scheme to get as many slaves to freedom as he could before the Democrats got into power. Douglass understood the import of the episode perfectly. "I refer to this conversation," he wrote in later years, "because I think that, on Mr. Lincoln's part, it is evidence conclusive that the Proclamation, so far at least as he was concerned, was not effected merely as a 'necessity.'" Lincoln and Douglass shelved their scheme as unnecessary in September after the fall of Atlanta, which changed public opinion in the North about Lincoln's handling of the war; the consequent promise of reelection more or less guaranteed freedom to the slaves without such risky measures.

At Lincoln's insistence the Republicans had already inserted a plank into their platform supporting a thirteenth amendment to the Constitution that would abolish slavery in the United States. Lincoln thought of it as the only sure way to protect emancipation from being undermined by later claims of unconstitutionality. He chose to press for congressional passage of the amendment in the lame-duck session of Congress immediately following the election. It might have been easier to wait for the more Republican Congress that would follow the sitting one (chosen in the off-year elections of 1862), but waiting would have delayed the assurance of freedom. Lincoln lent his talents of eloquence to this effort as well as his political skills, dealing in offices and projects dear to the hearts of wavering members of Congress. Success as a result did come early. The President approved the resolution submitting the thirteenth amendment to the states for ratification on February 1, 1865. He did not live to celebrate its ratification.

CHAPTER FIVE

A Free People Conduct
a Long War

Throughout his administration President Abraham Lincoln was preoccupied with two problems, military victory and race, and he consistently maintained after the summer of 1862 that they were so closely related as to come under the President's powers as commander in chief. He rarely focused long or hard on other problems of policy. Foreign policy, for example, the preoccupation of several twentieth-century American Presidents, Lincoln substantially handed over to his extremely able Secretary of State, William H. Seward. Likewise, it is not easy to characterize Lincoln's domestic policy under the sort of programmatic slogans that the more famous twentieth-century Presidents are identified with: "new nationalism," "new freedom," "new deal," or "great society."

In the absence of any such self-consciously systematic program, it is difficult to describe Lincoln's handling of the home front during the Civil War, and it will surely help, in beginning, to understand what the "home front" meant to Lincoln and his era.

Only the home front issues that directly affected mobilization of armies and navies attracted much attention from the President. Enlistments, conscription, desertion, and public opinion (insofar as it affected these) elicited from him and the Congress revolutionary and unprecedented policies along with careful explanations of them. But to leave those questions is to enter realms of activity—the economy, for example—to which Lincoln only sporadically paid attention and for which he could not be said to have developed any new systematic policies. He relied on the stock of old ideas he brought with him to Washington, and he had no time to develop new ones.

Indeed, Lincoln did not think of the North as the "home front." The very term, coined only in the Great War, was not available to Lincoln or his generation of political leaders, and neither was the concept. The North was what Lincoln and his generals protected—from occasional Confederate invasion or from sabotage and arson. The North was the public whose safety the Constitution required the President to protect in time of rebellion, but it was not to him a separate "front," where economic planning, government coercion, rationing, rules, regulations, and propaganda might help sustain victory and stave off defeatism. Congress shaped northern society by implementing political platforms forged in peace and now irresistible because a great part of the opposition political party was absent in the Confederacy. The Republican programs were not so much prompted by the needs of a society and economy at war as by the golden political opportunity afforded by the minority status of the Democratic party. The President drew on the North for men and materiel. But he did not mold or rearrange it.

What Lincoln had to do for the sake of the war effort often provoked sharp controversy at home. Some of the resistance revealed deeply rooted values and folkways that dwelt at an ineradicable level untouched by political argument or anything else in the arsenal of nineteenth-century political parties. By far the most unpopular policy of the Lincoln administration was the resort to conscription to fill the ranks of the armies of the United States. Conscription was surely inevitable. It was becoming the way modern nations fought great wars. Some Western European countries relied on it even in peacetime. The traditional hostility of republics to standing armies militated against its acceptance in the earliest days of the United States and lingered enough in public opinion to make it exceedingly unpopular. But the demands of mobilization for a modern war in a mass society overrode such traditions. The winds of modern change wafted through the slave South as well. The Confederacy, presumably more tender toward the liberties of white men than the northern government, nevertheless embraced conscription before the Lincoln administration did.

Lincoln decided to adopt conscription at a time when military misfortunes demanded revolutionary thinking in the administration and in the Congress. At the same July 22, 1862, cabinet meeting at which the President first presented the Emancipation Proclamation to his surprised ministers, Secretary of War Edwin M. Stanton proposed a draft of 50,000 men. No one present seemed startled by the proposal, and indeed Secretary of State William H. Seward suggested a draft of 100,000.

Only five days before, Congress had authorized a draft for nine months' service of the militia in certain prescribed circumstances. The legislators avoided the terms "draft" or "conscription," and, wary of old republican sentiment, they provided for the only kind of draft then known to American history, a militia draft, administered by the state governors. No such policy had been pursued since the adoption of the Constitution, but the Continental Congress had, at George Washington's request, passed a law permitting the draft of state militias during the darkest days of the American Revolution.

Lincoln was absorbed by the practical problem of raising troops of the proper sort to win the war. Without mentioning any constitutional, political, or legal dimensions of the subject, he told Stanton that the important consideration was to find recruits who could be placed in already existing regiments: such replacements were "nearly or quite equal in value to two in a new one." If that object could be advanced by initiating a militia draft, then Lincoln authorized the War Department to do so.

Sensing that conscription would meet resistance, the War Department devised drastic measures to enforce it. On August 8, 1862, Stanton issued a series of orders "to prevent evasion of military duty and for the suppression of disloyal practices." All persons liable to be drafted into the militia were forbidden to leave the country, and police authorities as well as federal officers were authorized to enforce this ban on travel, with special attention to ports and the Canadian border. Any person liable to the draft who left his state before the date of the draft could be arrested and placed on military duty at the nearest fort for the term of the draft. Five dollars would be deducted from his pay and given as reward to the arresting officer. And in the cases of all such persons arrested—in fact, of "all persons arrested for disloyal practices"—the writ of habeas corpus was suspended. Other orders issued that day authorized the arrest of persons discouraging enlistment, aiding or abetting the enemy, or engaging in any other disloyal practice and made violators liable to be tried by military courts.

The government thus unleashed every dogberry across the nation to make loosely defined arrests whose victims had no remedy by appeal to judges for writs of habeas corpus and might be tried essentially by court martial. For a month after the publication of these orders, civil liberties in the United States were perhaps as imperiled as they have ever been in the history of the country. Sweeping arrests made for ill-defined offenses, by men with no training or sensitivity for dealing with national issues, stained the American social fabric, and freedom of speech, not to mention the ability to travel, was severely curtailed.

There had never been anything remotely like it before. Under the notorious Sedition Act of 1798, there were only fifteen indictments and ten convictions. President Madison fought the War of 1812 incompetently and thus provoked great criticism, but he had a high tolerance for dissent and did nothing to limit civil liberties. Madison was, as one of his partisans said a generation later, "never once by the utmost exigencies of war, betrayed into a breach of the constitution," a statement no historian has ever made about Lincoln. Nor did President Polk make any moves to restrict civil liberties during the Mexican War, which was unpopular with Whigs (like Lincoln). Much more than the Civil War, both of these earlier wars were essentially wars supported by one political party and opposed by the other political party, but despite Lincoln's efforts to keep his war from degenerating into a Republican war exclusively and despite the loyalty of the Democratic party, he was the first President to embrace extreme curtailment of civil liberties in wartime. Of course, the threat to the existence of the republic Lincoln faced was without parallel before or since.

On September 8, 1862, with most of the state quotas for enlistment filled, a War Department official relaxed the enforcement of the orders. Though drastic and subject in execution to every abuse imaginable— partisanship, settlement of old scores, ethnic prejudice—the orders were sincerely meant to enforce the draft and were not a disguised method of crushing the opposition political party before election time later in the fall (relaxing them in early September left the last two months of the political campaign free from these extraordinary restraints).

Lincoln believed conscription was altogether proper and wholly necessary to raise men even for wars fought by republics. Shortly after making the July decision for the first national draft in American history, he explained to Gasparin:

> Be not alarmed if you shall learn that we shall have resorted to a draft . . . It seems strange, even to me, but it is true, that the government is now pressed to this course by a popular demand. Thousands who wish not to personally enter the service are nevertheless anxious to pay and send substitutes, provided they can have assurance that unwilling persons similarly situated will be compelled to do like wise. Besides this, volunteers mostly choose to enter newly forming regiments, while drafted men can be sent to fill up the old ones, wherein, man for man, they are quite doubly as valuable.

Lincoln always explained the draft in similarly logical, reasoned, and measured tones, and he seems never to have grasped the passion with which it was resisted by many Americans. Indeed, opposition on this question by political leaders usually made him suspicious and angry. It smacked of conspiracy. The administration's harshest measures were aimed at enforcing the draft and preventing or punishing desertion, and they stemmed in part from the President's belief in the necessity of force to maintain even republican armies and in the self-evident nature of the lawfulness and logic of conscription. Even so, American armies were notoriously ill-disciplined by European standards, and less than 6 percent of the Union army was filled by draftees.

Those who protested the draft probably came closer to the spirit of the founders of the republic. During the War of 1812, Daniel Webster, who was then a Federalist in opposition to the war measures of the administration, expressed the thinking of many when he said:

> Unlike the old nations of Europe, there are in this country no dregs of population, fit only to supply the constant waste of war, and out of which an army can be raised, for hire, at any time and for any purpose. Armies of any magnitude can here be nothing but the people embodied—and if the object be one for which the people will not embody, there can be no armies.

On September 24, 1862, two days after announcing the preliminary Emancipation Proclamation, the President himself proclaimed the suspension of the writ of habeas corpus nationwide and declared all persons who hindered the draft or discouraged volunteering liable to military trial. In June 1863 Lincoln sent a public letter to Erastus Corning and other New York Democrats who had protested the recent arrest and trial of the Democratic politician Clement L. Vallandigham of Ohio, an arrest made possible by the suspension of the writ of habeas corpus. Lincoln's letter was firm in its assertions of the administration's determination to quell subversive activities in the North. A much quoted passage expressed the President's determination to enforce mobilization:

> Long experience has shown that armies can not be maintained unless desertion shall be punished by the severe penalty of death. The case requires, and the law and the constitution, sanction this punishment. Must I shoot a simple-minded soldier boy who deserts, while I must not touch a hair of a wiley agitator who induces him to desert? . . . I think that in such a case, to silence the agitator, and save the boy, is not only constitutional, but, withal, a great mercy.

Lincoln knew that such measures were extraordinary, but he did not worry about their long-term effects on the republic as much as others did because he felt confident that they would disappear as soon as the war was over. In the letter to Corning, Lincoln said he was unable

> to appreciate the danger . . . that the American people will, by means of military arrests during the rebellion, lose the right of public dis-

cussion, the liberty of speech and the press, the law of evidence, trial by jury, and Habeas corpus, throughout the indefinite peaceful future . . . any more than I am able to believe that a man could contract so strong an appetite for emetics during temporary illness, as to persist in feeding upon them through the remainder of his healthful life.

The President proved essentially correct about that, but when it came to conscription, Lincoln did not read the public as shrewdly.

Horace Greeley could sense danger. On June 12, 1863, he wrote the Secretary of War, "It is folly to close our eyes to the signs of the times. The people have been educated to the idea of individual sover-eignty, & the principle of conscription is repugnant to their feelings & cannot be carried out except at great peril to the free States . . . Drafting is an anomaly in a free State; it oppresses the masses."

Greeley's letter was prophetic. The resistance anticipated in 1862 had never fully materialized, but after Congress enacted a conscription law on March 3, 1863, there occurred the greatest civil disorder in the nation's history, except for the Civil War itself—the New York City draft riots of July 13–17, 1863. Nicolay and Hay described the law succinctly as "the first law enacted by Congress by which the Govern-ment of the United States without the intervention of the authorities of the several States appealed directly to the nation to create large armies." The vehement resistance to the draft shows how close in some ways the American people of the mid-nineteenth century were to the origins of the republic, especially how suspicious they still were of distant and national power and how wed they were to the powers of the states. Moreover, like many other controversial events of the Civil War, this one was complicated by partisan politics.

Democrats had captured the New York state house in 1862. Gov-ernor Horatio Seymour immediately helped fill the Democratic lead-ership vacuum and became a contender for the Democratic nomination for president in 1864. He tailored his state messages and pronouncements to a national audience. Like many other Democrats, Seymour thought conscription unconstitutional, and he expected the courts soon to declare it so. Indeed, Chief Justice Taney was itching to do just that, if only a case would come before his court. Democratic workingmen in New York expected their governor and party to protect them from the draft. When the draft commenced as scheduled, a protest against it soon degenerated into wild racial and partisan rage against the Republicans and against innocent blacks, assumed to be the favored beneficiaries of Republican policies; victims were sometimes beaten beyond physical recognition by the furious mob. Soldiers and police put down the riot, but not before over a hundred people were killed, most of them rioters.

To say that party acrimony did nothing to prevent the riots is not to say that the Democrats incited them. On the contrary, Democratic politicians, including Seymour himself, tried to quell them. Seymour spoke to a hall full of restive workingmen, saying that he had requested postponement of the draft until the courts decided its legality. If it were declared legal, he would enforce it, he said, but he would find funds for the relief of those on whom it imposed hardship. Still, partisanship—along with urban concentration of population—helped account for the northern riots, for none occurred in the Confederacy. The draft was extremely unpopular there also, but there were neither political parties nor cities to focus resistance.

Later that year, when nullification by Pennsylvania courts was added to mob violence as an expression of the widespread resistance to conscription, Lincoln wrote a document about the problem of the draft. He thought realistically about the motives for volunteering to fight. He had volunteered himself as a young man, and he considered a broad range of them: "patriotism, political bias, ambition, personal courage, love of adventure, want of employment, and convenience, or the opposites of these." However these motives operated on individual Americans, they had apparently brought into the ranks about all who were going to come voluntarily. Still more men were needed to win the war. Naturally those who did not want to become soldiers would not like the draft law. But that did not "imply want of patriotism." "Nothing," Lincoln admitted, "can be so just, and necessary, as to make us like it, if it is disagreeable to us." On the other hand, people were "prone . . . too, to find false arguments with which to excuse ourselves for opposing such disagreeable things."

The argument that the draft was unconstitutional seemed obviously false to Lincoln. As a Whig, he had often faced such constitutional arguments from Democrats, who, to Lincoln's way of thinking, were searching for excuses to oppose policies they disliked for other reasons. Such arguments made him very impatient. The power to raise armies was expressly given in the Constitution—"fully, completely, unconditionally." It was "not a power to raise armies *if* State authorities consent; nor *if* the men to compose the armies are entirely willing; but it is a power to raise and support armies given to congress by the constitution, without an if." Lincoln thought "every patriot should willingly take his chance under a law made with great care in order to secure entire fairness."

Actually, the law contained at least two grossly unfair provisions, but Lincoln devised ingenious explanations of these. It allowed a draftee to send a substitute or to pay $300—a "commutation fee"—in lieu of service. Substitution, Lincoln admitted, favored the rich over the poor, but "it was a provision in accordance with an old and well known practice, in the raising of armies" and was little objected to. To Lincoln the commutation fee, which was much objected to, ameliorated "the inequality" that substitution introduced. Without the commutation provision, competition among wealthy men for substitutes probably would raise the price "above three hundred dollars, thus leaving the man who could raise only three hundred dollars, no escape from personal service." Lincoln's reasoning was surely faulty: per capita income during the Civil War was only about $150 a year. His argument ultimately rose or fell on how deeply embedded in folkways was the custom of substitution. "The inequality," he said in his plea for the superiority of half a loaf to none, "could only be perfectly cured by sweeping both provisions away. This being a great innovation, would probably leave the law more distasteful than it now is."

Lincoln's history, though stirring, was no better than his social reasoning:

The principle of the draft, which simply is involuntary, or enforced service, is not new. It has been practiced in all ages of the world. It was well known to the framers of our constitution as one of the modes of raising armies, at the time they placed in that instrument the provision that "the congress shall have power to raise and support armies." It had been used, just before, in establishing our independence; and it was also used under the constitution in 1812. Wherein is the peculiar hardship now? Shall we shrink from the necessary means to maintain our free government, which our grandfathers employed to establish it, and our fathers have already employed once to maintain it? Are we degenerate? Has the manhood of our race run out?

Conscription may have been known to the framers, but it was hardly approved by them. The Revolutionary War measure was a militia draft, through the states, like the one of the summer of 1862, not a national draft of the sort instituted in 1863. In the desperate War of 1812, though a draft was proposed, it was rejected by Congress. New England states threatened to resist, and Daniel Webster recommended state nullification of any federal draft. The state of New York employed conscription in the War of 1812, but that was not a national measure and could hardly be described as having been enacted "under the constitution." States could do many things under the Constitution that the national government could not: for many Americans, that was the point of the Constitution.

One thing Lincoln had learned as a lawyer was the effective pleading of the cause of even the sorriest client. And his political instincts remained excellent: he worked hard on his defense of conscription, but ultimately he never made this document public. Though conscription was certainly necessary and probably the fairest way to apportion military service in a mass society, the law of Congress of March 3, 1863, left much to be desired.

Conscription was the most momentous issue for the Lincoln administration after slavery and race, but the President's handling of it was not much different from his handling of other controversial issues that impinged on northern society. Winning the war was uppermost in his mind, and temporary measures that were deemed necessary to bring about victory, no matter how unprecedentedly drastic they might be, were willingly embraced without much agonizing over their constitutionality.

Such was the case with civil liberties. The Constitution provided that the "privilege of the writ of habeas corpus shall not be suspended, unless when in cases of rebellion or invasion the public safety may require it." Despite its explicit constitutional justification, Lincoln's suspension was much criticized at the time and ever since. Many thought then that Lincoln had no power to suspend the writ, for although the Constitution was explicit on the point in case of civil war, it did not say with whom the power lay. The statement appeared in the section of the document dealing with the powers of Congress, however, and was regarded by most antebellum legal commentators as a legislative prerogative. Chief Justice Taney, a pro-slavery Democrat bitterly opposed to coercion of the southern states, wrote an opinion in May, called *Ex parte Merryman,* in which he stated that Congress and not the President held the power.

Lincoln simply seized the doubtful power. The wartime Presidents who preceded Lincoln acted differently. Polk, who fought a foreign war, had not the constitutional power that Lincoln did; Madison, facing invasion, had the same powers under the Constitution as Lincoln, but was one of the original founders of the republic and was not as willing to employ government power. Lincoln first suspended the writ of habeas corpus very soon after the firing on Fort Sumter. The situation in Washington at that time seemed desperate to many, for the nation's capital was precariously surrounded by slave states. No one knew then what is etched indelibly in American collective memory now: that only eleven states would secede from the Union. For all that Lincoln and the other officials in Washington—or Jefferson Davis and the officials in Richmond—knew, the rest of the slave states, including nearby Maryland, would secede from the Union, too.

If Maryland seceded, Washington would be a Union island within the Confederacy, and while waiting for the Maryland legislature to meet and possibly consider a secession ordinance, the capital was virtually in that situation anyway. After a riot in Baltimore against Massachusetts troops trying to reach the largely unprotected capital, the Baltimore authorities burned the railroad bridges to the city, cutting Washington off from the North. The President, the general-in-chief, and many others grew anxious lest the capital fall to a quick rebel attack. Nicolay and Hay recalled that Lincoln, though "by nature and habit . . . calm . . . equable . . . undemonstrative," paced the floor for nearly half an hour on the afternoon of April 23, 1861, and then "stopped and gazed long and wistfully out of the window down the Potomac in the direction of the expected ships" coming to the capital's rescue. Unaware that one of his secretaries lingered in the room, the President "broke out with irrepressible anguish in the repeated exclamation, 'Why don't they come! Why don't they come!'"

On the same day General Scott informed Lincoln that the Maryland legislature was to convene three days later. Lincoln knew it was not improbable that they would take steps toward secession, but when Scott asked for permission to arrest the legislators and prevent their meeting, Lincoln refused. The next day, however, he suspended the writ of habeas corpus along the transportation routes to Washington through Maryland. Generally, that was the way Lincoln dealt with restrictions of civil liberties: he acted to curtail them for reasons of military necessity and attempted to avoid restrictions imposed to influence political events or decisions. Such a distinction could by no means always be maintained, and months later, in September, when Maryland seemed rather securely within the Union, he permitted the arrest of a number of the state's legislators on the strength of reports, never divulged to the public and not extant today, that they were to enact a secession ordinance or cooperate with a Confederate invasion scheme.

Lincoln's policies on civil liberties were not consistent. He did not really have a policy on civil liberties. Instead, he deemed it his duty as President to win the war and felt the Constitution empowered him to restrict civil liberties when and where they threatened to interfere with that goal. For Lincoln it was a matter of reacting to particular situations and leaving it to subordinates to act in the many far-flung instances beyond his purview. Sometimes a class of actions demanded attention, like draft resistance or desertion. Sometimes an area of the country, like Missouri or Kentucky, demanded attention; sometimes, one individual, like Clement L. Vallandigham.

Vallandigham, arrested in Ohio on May 1, 1863, for giving a speech that allegedly discouraged enlistments, was tried the next day by a military commission and sentenced to imprisonment for the duration of the war. The administration learned of the arrest after the fact, and though Lincoln and his cabinet regretted its having been done, they felt that they must back the general who ordered it. The President decided to commute Vallandigham's sentence to banishment within Confederate lines.

Numerous public protests followed the arrest, and Lincoln felt compelled to respond to them in the public letter to Erastus Corning and New York Democrats referred to earlier. The letter proved effective, and Lincoln had already somewhat blunted the criticism of Vallandigham's arrest by altering the punishment meted out by the military commission. Yet Lincoln had allowed himself to be forced into defending an arrest of which he did not wholeheartedly approve. His rare public letter—the first pronouncement on the subject since his special message to Congress of July 4, 1861—was perhaps ultimately unfortunate for his later reputation because it has ever since distorted perceptions of civil liberties under the Lincoln administration. In order to defend the Vallandigham arrest, he had to take the broadest ground for restricting political speech, and he had to endorse the use of the military tribunal that condemned the Ohioan. In fact, he was defending the military's restraint of an active politician of the opposing party who was arrested for words spoken in a political speech.

Lincoln distinguished between national interests and the mere reputation of the administration. He admitted it would have been wrong to arrest Vallandigham because his speech "was damaging the political prospects of the administration." Otherwise, the President was left on ground not of his own choosing. He maintained that Vallandigham in fact discouraged enlistments and encouraged desertions by avowing his hostility to the war. "He was warring upon the military," Lincoln said, "and this gave the military constitutional jurisdiction to lay hands upon him. If Mr. Vallandigham was not damaging the military power of the country, then his arrest was made on mistake of fact, which I would be glad to correct, on reasonably satisfactory evidence." Yet Lincoln did not go into what Vallandigham had said or where he had said it. Instead, he followed this with the vivid example of the simple-minded soldier boy and the wily agitator.

The New York Democrats' protest conceded the propriety of military arrest in areas of military occupation and actual insurrection (where most of them took place in fact), but they condemned arrests made far behind such lines. Here the peculiarities of the Vallandigham case made Lincoln's task more difficult. The President replied that the Constitution made no such distinction as the Democrats were making. "Public safety" and not proximity to the front was the criterion set by the founders for suspending the writ of habeas corpus. Lincoln was technically correct about that, but the two were clearly related. "Public safety" seemed to connote dangers of sabotage, terrorism, or assassination more than what Lincoln described at one point as "mischievous interference with the raising and supplying of armies" or "enticing men out of the army." At least one of Lincoln's assertions was chillingly broad: "The man who stands by and says nothing, when the peril of his government is discussed, can not be misunderstood. If not hindered, he is sure to help the enemy. Much more, if he talks ambiguously—talks for his country with 'buts' and 'ifs' and 'ands.'" The President seemed more appealing when, as in the case of his arguments for conscription, he made allowances for the inevitable "ifs" and "buts" of a democracy. Lincoln had not questioned the patriotism of those citizens who would serve "if" everyone else had to run the risk of serving as well, for example.

Each time a crisis occurred, Lincoln reacted anew, fashioning yet another proclamation suspending the writ of habeas corpus, when from all appearances it had already been done for the whole nation by September 24, 1862. In the end, tens of thousands of civilians were at one time or another arrested and put in military prisons in the

North, usually for brief periods. But the large number of civilians in northern prisons does not provide a true index of the extent to which dissent was crushed in the North, for most of the prisoners were not dissenters or political prisoners in the modern sense. Many were not northerners, either. A great number of Confederate refugee citizens, civilians caught between the lines of the contending armies, and other persons from territory occupied by federal forces wound up in northern military prisons. Our misperception of the average victim of military arrest during the Civil War stems from our continuing national innocence: we have no experience of great wars fought on our own soil in over 125 years and have happily forgotten the inevitable entanglements of civilian lives with military events. Critics of tender conscience still detect a pattern of dictatorship in Lincoln's internal security measures, and the President's defense of the Vallandigham arrest has consistently misled historians into thinking the typical arrest involved political speech.

Other civilian prisoners had been caught running the Union blockade. Some had been imprisoned for nefarious practices that America's peacetime code seemed inadequate to police: defrauding veterans' widows of their pensions, absconding with military payrolls, or forging military passes. Great numbers of the northern citizens arrested came from border states, especially Missouri, which were scenes of unrestrained guerrilla war. A few prisoners had engaged in practices probably harmful to the war effort that were legal but not much admired by the puritanical Republicans. Men and women who sold liquor to Union soldiers, for example, were subject to arrest. The army also went after fraudulent contractors without much regard for their civil liberties. And deserters and bounty jumpers (young men who enlisted in order to receive the lucrative bounties offered by national, state, and local governments to stimulate recruiting, and then deserted with the cash) enraged the federal authorities so much that for a time they used torture to extract confessions from suspects.

The overt purpose of the arrests was not to stifle dissent, and indeed dissent was anything but stifled. Rancorous partisan abuse continued in the press and on the hustings. After Lincoln's reelection in 1864, for example, a Wisconsin newspaper's headline ran: "The Union of States is gone forever. The South never will be subjugated. A revolution, already rife in the North, will burst with bloody fury at no distant day. A Central and Northwestern Confederacy will surely be established. The Northwestern Confederacy will join hands with the South, regardless of politics, for commercial interests." Newspaper coverage of the Union armies was so extensive that Robert E. Lee made a point of reading northern papers to gain intelligence about the enemy.

Despite party discipline, some Republicans in Congress added to the volume of dissent. Men like Lincoln's old rival Lyman Trumbull were genuinely troubled by the administration's restrictions on civil liberties and attempted to restrain government power. Conversely, some Democrats at first endorsed restrictions on civil liberties; the party's presidential nominee for 1864, George B. McClellan, had a hand in the arrest of the Maryland legislators in September 1861. Nevertheless, the imperatives of partisanship dictated criticism: the Democrats were bound to criticize, and their ability to keep the issue before the people doubtless helped keep in check Republicans who might otherwise have been careless of the people's liberties.

Though critical, the Democrats remained loyal. During the war and long afterward it was commonly believed that there were vast organizations in the North whose members were disloyal Democrats, whom the Republicans called "Copperheads." One of the most important historical discoveries about the Civil War made in the twentieth century is that the Copperhead menace was wildly exaggerated by Republican fears; the Democratic party constituted a loyal opposition. The tens of thousands of civilians arrested by military authority seemed easily explained when Republican assertions about the Copperhead menace could be taken seriously. They no longer can be, and that means that the vast majority of the people arrested were not disloyal northerners. Among the northerners imprisoned, probably only a few held genuinely disloyal sentiments, and of those, even fewer had engaged in any disloyal activity. The handful of internal security successes of the Lincoln administration—the arrests of real saboteurs or spies like Rose O'Neal Greenhow, or the arrests of swindlers and embezzlers—could not be interpreted by even the most enthusiastic patriot as worth the cost in innocent civilians mistakenly or needlessly arrested well behind the lines and away from the precarious border states.

One of the modern myths about civil liberties during the Civil War suggests that the pattern of military arrests of civilians was essentially political, that is, that they were timed shortly before elections and amounted in some cases to rounding up the Democrats until election day and then letting them go afterward. There is not a scintilla of proof of that assertion and much evidence to the contrary. The arrests of the late summer of 1862, for example, though sweeping, were timed to enforce the draft call and were sharply curtailed by the government when the quotas were filled—just after the first week of September and a month or two before election day. Many of the civilian prison-ers—blockade runners from England, for example, or refugees from the Confederacy—were not eligible to vote in northern states anyway. Lincoln's internal security program was not conducted for partisan political advantage. Gaining a reputation as a tyrant is no way to win elections in the United States.

Aside from internal security, other programs commonly thought of as essential to modern war efforts are difficult to find in the Lincoln administration. Conspicuously absent were attempts to manage the American economy. This may seem surprising in light of Lincoln's lifelong interest in economic policies; indeed, he entered politics—or at least chose the particular party he did upon entering—because he wanted to improve the underdeveloped economy of the western areas in which he grew up. Moreover, the Republican party, Lincoln's new political home in the 1850s, though focused as far as Lincoln was concerned primarily on the problem of the expansion of slavery in the United States, also embraced a powerful economic vision. Lincoln had articulated its capitalist critique of slavery as well as any Republican in the 1850s.

In part Lincoln did not exert himself on economic matters because he did not have to. He enjoyed the luxury of Republican control of

Congress and could watch his old Whig economic program enacted without struggle. In the winter of 1862–1863 the President did work publicly and behind the scenes to bring about legislation establishing a national bank and with it, eventually, a national currency instead of the myriad state bank notes that circulated as local currencies. Otherwise, Congress on its own, seizing the opportunity offered by the departure of southern Democrats, raised tariffs four times, so that some duties stood at 100 percent by 1865. Likewise, vast economic and legal encouragement was given by Congress to the construction of a railroad connecting the Pacific West with the rest of the country. The Homestead Act of 1862 gave public lands to settlers, and also to states to fund the establishment of agricultural and mechanical colleges under the Morrill Land Grant Act passed the same year. Some of these measures, such as tariffs, raised revenues for the war effort; others, such as colleges and western settlement, were no help in war, dispersing population and diverting men from military service. Taken as a whole, the domestic policies of the Lincoln administration embody a Republican economic program rather than a warfare state.

Lincoln did not have to exert himself much as well because he was President of the belligerent with the superior industrial economy. That meant few adjustments had to be made in his conventional capitalistic ideas to make his country's economy equal to the demands of the war effort.

But the most important reason for his inattention to matters of economic planning or mobilization was the kind of war Lincoln had to fight. The Civil War was not a war that demanded elaborate economic mobilization. It was a "modern" war fought by mass armies motivated less by harsh discipline than by national feeling and armed with the products of the industrial revolution or machine age. But it was not a "total" war.

The railroads illustrate this well. Although Congress in January 1862 gave the President authority to seize and operate any or all railroads "when in his judgment the public safety may require it," Lincoln and the War Department seldom did so. Thus General McClellan wrote to the president of the B & O Railroad in September

1862, asking "if you could immediately have the railroad bridge over [the] Potomac, at Harper's Ferry, fully repaired" so that he could pursue Robert E. Lee on his retreat to Virginia after Antietam! There had been no previous railroad-era wars in American history, of course, but in our century, President Woodrow Wilson, calling the Great War "a war of resources no less than of men, perhaps even more than of men," seized the railroads. A government board operated them during most of the war. Lincoln's era would not have understood the idea of economic mobilization for a "war of resources."

As a war President, Lincoln was obliged to interrupt normal economic development to divert resources—millions of dollars a day, he calculated—to armies and navies and their voracious need for food, uniforms, shoes, harness, weapons, horses, flags, wagons, ships, and fifes and drums. Naturally the war, which gobbled up resources to power tens of thousands of men who often marched fifteen miles a day and wantonly destroyed other resources, impeded and distorted American economic development. But the astonishing point is how little that was the case—so little that some argue that the war aided industrial development in the United States. Lincoln himself marveled at how little retarding effect the war was having on economic growth and pointed to it as proof that the rebellion was doomed to failure. "The important fact remains demonstrated," the President boasted in his annual message of December 6, 1864, "that we have *more* men *now* than we had when the war *began;* that we are *gaining* strength, and may, if need be, maintain the contest indefinitely. This as to men. Material resources are now more complete and abundant than ever . . . The national resources . . . are unexhausted, and, as we believe, inexhaustible." The Civil War had so little effect on economic development that the Democratic party, which since its origins during the Bank War of the 1830s focused on complaining about the economy, was for the most part robbed of this familiar issue. The Democrats' 1864 national platform contained not a single economic plank and made only brief passing reference to "the material prosperity of the country," saying it was "essentially impaired."

Not only did the war not greatly impede growth, but it did not even distort the economy unduly. The simple armies of Lincoln's day needed more of what was already being produced rather than new categories of hefty goods not ordinarily produced in peacetime, like tanks or military aircraft. Moreover, clever managers made adjustments in production that left the same firms and factories producing, but now turning out army tents instead of sailcloth.

The role of technology in the war has been exaggerated. In the 1860s, technology was important in war, but terrain was much more important. When, for example, Union armies attacked in the Wilderness—the wooded area of Virginia south of the Rappahannock River and west of Fredericksburg—they did not conquer the Confederate armies, though Lee's forces were much smaller in size. Under Hooker in 1863 and Grant in 1864, the Union armies were stymied in the wilderness and to a great degree by the wilderness. Artillery could not be employed to full advantage, and the infantry, instead of maximizing range and accuracy in their fire, often resorted to using buckshot. Indeed, the importance of industrial technology in mid-nineteenth-century war went unrecognized to a surprising degree by people at the time. They associated military prowess with an agrarian lifestyle, where the ability to walk long distances, ride horses, and shoot were naturally cultivated. Old-fashioned republicanism lingered in widespread American suspicions of the weakening effects of cities and the lifestyles of bureaucratic capitalism.

The head of the army's ordnance bureau, General James W. Ripley, took little interest in technological innovations in weaponry. On the whole, the army assumed that no innovation, however potent, could be developed and mass-produced quickly enough to influence the outcome of this war. They did not know how long the war would last, and except for the rare pessimist like William T. Sherman, most generals were optimists who thought the war could be won in the next season's campaign.

Lincoln was optimistic, too, but he was nevertheless interested in technological innovation. Indeed, he was fascinated by it and even owned his own patent on a device he invented in 1849 for getting river vessels over shallow water. Interest in technology was a crotchet of the President's, unrelated to his strategic ideas. Like his sense of humor, it was something Lincoln could not help indulging.

The real sources of Lincoln's interest in technology lay less in his military notions than the economic ideas he had held from earliest maturity. Technological innovation, he thought, was a mark of the progressive races in world history, and groups like Indians and Mexicans, he said, simply lacked the enterprising outlook of the "Yankee." To him all creation was "a mine" and man, a "miner," not a mere "lodger" in or "feeder" on creation. Ants and beavers worked, but only man improved on his workmanship.

Inventors—and America was replete with them—quickly came to understand that even if the army showed little interest, they could often gain a hearing and a test of their devices if they went to see the President first. A vivid example is provided by Thaddeus S. C. Lowe, a 28-year-old balloonist who came to Washington in 1861 to propose a balloon corps for aerial observation. Armed with a letter from the head of the Smithsonian Institution, Joseph Henry, Lowe went to see Lincoln, who sent him to General-in-Chief Winfield Scott. Scott was too old to take seriously the idea of using balloons for military observation, and turned Lowe down. A month later, after the Battle of Bull Run, Lowe decided to try again. Lincoln again sent him to the general's office, where he was informed that Scott was busy and he would have to wait. Lowe waited a couple of hours, but the general went to lunch. When he returned, he took his afternoon nap. Exasperated, Lowe went back to the President's office, and Lincoln decided to walk over to Scott's office with him. Scott then heard Lowe out and endorsed the experiment. By 1862 Lowe had seven balloons and a naval vessel. The air unit provided valuable observations of the enemy in Virginia, but gradually the idea fizzled. Lowe was a civilian, and the army had trouble working with him. He quit, and the balloon corps was disbanded in 1863.

President Lincoln never went on a balloon ascension, but he did test some weapons personally at the Navy Yard and observe the tests of others. On one occasion, he proved himself a good marksman with a breech-loading rifle. On another, along with Secretary of State Seward and Secretary of the Treasury Chase, he might easily have been killed by a rocket that misfired. The President promoted the testing and use of several forward-looking weapons of war: breech-loading firearms, rifled artillery, and early machine guns, for instance. But the army was ultimately correct. Taken all in all, technological innovations devised during the war had little impact on the outcome of land battles or campaigns, though breech-loading carbines improved the performance of the Union cavalry by the end of the war.

Naval warfare was a different matter. Terrain is not a factor on the wide seas, and technology looms correspondingly larger. Oddly enough, the technologically backward Confederacy led the way here in a flurry of experimentation bred of desperation (they began the war with only one naval ship afloat and no shops or yards capable of building a man-o'-war). The developments were attributable more to Stephen Mallory, the ingenious Confederate Secretary of the Navy, than to Lincoln's presidential counterpart, Jefferson Davis. The Union met the challenge of the Confederacy's new ironclad vessels with its own ironclad, the *Monitor*, which Lincoln advocated, but the Union was never able to overcome the enemy's naval innovations. The Confederates' mines and ironclad batteries, for example, protected ports from which blockade runners operated until land forces helped the navy capture them.

Although the war remained technologically in the Napoleonic era and the American economy was not dramatically transformed by the Union war effort, the vast changes of scale in government purchasing did invite corruption, an economic problem that Lincoln as President dealt with directly and often. He handled it well enough that the Democratic opposition was never able to pin the label of corruption on the administration. Lincoln's own character pointed the administration toward financial rectitude, but his political background held potential for sordid plunder. Thus he might have led the country back to the idealistic republican virtue of the founders or forward to the disgraceful "Great Barbecue" of America's postwar Gilded Age. Lincoln was personally ethical, especially in money matters; his wife, who indulged an easier conscience in that realm, thought him "almost a monomaniac on the subject of honesty," and the campaign nickname "Honest Abe," like his legendary birth in a log cabin, was no myth concocted for the canvass. Yet from his entry into politics, Lincoln had been associated with doctrines of economic development that brought him into regular contact with bankers, railroad managers, and other businessmen, some of whom had more relaxed views of economic virtue than he. As a politician, Lincoln understood the temptations of pecuniary gain; he was inclined to compromise and seek practical solutions to problems of placing private gain ahead of public interest.

Arriving in Washington on the heels of the notoriously corrupt Buchanan administration, "Honest Abe" Lincoln could hardly afford to allow his administration to gain a similar reputation. War threatened virtue, however. Emergency measures had to be taken to defend the country, and, as luck would have it, the cabinet member with the shadiest reputation, Simon Cameron of Pennsylvania, sat at the center of the demand for contracts for war goods, the War Department. Cameron did not last a year in his job before being replaced by Edwin M. Stanton. The House of Representatives, which was controlled by his own political party, eventually censured Cameron. The President, however, felt called upon to defend him in a message he sent to Congress on May 26, 1862.

In it Lincoln described Washington in the two weeks following the firing on Fort Sumter as essentially in "the condition of a siege," with "all the roads and avenues" to the city "obstructed" and the forces called upon for defense "prevented from reaching the city by organized and combined treasonable resistance in the State of Maryland." Congress was not in session, and there was no time to call it, so Lincoln decided to act. In a historic cabinet meeting held on Sunday, April 21, 1861, the President, with the "unanimous concurrence" of the cabinet, gave orders to expand the army and navy without congressional approval, made arrangements with private parties for transportation and supply of troops, entrusted persons who were not government employees with millions of dollars of public money, and transmitted his orders by private messengers "who pursued a circuitous way to the seaboard cities, inland, across the States of Pennsylvania and Ohio and the northern lakes." "I believe," the President said, "that by these and other similar measures taken in that crisis, some of which were without any authority of law, the government was saved from overthrow." Cameron's part in these transactions was a part only, Lincoln explained; the President had initiated everything and all the other department heads in addition to Cameron concurred in the measures.

It had indeed been a harrowing time: Secretary of the Navy Gideon Welles recalled the historic cabinet meeting as one where measures were enacted for which they might have been hanged, for all they knew of the possible outcome. Lincoln's willingness to take responsibility and not to let the already discredited Cameron bear the burden for the administration naturally gained the Pennsylvanian's deep gratitude. Years later, when Mrs. Lincoln was a confused and shattered widow, Cameron would be one of the few of the President's former close associates to answer her pleas for assistance.

Excusing financial irregularities by pleading disorganization and desperation would not work forever, of course, and the administration, particularly the War and Navy departments, had to take measures to organize, regularize, audit, and investigate. Gradually they did so, and one of the reasons the Democrats did not succeed in labeling the administration as corrupt is that the administration policed itself. Scandals were bound to occur, but the administration often detected them first, caused them to cease, and sometimes punished the culprits by imprisonment in military prisons. Stanton was apparently incorruptible, and some of the men who worked for him gained reputations as detectors of fraud. One of these was Assistant Secretary of War Peter H. Watson, who in 1863 detected corruption in government purchases of forage on the Philadelphia corn exchange. Civil War horses and mules were fed a mixture of oats and corn, two grains of different weights and different prices. By altering the proportions in the mixture, a merchant stood to gain much in selling the large quantities purchased by the government for the war.

Watson detected irregularities in the mixture, had some Philadelphia merchants arrested, and then left for New York on other department business. In his absence the president of the corn exchange and other merchants came to Washington to make a deal. They offered $65,000 to cover the amounts plundered by two of the accused in exchange for the release of the rest of the prisoners and for the papers seized by the War Department. Meanwhile, Senator David Wilmot of Pennsylvania came to see Lincoln and persuaded him to talk to Watson. Lincoln did so, pointing out to the assistant secretary that much of the money had been refunded, that a steady flow of grain was essential to the war effort, and that political unity in Pennsylvania was necessary to the war effort as well. Watson refused to release the prisoners on a verbal order; he insisted on having it in writing from the President. Lincoln returned to his office and informed Wilmot that there was nothing he could do in the case. Eventually the matter was resolved by compromise, and the Philadelphia merchants avoided being tried in a military court.

If corn and oats could tempt merchants in the City of Brotherly Love, it is not difficult to imagine the soul-destroying lure of cotton in Union-occupied towns in the Mississippi River Valley. The hunger in the North for southern cotton was very great indeed once the supply was cut off by war, and the government made the decision to license trade in it. The Treasury Department issued permits to sell cotton, and they were sought after avidly, by fair means and foul. Even southerners could take an oath of allegiance and acquire a permit. Memphis, Tennessee, was the corrupt center of the trade after 1862. The President and the Congress refused to clamp down on the system, imbued as they were with the outlook of old Whigs, who thought of commerce and trade as something that united classes and nations and not something that divided them into rich and poor. To them, Union, liberty, and prosperity were closely intertwined concepts; slavery bred disunion and poverty; and it was easy to think of reconstructing southern loyalty through commercial lures.

In the midst of the war effort, the President was sometimes called upon to mediate conflicts between economic classes. For example, in

Philadelphia in the summer of 1864 some 20,000 working women—seamstresses making army uniforms—protested to the Secretary of War that the wages paid in government arsenals had fallen 30 percent while the cost of living had risen by 75 percent. While the roughly 80 percent inflation rate for the North during the war compares very favorably with inflation rates in twentieth-century wars, it seemed unmanageable to the hard-pressed working women of Civil War Philadelphia. The women denounced "a large number of men in this city who are making immense fortunes off the Government by their contracts." They thus subscribed to the myth of a "shoddy aristocracy," a new class of rich Americans. "Shoddy"—an inferior wool made from reworked rags and used to make uniforms that came apart in the rain—became a slang term for inferior goods supplied by government contractors rather than high-quality ones. Corruption existed, but not enough to create a new aristocracy of ill-gotten wealth: income redistribution in the North during the war was not great, and classes did not change much in composition.

It was true, however, that private uniforms contractors consistently paid a lower scale than that offered in the government factories making uniforms. The women also asked that production by the government factories be increased, "whereby four times the number of women now engaged might be employed, and millions of dollars annually saved the Nation." The Republican governor of Pennsylvania forwarded their letter to the Secretary of War, and he in turn referred it to the President. "I know not," Lincoln said, "how much is within the legal power of the government in this case; but it is certainly true in equity, that the laboring women in our employment, should be paid at the least as much as they were at the beginning of the war." The arch-capitalist Lincoln administration was not likely to do anything about wages paid by private contractors, but Stanton did require the government works to hire more women and to raise their wages 20 percent.

Conditions for the women worsened anyway, and in February 1865 they held mass meetings where they decided to send delegations to the President to plead their cause. Lincoln patiently heard them out and promised to run the government factories at full capacity. He could not alter the existing contracts with private employers.

Lincoln believed in the right to strike. He had affirmed it publicly on the eve of his presidential nomination in 1860. Speaking in Connecticut at the time of a major strike in the shoe industry, Lincoln said, "I am glad to see that a system of labor prevails in New England under which laborers CAN strike when they want to." In part, he meant the words as a criticism of slavery, but they were also a genuine affirmation of the rights of working people. He remembered his humble origins, though he was not a systematic thinker on economics or any other subject. Less than a year before the Connecticut speech, he had endorsed, again by way of attacking slavery, the free labor system of the North: "If any continue through life in the condition of the hired laborer, it is not the fault of the system, but because of either a dependent nature . . . or improvidence, folly, or singular misfortune."

Abraham Lincoln held a conventional male attitude toward women. Both politics and the law, especially the brand of law Lincoln practiced on the convivial circuit, smacked of the fraternity—practical jokes, risqué humor, and among most practitioners (but not Lincoln), drinking. The famous (though questionable) anecdote that Lincoln referred to Harriet Beecher Stowe, the author of *Uncle Tom's Cabin,* as "the little woman who made this big war," does exemplify Lincoln's attitude toward women. Yet he had mentioned women's suffrage in his 1836 campaign statement, and his wife took an extraordinary interest in politics for a woman of her era, was better educated than most women of the time, and qualified to be termed by some historians a "domestic feminist" because of the amount of control she exerted within the marriage and home.

The incident of the Philadelphia working women illustrates the way that social groups which would become objects of intense scrutiny by twentieth-century historians were brought to the attention of Abraham Lincoln in a century that was not as concerned about them. He saw them only briefly in incidents that threatened the war effort and demanded immediate attention. Such incidents did not evoke long-range policies or systematic thought from the harassed President.

Indian policy provides another example. It was hardly a primary focus of Lincoln's, but in August 1862 a major uprising among the Sioux in Minnesota briefly demanded his attention, because it threatened to siphon troops from the Confederate front. The Indian rebellion was quickly crushed, and a military tribunal, established by General H. H. Sibley, sentenced 303 captured Sioux warriors to hang for "participation in . . . murders and outrages [rapes]" in the brief war. Death sentences by military commissions had to be reviewed by the President, and after discussion in the cabinet on October 14, Lincoln ordered the executions postponed. Eventually he pardoned all but 38, attempting to distinguish between warriors who fought in pitched battles against white soldiers and those who ambushed unarmed civilians and committed rapes. On December 26 the 38 Sioux were hanged publicly in Mankato, Minnesota.

With Indian relations thus briefly and spectacularly called to his attention, Lincoln, in his annual message to Congress of December 1, 1862, mentioned "reform" of the system of dealing with the tribes. It is not possible to tell precisely what he meant, and, as his attention refocused on the Civil War and emancipation, Lincoln left policy to his Indian commissioner William P. Dole, to the Interior Department in which Dole worked, and to the army.

Lincoln's views on Indians were perhaps mild for a son of the frontier whose grandfather had been murdered by Indians and whose father's life was ever after stunted by the resulting poverty, dislocation, and lack of education. Whiggish benevolence was at odds with Whiggish economic views in Lincoln, and the latter held sway in his image of the native Americans. When he met with a group of chiefs on March 27, 1863, the President contrasted the prosperity and superior population of the whites to the Indians' sad lot, and attributed the happier station of the "pale face people" to their practice of agricultural pursuits rather than reliance on "wild game for subsistence." If he did not think of them as savages, he did retain a belief in their innately warlike nature and could, without conscious irony, tell the Indian delegation, in the very midst of the Civil War, that the whites were "not, as a race, so much disposed to fight and kill one another as our red brethren." He spoke to them in the patronizing pidgin English customarily invoked by white authorities in addressing Indians.

The war also brought the problem of anti-Semitism to the President's attention. General Grant's notorious General Orders, No. 11, issued December 17, 1862, expelled the "Jews, as a class . . . from the Department" of the Tennessee because they were "violating every regulation of trade established by the Treasury Department and also Department orders." Outraged Jews sent letters of protest, but no one in the administration took a great interest in the problem until Caesar J. Kaskel, of Paducah, Kentucky, called on the President in person to protest. The next day, January 4, 1863, General Halleck revoked the order; Halleck explained to Grant later that "the President has no objection to your expelling traders & Jew pedlers, which I suppose was the object of your order, but as it in terms prescribed an entire religious class, some of whom are fighting in our ranks, the President deemed it necessary to revoke it." The professional officer class in the United States, like that in Western Europe, was considerably tinged with anti-Semitism. Lincoln was clearly more tolerant, as was Congress, whose law permitting Jews to serve as army chaplains led Lincoln to appoint the first Jewish chaplain in American history on September 18, 1862. Despite a tolerant outlook, Lincoln could still refer to the United States in official documents as "a Christian people."

The myriad problems that beset the President left him little time for his wife and children. His family and personal life came under more scrutiny in Washington than in Illinois, but it still reveals little of interest. Life in Washington for Lincoln and Mrs. Lincoln grew quite unhappy, especially after the death of Willie Lincoln, aged eleven, on February 20, 1862. Lincoln's strenuous work schedule thwarted any close family life. Most days he worked from seven in the morning until eleven at night, with time out for brief meals. Mrs. Lincoln, who was not given to exaggerating the degree of separation between her and Mr. Lincoln, wrote a friend during the war, "I consider myself fortunate, if at eleven o'clock, I once more find myself, in my pleasant room

& very especially, if my tired & weary Husband, is *there*, resting in the lounge to receive me—to chat over the occurrences of the day."

War, as Lincoln had pointed out to Thomas Clay, did not admit of holidays, and the commander in chief took none. He worked even on Christmas Day—a key four-hour cabinet meeting on a serious crisis, for example, occurred on December 25, 1861—and enjoyed no privileges at any presidential retreat, except the Soldiers' Home on the edge of Washington, where the Lincolns dwelled in summer to escape the oppressive heat of downtown Washington.

Lincoln's endurance was aided by his excellent health. He retained his railsplitter's strength, and his abstinence from alcohol and tobacco eliminated threats to his health from so-called "diseases of choice." As for other diseases, he managed to avoid most of them, except varioloid, a mild form of smallpox that struck him on the train ride home from Gettysburg in November 1863. (Lincoln thus fell victim to an epidemic that swept through northern prisoner-of-war camps in 1862 and 1863.) The White House was quarantined for a time, and Lincoln was in and out of bed for about two weeks.

If nothing else, Lincoln's excellent health gave him an edge over Jefferson Davis, who suffered from numerous maladies, including recurrent malaria, seriously impaired vision in one eye, and a variety of less well defined conditions like facial neuralgia, earaches, and bad nerves. Physical exhaustion takes its toll in war. Stonewall Jackson fell asleep with a biscuit in his mouth while eating with his staff during the Seven Days' Battles, and his performance in that campaign was markedly below par. The strains on the commanders in chief did not equal the physical rigors of a military campaign, traveling on horseback and sleeping often on the ground, but they were great all the same, and Jefferson Davis very often appeared gaunt and under stress—Lincoln, less often so.

Most historians would say that Lincoln held another edge over his rival: his eloquence as speaker and writer. The language Lincoln employed in dealing with the American people at home has evoked praise and wonder and imitation. The President carefully shaped his words in public letters, papers, and proclamations meant to explain the purpose of the war and to inspire devotion to it. His stylistic success should not blind us to the rather limited nature of these communications. Neither Lincoln nor his era had any sense of propaganda and a rather limited one of shaping public opinion. The very term "propaganda" took on its modern meaning in the twentieth century, when government organizations acted deliberately to mold attitudes, and after advertising became an "industry" and could provide the techniques.

Lincoln acted to shape opinion only occasionally. He was more often reacting, answering a crisis or challenge, as in the Corning letter; responding, sometimes reluctantly, to an invitation from friendlier groups, as in the Gettysburg Address and in responses to serenades; or dutifully fulfilling an official function, as in his long annual messages to Congress. One can detect no "program" or "orchestration" of efforts, but he had a sense of timing and propriety that influenced, for example, the decision not to issue the paper on the draft discussed at the beginning of this chapter.

The point can be made clearer, perhaps, by glancing at the visual media of the day. The United States government employed no official artists either to record or glorify battlefield events or landmarks of administration history. The famous painting of *The First Reading of the Emancipation Proclamation to the Cabinet*, painted by Francis B. Carpenter while resident in the White House in 1864, was entirely Carpenter's brainchild and had no personal or partisan origins or uses within the administration. The many photographs of Lincoln were taken, for the most part, at the instigation of others, often artists. Indeed, Carpenter, who conducted Lincoln to Mathew Brady's gallery in February 1864 to pose for photographs on which to base his artwork, was indirectly responsible for the most famous of the Lincoln images that remain American icons: the "five-dollar bill" pose, the profile on which the Lincoln penny was later based, and the much loved picture of Lincoln and his son Tad looking at a photo album together. An artist was responsible, not the President or his political party. Lincoln occasionally signed photographs for personal friends or, when requested, for sale at Sanitary Fairs that raised money for medical supplies for the troops, but he did not keep a supply on hand to give admirers.

The United States government did not produce any posters to speak of; even most recruiting posters, in keeping with the practice of raising troops by private and state efforts to be accepted later into U.S. service, were produced privately and outside Washington, D.C. By contrast, the countries engaged in the Great War produced hundreds of millions of posters, with the United States producing more than all the other nations put together. They usually conveyed simple messages: protect this beautiful country; kill the ugly monsters attacking it. Lincoln aimed higher. To the northern public he addressed a different message that continues to be quoted, invoked, and studied as a useful expression of the American purpose.

Lincoln's task was to define the political side of war in such a way that the people in the North would support it. His forte lay not in invoking the traditional image of military glory or ruin, like the retreat from Moscow, but in creating redeeming political images. The Gettysburg Address and the Second Inaugural Address offer the two best examples of these efforts.

Contrary to popular myth, Lincoln's words at Gettysburg were not the result of last-minute inspiration. He had been thinking for a long time about the political meaning of the war when the invitation to speak at Gettysburg gave him an opportunity to distill his ideas into a formal and public prose.

Lincoln was a poor extemporaneous speaker and knew it. His whistle-stop tour across the North en route to his inauguration back in 1861 had revealed this failing to him and to the country. He had said things then that hurt him politically. By the end of the journey, he would apologize after speaking extemporaneously and wonder aloud whether he had said "something indiscreet." Lincoln remembered such lessons and as President generally avoided making impromptu speeches. Press conferences were unheard of, and newspaper interviews infrequent. He had no "press secretary" or "managers" of any sort. The White House staff consisted of two secretaries (who occasionally employed an assistant) and two doormen.

To the quaint nineteenth-century practice of the serenade, we owe our rare glimpse of Lincoln's mind at work on the ideas in the Gettysburg Address. Unimaginable in the modern era of Secret Service security and a White House staff numbering over a thousand, the serenade brought to the President's balcony a little musical band and a group of well-wishers to solicit a few remarks. On July 7, 1863, Lincoln responded to a serenade celebrating the Fourth of July and the recent victories at Gettysburg and Vicksburg. "How long ago is it?" Lincoln asked, "—eighty odd years—since on the Fourth of July for the first time in the history of the world a nation by its representatives, assembled and declared as a self-evident truth that 'all men are created equal.'" By November 19, when Lincoln spoke at the dedication of the soldiers' cemetery at Gettysburg, that idea had become: "Four score and seven years ago our fathers brought forth upon this continent, a new nation, conceived in Liberty, and dedicated to the proposition that all men are created equal."

Lincoln had refined the idea of soldierly sacrifice—the ultimate meaning of the war—as well. The speech is so eloquent and economical of language that any attempt at summary would be humiliatingly inadequate. Here is the rest of the address:

Now we are engaged in a great civil war, testing whether that nation, or any nation so conceived, and so dedicated, can long endure. We are met on a great battle-field of that war. We have come to dedicate a portion of that field, as a final resting place for those who here gave their lives, that the nation might live. It is altogether fitting and proper that we should do this.

But, in a larger sense, we can not dedicate—we can not consecrate—we can not hallow—this ground. The brave men, living and dead, who struggled here, have consecrated it, far above our poor power to add or detract. The world will little note, nor long remember, what we say here, but it can never forget what they did here. It is for us, the living, rather, to be dedicated here to the unfinished work which they who fought here, have, thus far, so nobly advanced. It is rather for us to be here dedicated to the great task remaining before us—that from these honored dead we take increased devotion to that cause for which they here gave the last full measure of devotion—that we here highly resolve that these dead shall not have died in vain—that this nation, under God, shall have a new birth of freedom—and that, government of the people, by the people, for the people, shall not perish from the earth.

Lincoln had consistently defined the war's purpose as saving the "Union," and he never deviated from that. However, he likewise never deviated from defining the Union, or describing it, so that there could be no mistaking its identification with freedom more than with geographical boundaries. Thus the most important line in the speech is the first one, dating the country's founding, not from the Constitution of 1787 but from the Declaration of Independence of 1776.

Gettysburg's dead lost their lives that the nation might endure, but the nation was one dedicated to the proposition that all men are created equal, and continued national life meant "a new birth of freedom" rather than mere survival. The President spoke again of the war's ultimate meaning and purpose in his Second Inaugural Address, delivered March 4, 1865. This was a less characteristic speech in that it sounded more like a sermon than a secular political appeal. Lincoln also exercised in the address one of his greatest powers as a speaker: he was willing and able to tell people what they did not want to hear. The President reviewed the history that had intervened since his First Inaugural Address:

Four years ago, all thoughts were anxiously directed to an impending civil-war. All dreaded it—all sought to avert it . . . Both parties deprecated war; but one of them would *make* war rather than let the nation survive; and the other would *accept* war rather than let it perish. And the war came.

One eighth of the whole population were colored slaves . . . These slaves constituted a peculiar and powerful interest. All knew that this interest was, somehow, the cause of the war. To strengthen, perpetuate, and extend this interest was the object for which the insurgents would rend the Union, even by war; while the government claimed no right to do more than to restrict the territorial enlargement of it. Neither party expected for the war, the magnitude, or the duration, which it has already attained. Neither anticipated that the *cause* of the conflict might cease with, or even before, the conflict itself should cease. Each looked for an easier triumph, and a result less fundamental and astounding.

Although few white southerners would have admitted that their purpose was to "strengthen, perpetuate, and extend" slavery, Lincoln's was otherwise a dispassionate description of the war, more often described at the time in bitter terms of conspiracy.

Lincoln followed with what his audience surely did not want to hear:

Both read the same Bible, and pray to the same God; and each invokes His aid against the other. It may seem strange that any men should dare to ask a just God's assistance in wringing their bread from the sweat of other men's faces; but let us judge not that we be not judged. The prayers of both could not be answered; that of neither has been answered fully. The Almighty has His own purposes.

Then Lincoln continued with a blistering appraisal of the war's cost, and suddenly concluded with a soothing appeal to Christian charity:

Fondly do we hope—fervently do we pray—that this mighty scourge of war may speedily pass away. Yet, if God wills that it continue, until all the wealth piled by the bond-man's two hundred and fifty years of unrequited toil shall be sunk, and until every drop of blood drawn with the lash, shall be paid by another drawn with the sword, as was said three thousand years ago, so still it must be said "the judgments of the Lord, are true and righteous altogether".

With malice toward none; with charity for all; with firmness in the right, as God gives us to see the right, let us strive on to finish the work we are in; to bind up the nation's wounds; to care for him who shall have borne the battle, and for his widow, and his orphan—to do all which may achieve and cherish a just, and a lasting peace, among ourselves, and with all nations.

Afterward, Lincoln showed conscious recognition of his achievement in the address. Responding to a complimentary letter, the President expressed his belief that the speech would "wear as well as—perhaps better than—any thing I have produced." But, he added, "I believe it is not immediately popular. Men are not flattered by being shown that there has been a difference of purpose between the Almighty and them. To deny it, however, in this case, is to deny that there is a God governing the world. It is a truth which I thought needed to be told; and as whatever of humiliation there is in it, falls most directly on myself, I thought others might afford for me to tell it."

Abraham Lincoln's carefully crafted nationalism, a notable and consistent strain in his thought from the early 1850s to the end of his life, was present as well in that famous passage from the second Message to Congress, of December 1, 1862, which provides the title of this book:

> Fellow-citizens, *we* cannot escape history . . . The fiery trial through which we pass, will light us down, in honor or dishonor, to the latest generation . . . We know how to save the Union. The world knows we do know how to save it . . . In *giving* freedom to the *slave,* we *assure* freedom to the *free*—honorable alike in what we give, and what we preserve. We shall nobly save, or meanly lose, the last best, hope of earth. Other means may succeed; this could not fail. The way is plain, peaceful, generous, just—a way which, if followed, the world will forever applaud, and God must forever bless.

CHAPTER SIX

Politics as Usual

Abraham Lincoln may not have had a systematic policy to meet every problem his country faced, but when problems arose, he possessed the political skills to deal with them. In this realm, both friend and foe, sanctifier and critic, have agreed that Lincoln was truly gifted. His detractors have often thought of him as *only* a politician, but in so doing even they have tacitly acknowledged his mastery of the American party system. His admirers argue that only constant attention to politics allowed him to win the war and emancipate a race.

"A free people, in times of peace and quiet—when pressed by no common danger—naturally divide into parties," Abraham Lincoln believed. And "at such times," he added, "the man who is of neither party, is not—cannot be, of any consequence." Lincoln's candid acknowledgment of belief in the two-party system left no room for doubt about his willingness to use partisan techniques to realize his ambitions, but an important question about his presidency remained unanswered. What role would political parties take in time of war, when the nation was "pressed by . . . danger"?

American politics, always hard fought and often laced at election time with allegations of bastardy, larceny, and antirepublicanism, took on dangerous overtones of treason and Caesarism in wartime. The continuity of robust two-party politics in the North throughout the war was a triumph of the American political system consciously sought by the President, but it put strains on the republic and its politicians that have too often been ignored. The political achievements of the era can be properly appreciated only by recognizing the genuine tension caused by issues of dissent and loyalty played out in an era of sharp partisan confrontation. Modern terms for analyzing public speech and government policy such as "discourse," "conversation," or "dialogue" seem inadequate to describe the suspicion and paranoia induced in even the most practiced politicians by the war's partisan struggles. War seemed to return the country to the shrieking fevers of anxiety about the fragility of freedom and the dangers of despotism that animated the founders of the republic. Occasionally even Lincoln, who was not as sure of the role of parties in war as he had been in peace, was seized by these fears.

Though a politician throughout his adult life and a dedicated party adherent, Lincoln retained a firm understanding of the line separating party loyalty and patriotism. On the one hand, he sought partisan advantage mercilessly when he could; on the other, he usually realized that opposition to him was not necessarily unpatriotic. Both sides of Lincoln's political personality are apparent in a long letter he wrote to the German-American Republican politician and general Carl Schurz on November 10, 1862, answering his complaints about the Republicans' performance in the recently completed off-year elections. Schurz said the Democrats had gained because the administration allowed its opponents into its councils. Lincoln, the dedicated partisan, could easily point out that the administration "distributed to its party friends as nearly all the civil patronage as any administration ever did." But when the war came, Lincoln the sensible patriot argued, "The administration could not even start in this, without assistance outside of its party. It was mere nonsense to suppose a minority could put down a majority in rebellion." He knew that "the war should be conducted on military knowledge" rather than "on political affinity."

Both Democrats and Republicans had to be appointed to lead the armies, and Lincoln was honest enough to say of the generals who shared his party affiliation, "I do not see that their superiority of success has been so marked as to throw great suspicion on the good faith of those who are not Republicans." Lincoln often stood above the suspicious partisanship of men like Schurz, who responded to Lincoln's letter with further accusations, including an allegation that subordinates of the Adjutant General of the United States Army had supplied the Confederates with information. (Lincoln denied this and suggested that Schurz had better come to Washington with proof of such a serious charge, if he had any.)

Schurz was not the only partisan with such suspicions. The Civil War presented one of the situations most feared by adherents of classical republicanism. The country seemed rife with potential Caesars. Tradition held that republics were notoriously ill-suited to waging wars, and as a consequence the need for military efficiency might give rise to demands for dictatorship. South Carolina's shrewd diarist, Mary Boykin Chesnut, as early as August 29, 1861, heard that a British journalist covering the American war was saying that "the tramp of the man, who ever he may be (McClellan?) is already heard who is to be their *despot. Then* our trouble comes. We can easily fight the 'many headed monster thing' now pretending to govern." Conversely, northerners betrayed their belief in the unsuitability of republican governments for war when they attributed, without any proof, the military success of the Confederacy to its being a virtual military despotism. Among the most widely circulated of political pamphlets was Charles J. Stillé's *How a Free People Conduct a Long War,* which attempted to calm fears about this republican failing by comparing American experience with Great Britain's in the wars against Napoleon: "In the commencement, there was the same wild and unreasoning enthusiasm with which we are familiar; the same bitter abuse and denunciation of the government at the first reverses; the same impatient and ignorant criticisms of military operations; [and] the same factious and disloyal opposition on the part of a powerful party."

In truth, almost no one, in or out of the army, in either the Confederacy or the Union, really desired the imposition of a dictatorship for the war. But fear of the possibility occasionally poisoned the atmosphere of politics in the North. Democrats complained of the excesses of power wielded by the Lincoln administration in predictable ways, adhering to the pattern of classical republicanism. They expressed fears that wars provided pretexts for governments to encroach upon and eventually crush the people's liberties. Despite being the government party, some Republicans shared these fears: they thought their own army might be turned against them. Carl Schurz's belief in rumors of treason in the army was of a piece with this.

Most such rumors in the Republican party focused at first on the man Mary Chesnut mentioned, George B. McClellan. Allegations of despotic tendencies were completely unfounded and unfair. McClellan was a partisan Democrat but a thoroughly democratic American. His reaction to losing the election of 1864 typifies the general's adherence to the values of the American republic. To his brother he wrote a few days after the election, "Until we meet it is hardly worth while to discuss the late election further than to say that it was very close so far as the popular vote was concerned; & that as we were defeated we have nothing to do but to acquiesce in the result & pray that the country may pass safely through the ordeal of the next four years." McClellan never cried foul; instead he readily admitted that "the people have decided with their eyes wide open."

Lincoln must not have believed the rumors about McClellan or he would not have brought him back to command the Army of the Potomac again in 1862 after the Second Battle of Bull Run. Yet even Lincoln, with his clear-headed sense of the limits of partisanship in war, eventually fell prey to the fevered fear of possible dictators. Soon after Lincoln appointed Joseph Hooker to replace Ambrose Burnside at the head of the Army of the Potomac, the President on January 26, 1863, wrote Hooker a now famous letter:

> I have heard, in such way as to believe it, of your recently saying that both the Army and the Government needed a Dictator. Of course it was not *for* this, but in spite of it, that I have given you the command. Only those generals who gain successes, can set up dictators. What I now ask of you is military success, and I will risk the dictatorship.

The letter is often cited as proof of Lincoln's willingness to tolerate in high places men of ambition and strength who might threaten his own power and position. But it reveals something less attractive as well: Lincoln himself occasionally believed the rumors of plots to overthrow the republic. Such suspicions gained the upper hand only when Lincoln was under great stress and especially aggravated, but he was under stress a great deal of the time.

Interpretations of military actions were particularly susceptible to partisan suspicion. In the aftermath of the Battle of Gettysburg, when Lee's army got over the Potomac and the last hope of decisive pursuit was gone, the President grew very angry. On Tuesday, July 14, 1863, a regular day for the cabinet to meet, Lincoln disbanded the meeting, saying he was not in a proper frame of mind for deliberation. As the Secretary of the Navy walked across the lawn back to his department to work, the President hastened to catch up with him. Welles recalled:

> He said, with a voice and countenance which I shall never forget, that he had dreaded yet expected this; that there has seemed to him for a full week a determination that Lee, though we had him in our hands, should escape with his force and plunder. "And that, my God, is the last of this Army of the Potomac! There is bad faith somewhere. Meade has been pressed and urged, but only one of his generals was for an immediate attack, was ready to pounce on Lee; the rest held back. What does it mean, Mr. Welles? Great God! what does it mean?"

Lincoln seldom lapsed into the belief that military failure was attributable to "bad faith," but it was a common tendency of the partisan age and one especially prevalent in the ranks of the so-called radical Republicans, the members of his party with the most zealous antislavery convictions. They often assumed that Union defeats resulted from the inadequate antislavery zeal of certain generals, men who were politically disinclined to harm the slavocracy. Such views led them to champion officers, as Lincoln put it, more on grounds of "political affinity" than "military knowledge."

Democratic generals did not worry Lincoln as much as Democratic politicians did. A serious incident, involving more than temporary pique, occurred later that same summer and threatened to complicate the war effort if not to divide the forces for Union absolutely in two.

On Monday morning, September 14, President Lincoln convened a special session of the cabinet to deal with a crisis in Pennsylvania. He told them that military officers in Pennsylvania were complaining that judges were issuing writs of habeas corpus to free recruits and draftees. The officers were compelled to appear in court to explain why certain men were held in the army. The practice had become so common of late that it threatened to halt the business of mobilization in the state.

Attorney General Edward Bates thought Lincoln "more angry than I ever saw him." The President, Bates recalled, "declared that it was a formed plan of the democratic copperheads, deliberately acted out to defeat the Gov[ernmen]t, and aid the enemy. That no honest man did or could believe that the State Judges have any such power." Lincoln vowed to enforce the law and to send any interfering judges after Vallandigham, that is, to banish them to the Confederacy as he had the Ohio martyr to free speech.

When the cabinet and the President met again to discuss the problem the next day, Lincoln brought with him a toughly worded order instructing officers to respond to writs of habeas corpus by indicating to judges that the prisoners were held by presidential authority, and "if said court or judge, shall issue any process for his, said officer's arrest, he refuse obedience thereto; and that, in case there shall be any attempt, to take such person from the custody of such officer, or to arrest such officer, *he resist such attempt, calling to his aid any force that may be necessary to make such resistance effectual.*"

Secretary of the Treasury Chase feared that the order would initiate civil war in the free northern states. Lincoln was wrong about the law: Montgomery Blair himself, for one, had as a state judge issued writs of habeas corpus to release soldiers from military service. It was a matter of established precedent in the United States, where the civilian authority was superior to the military. Lincoln was wrong about the facts, too. The problem did not lie with state judges alone; two of the worst offenders, in Secretary of War Stanton's view, were federal judges appointed by President Buchanan.

What the judges had in common was their affiliation with the Democratic party. But the President was surely wrong to think these occurrences stemmed from a Democratic conspiracy. Like many other Democrats, the judges in Pennsylvania believed conscription unconstitutional, and they happened to be in positions to do something about the problem. By employing writs of habeas corpus to frustrate the conscription system enacted by Congress in 1863, judges were engaging in a form of piecemeal legal nullification. It was probably inevitable in republican America, whose judiciary was the most powerful in the Western world—President Jefferson Davis faced the very same problem in the Confederacy.

The cabinet calmed Lincoln down and persuaded him to issue another proclamation suspending the writ of habeas corpus that would warn against the practices of the Pennsylvania judges. Then he could issue his more drastic enforcement orders quietly. By preparing public opinion first, the policy worked.

Though he could understand objections to conscription of many sorts, Lincoln could never understand arguments that it was unconstitutional. "It is the first instance, I believe," Lincoln wrote, "in which the power of congress to do a thing has ever been questioned, in a case when the power is given by the constitution in express terms." Little wonder, then, that in exasperation he was tempted to attribute frustration of the draft by the judiciary to disloyal partisan malice. The ability of the judiciary to halt an army on the march was perhaps more than any commander in chief could bear.

Other members of Lincoln's party were much quicker than he to make evil assumptions about the Democrats and in the process to threaten democratic government. For a substantial part of the war, not only was Missouri ruled by an illegal usurping government, but two other states in the North, Indiana and Illinois, were governed by the executive without any legislative check. In Indiana, Governor Oliver P. Morton, a Republican who always seemed to Lincoln to be unnecessarily fearful of enemy attack or fifth-column movements, engaged in a bitter political struggle with the Democratic legislature elected in 1862. When the Democrats seemed likely to pass a militia bill that threatened the governor's extensive military powers, the Republican members walked out and prevented a quorum. From early 1863 to early 1865 Morton governed the state from his office, and since the legislature had not yet made the annual appropriations, he raised the requisite money through loans from the War Department in Washington and from wealthy Republican citizens. Because the Indiana state treasurer was a Democrat, Morton disbursed those funds directly from a safe in his office. His sympathetic biographer entitled the Civil War section of his life "I Am the State."

In Illinois, the Republican governor Richard Yates, an alcoholic who harbored frenzied fears of fifth-column movements, discovered an obscure provision of the state constitution, never used before or since, that allowed him to "prorogue" the legislature if the two houses could not agree on a date for adjournment. Faced with a disagreeable Democratic legislature, he seized the opportunity and thereafter governed alone.

Other border states where there were military operations experienced some electoral irregularities, but nowhere in the North were elections canceled, and when the time came, free elections were held even in Missouri, Indiana, and Illinois. The national elections were never in question, and the story of Civil War politics was politics as usual.

The most important example of that was the presidential election of 1864, which, with the exception of the part of the country in rebellion, proved to be a full-fledged political campaign of the freest sort, the kind of colorful party contest that could be found nowhere else in the world in the middle of the nineteenth century, let alone in the middle of a war. It was not without precedent: during the War of 1812, James Madison had run for reelection in a free and open contest.

Before the election of 1864, Lincoln had as a principal task keeping the Republican party together to enjoy its new majority status in the North. From all appearances, this should have been unusually easy. The Democratic party had split in 1860, and by 1861 most of the southern wing was no longer participating in elections under the United States Constitution. In Congress the opposition party was now a pathetic minority left leaderless in 1861 by the death of Stephen A. Douglas. President Buchanan retired to Pennsylvania, tarnished by the scandals that had rocked his administration and by his own feeble performance in the secession crisis. Much of the rest of the leadership of the old Democratic party was in the south.

The Democrats proved remarkably resilient under the circumstances. They quickly rallied to contest elections effectively in most northern states. It would not have been difficult to let the party die, with so many disadvantages and with such a vacuum of leadership, but the Democrats made few serious mistakes during the war. Most important, they formed a loyal opposition—a fact sometimes lost sight of after the Civil War. They were unable to regain their old electoral majority, but they remained genuinely competitive.

The President never underestimated them. He knew that he had been elected by a minority; and despite the departure of the bulk of the southern Democrats in the Confederacy, Lincoln could not be certain of Republican political superiority. He worked mainly to keep his party together as an effective vote-getting organization, not to purify its principles or conduct.

Besides, the Republican party was his principal organ for governing the nation, and he needed to retain its talented members for serious work in governance in the difficult situation that faced him. From the start Lincoln had recruited the party's ablest members to work for the administration. It did not matter if they happened to be potential rivals for party leadership—or for the presidential nomination in 1864. Lincoln enjoyed the deepest form of self-confidence: he knew no fear of the talents of others. When he selected his cabinet, he absorbed those who had been his strongest rivals for the nomination in 1860: Seward, Bates, Chase, and Cameron. He needed talent, and he sought unity.

Party unification proved difficult for Lincoln because of rivalries between former Whigs and ex-Democrats. Lincoln had been a lifelong Whig—in fact, a Whig for the life of that party—and he retained the economic principles of its old platform. A majority of Republicans, including many strong men in the party, were old Whigs, too, but they tended to forget, in the enjoyment of victory over the Democrats for the first time in a decade, that ex-Democrats constituted the Republicans' winning margin.

William H. Seward and his political advisor Thurlow Weed wanted a strong cabinet as much as Lincoln did, but they tended to equate strength with a long-standing adherence to essential principles of the Republican party, which were almost always Whig in origin. Weed traveled to Springfield to confer with the President-elect about the shape the new cabinet was taking. Lincoln had decided on three ex-Whigs (Bates, Seward, and Caleb B. Smith, of Indiana) and four ex-Democrats (Blair, Welles, Cameron, and Chase). Weed had come to urge an ex-Whig for the Treasury Department, rather than Chase, because of the importance of that position to the old Whig schemes of economic development. Lincoln pointed out to Weed that the party consisted of two elements, ex-Whigs and ex-Democrats, and that these had to be balanced. Weed saw an opening and pounced: the problem was that the ex-Democrats outnumbered the ex-Whigs four to three. Lincoln replied that Weed's calculation left the President out of the equation; he would be present at the cabinet meetings, too, and that put the balance at a perfect four and four. Lincoln, by keeping a careful eye on such things within the Republican Party, was able to form a cabinet with extremely able people to run their departments.

Democrats, unlike ex-Democrats, were shown little mercy. The Lincoln administration predated civil-service reform, and the President was capable of wielding the patronage with skill and impunity. By the spring of 1861 Lincoln had completed the most sweeping removal of political opponents in U.S. history: 1,195 of 1,520 Democratic office-holders were relieved of their posts to make way for loyal Republicans. Many southern offices remained unfilled, thus accounting for most of the other 325 jobs.

Lincoln's ability to maintain the balance in his party and keep the talent working for the administration is nowhere better illustrated than in his adroit handling of the cabinet crisis of December 1862. It came at a new low point for the administration: the Battle of Fredericksburg had been lost on December 13, and Republicans had recently seen five states that went for Lincoln in 1860 return Democratic congressional majorities in the off-year elections (New York, Pennsylvania, Ohio, Illinois, and Indiana). Many Republicans in Congress grumbled that the cabinet ought to be shaken up so that there could be a more vigorous prosecution of the war. Criticism focused on Seward, who was thought to have a paralyzing effect on Republican policy. Republican suspicions about the Secretary of State were apparently being fed by the Secretary of the Treasury, Chase, who leaked stories of what went on at cabinet meetings. The crisis was not necessarily a Chase conspiracy. He happened to be the sort of antislavery enthusiast some of the Republicans thought would bring proper zeal for a vigorous prosecution of the war, and he was discontented with the cabinet meetings, which did not determine major policies.

On December 16 and 17, 1862, Republican members of Congress who had heard Chase's indiscreet remarks met in caucus and drafted a protest that denounced Seward by name and suggested a reorganization of Lincoln's cabinet. When Seward heard about it, he assumed he was finished: he and his son Frederick, the Assistant Secretary of State, submitted their resignations and began packing their private papers to leave Washington.

For Lincoln the crisis posed two problems: it challenged his leadership of the party, and it threatened to rob him of the considerable talents of William H. Seward. He invited a committee of disgruntled Republican Senators to the White House for a meeting on the night of December 18. They presented their grievances and made their case against Seward. Lincoln asked them to return the next night, December 19. On the morning of the 19th he assembled the cabinet and told them he was surprised to hear that the Republican Senators had an impression that the cabinet was divided. He then asked all the cabinet members except Seward to come to the meeting that night.

When the Senators arrived, they found Lincoln, Chase, and the rest of the cabinet waiting for them. Now the Senators were in the position of denouncing the cabinet to their faces. And Chase was in the excruciatingly uncomfortable position of telling those to whom he had previously been complaining in private that there were no problems in the cabinet. The Secretary of the Treasury was embarrassed and half-heartedly offered his resignation the next morning. Lincoln's eyes lit up. "Where is it?" he asked. When Chase brought it to the President, Lincoln said, "I can see my way clear. Now I can ride. I have a pumpkin in each end of my bag." On the 20th Lincoln refused both resignations and the crisis was over.

A year later Lincoln faced a different political problem with Chase and other discontented Republicans, many of them radicals: he needed to maintain party unity, and he needed to unite the party behind him so that he could be renominated and win the 1864 election. (Lincoln gave up advocating "the limitation of the presidential office to one term," a position he took in 1844.) Seward appears to have renounced his presidential ambitions, but Chase's never abated. As Secretary of the Treasury, he occupied a strategic base from which to build a political machine for the presidency. The United States customhouses and revenue offices held many federal appointees, every one of whom was a potential voter and, more than that, a potential campaign worker or contributor. Any person who held a job from the Lincoln administration might expect to contribute as much as 10 percent of his wages to the party coffers. The New York customhouse alone employed more than 1,000 people and was the focus of unseemly squabbling among political factions in New York during most of the war.

Chase's presidential ambitions were undermined by premature exposure, indecisiveness, and inability to shore up his geographical base. In February 1864 Kansas Senator Samuel C. Pomeroy mailed a printed circular to about 100 Republicans, urging the one-term principle for the presidency. The government, Pomeroy asserted, was so bloated with patronage because of expansion for the war that it could be used as a machine of despotism by the incumbent. Moreover, the war was languishing, and Chase should be the Republican nominee. Both Chase and Lincoln said that they read about the circular only in the newspapers, but years later, insiders recalled variously that Chase was behind the letter or that it had been published by Chase supporters to force him to decide to run. Whatever its origins, its results were disastrous for Chase. The public thought it disloyal for a cabinet member to be scheming for the presidential nomination. When a Republican caucus in the legislature in Chase's home state, Ohio, declared for Lincoln, the Secretary of the Treasury decided to remove speculation about his candidacy, and a public letter on March 5 with-drew his name from consideration.

Relations between Chase and Lincoln were strained, though Chase stayed on in the Treasury until July, when, in yet another squabble over the New York customhouse, he again offered his resignation. This time Lincoln accepted. Chase left the government but campaigned for Lincoln's reelection in the fall and was eventually rewarded with ap-pointment as Chief Justice of the United States Supreme Court.

Chase may have been the focus of discontent, but he was not its only cause, for a third party was formed in June, called the Radical Democrats, led mainly by German-Americans; they nominated John C. Frémont for President. Lincoln easily regained nomination at the Republican convention in Baltimore in June, but as long as the third-party ticket was in the race, unity was still denied him. After military fortunes—and with them the hopes of the administration—turned for the better in September, Frémont withdrew from the race. The day after, Lincoln asked Montgomery Blair, Frémont's archenemy and the focus of hatred by many of the more radical elements in the Republican party, to resign.

With unity in the party achieved, the Republicans ran their accus-tomed vigorous campaign, as did the Democrats. It was politics as usual, with torchlit parades, fireworks, party songs, barbecues, and rallies. The Republicans took a number of steps that contributed to a campaign strategy a little different from the one adopted four years earlier. None of these can be definitely attributed to Lincoln's instiga-tion, but they added up to victory for him in November.

Perhaps the most dramatic was the change of the party's name from Republican to National Union, usually shortened to "Union." In truth the Republican party had been known by other names throughout its brief and turbulent life. In Pennsylvania, where the party had avoided any taint of antislavery radicalism, it was called the People's party. The Union party name came into use in some areas as early as 1861. This tactic was always an attempt to avoid association with radical antislav-ery sentiments, to attract War Democrats to the ticket, *and* to suggest that the opposition party was opposed to the Union. On July 25, 1864, Lincoln wrote a Republican in New York suggesting that the Confederate agents in Canada, across from Niagara Falls, were there "to assist in selecting and arranging a candidate and a platform for the Chicago [Democratic] Convention." "Thus," Lincoln concluded, "the present presidential contest will almost certainly be no other than a contest between a Union and a Disunion candidate, disunion certainly following the success of the latter. The issue is a mighty one for all people and all times." In keeping with the new Union party image, Vice President Hannibal Hamlin was replaced on the ticket by Andrew Johnson, a War Democrat and a southerner.

Both parties ran more issues-oriented campaigns than in 1860. The principal evidence of this was a massive effort at production of partisan pamphlets on the issues. The Loyal Publication Society, a volunteer organization, solicited writers and printed some 470,000 documents for the election. Typical was Francis Lieber's *No Party Now But All for Our Country.* The Democrats' Society for the Diffusion of Political Knowledge offered literature for partisans of the other faith. The greatest effort came from the National Union Congressional Committee, which managed to distribute some six million documents, nearly three for every vote Lincoln got in November.

Though hardly uniform in content, the Republican (or Union) literature and the other moves made by party adherents constituted a consistent campaign strategy of wrapping themselves in the flag and tarnishing the Democrats with charges of disloyalty. In fact, what the Union party did was to run a campaign that, like Francis Lieber's pamphlet, suggested that party opposition to the government in war was illegitimate. The survival of the two-party system in the Civil War is a triumph of representative democracy, but it was difficult for people at the time to see any advantages. Everyone defended free elections. No one particularly praised party spirit.

As the Republican campaign unfolded, first there were noisy debates in Congress over the expulsion of a Democratic member of the House of Representatives named Alexander Long for advocating peace. Then in June General William S. Rosecrans published a report on secret societies in Missouri that were allegedly organized to bring about secession from the northern war effort and the formation of a Northwest Confederacy. The idea of a conspiracy to form a Northwest Confederacy became a great northern bugbear, widely feared but advocated by almost no one. Nearer election time, in October, the Judge Advocate General of the Army, a tough-talking Kentucky Unionist named Joseph Holt, published an exposé of an organization called the Sons of Liberty, describing it as a vast disloyal network with tens of thousands of members in northern states like Missouri, Indiana, and Illinois.

Lincoln's role in setting the tone or strategy for the campaign is not easy to determine. For one thing, he continued to adhere to the traditional role of a presidential candidate and avoided public pronouncements on the issues. Lincoln said he believed "it is not customary for one holding the office, and being a candidate for re-election," to write public letters to be presented at political meetings. Moreover, Lincoln was located in Washington for this campaign instead of Springfield, and did not have to communicate with the party's congressional leaders by letters that would later prove useful to historians. Presidential campaigns were not as centralized then as now, either, and powerful state party operatives made their own decisions about campaign matters, with the result that different areas of the country emphasized different aspects of the Union party message.

Among the clues Lincoln left history were some that suggested a personal preference for a rather different approach to the campaign. When he gave his official response to the notification of nomination on June 9, for example, the President chose to stress his approval of the platform plank urging an amendment to the Constitution abolishing slavery forever in the United States. This was not consistent with the Union party strategy, in that it stressed the divisive issues of slavery and race rather than the safe pieties of nationhood. Moreover, Lincoln was personally skeptical of the allegations of the strength of the Sons of Liberty and other secret disloyal organizations. He had at first been alarmed enough about the reports to send his trusted secretary John Hay to Missouri to investigate their strength. But Hay's report and whatever the President knew from other sources convinced him that there was about as much "puerility" as effective malice in these opéra-bouffe organizations.

And yet, by late summer, as his political fortunes sank, even Lincoln was beginning to act on fears that the opposition party might willingly surrender the republic to disunion. That was surely part of the meaning of the famous blind memorandum of August 23, in which the President wrote: "This morning, as for some days past, it seems exceedingly probable that this Administration will not be re-elected. Then it will be my duty to so co-operate with the President-elect, as to save the Union between the election and the inauguration; as he will have secured his election on such ground that he can not possibly save it afterwards." At the regular cabinet meeting that day the President asked the members present to sign the folded sheet without knowing what was written on the inside. The remarkable document testifies to Lincoln's sincere belief that he would lose the election. And that in turn provides dramatic proof of his belief in the soundness of republican institutions: he never dreamed, as any potential dictator might, of postponing or disrupting or stealing the election. Still, he did not fully believe in the naturalness of political parties in time of war, when the country was "pressed by . . . danger." To Lincoln, in his despondent mood, the Democrats constituted a party that would win the election on grounds that would make it impossible for them to save the Union.

Such a belief maligned the Democrats, of course. They drafted a platform declaring the war a failure and calling for an armistice preparatory to restoring the Union by negotiation. Then they nominated a war hero, McClellan, who felt compelled after some vacillation to repudiate openly the so-called peace plank of the platform. He eventually stated that he could not pronounce as a failure what his men in the Army of the Potomac had fought so hard for. The Democrats were a loyal opposition, but many Republicans feared otherwise and were prepared to act vigorously on their fears. In June Indiana's always nervous Governor Morton ordered a raid of the office of Harrison Dodd, a leader of the Sons of Liberty in that state. Dodd had actually contacted Confederate agents in Canada about liberating Confederate prisoners of war and setting up a Northwest Confederacy. His office held a cache of arms and correspondence with Democratic politicians in the state (who were not linked to the scheme necessarily, only to Dodd, who was a prominent Democrat). Others were arrested as well, including Lambdin P. Milligan, taken from sickbed in the night in Huntington, Indiana, and smuggled to Indianapolis. Dodd escaped his cell to Canada, but others stood trial before a commission of generals and colonels of the United States Army. Milligan was sentenced to hang.

Such serious actions cannot fairly be interpreted as Republican dirty tricks to win the election; many sincerely believed in the Northwest conspiracy. Still, tarring the Democrats with treason did help the Republican cause, and it fit with what can only be called a pattern or strategy of making the Democrats appear to be opposed to the Union. The strategy worked so well that the President, at least, found himself pulling away from it a bit by election time, soothing fears on both sides. Responding to a serenade on the night of October 19, Lincoln employed the occasion to say something substantial, which he wrote out in advance:

> Something said . . . has been construed by some into a threat that, if I shall be beaten at the election, I will, between then and the end of my constitutional term, do what I may be able, to ruin the government.
>
> Others regard the fact that the Chicago [Democratic] Convention adjourned, not *sine die,* but to meet again, if called to do so by a particular individual, as the intimation of a purpose that if their nominee shall be elected, he will at once seize control of the government. I hope the good people will permit themselves no uneasiness on either point.

"I believe," Lincoln concluded after a little hedging, " . . . they are still resolved to preserve their country and their liberty; and in this, in office or out of it, I am resolved to stand by them."

When the election was over and Lincoln's victory was assured, the

President sounded even more confident and at last added political parties to the normal course of wartime events in a republic. Once again, Lincoln drafted remarks in advance as a response to a serenade:

> It has long been a grave question whether any government, not *too* strong for the liberties of its people, can be strong *enough* to maintain its own existence in great emergencies.
>
> On this point the present rebellion brought our republic to a severe test; and a presidential election occurring in regular course during the rebellion added not a little to the strain. If the loyal people, *united,* were put to the utmost of their strength by the rebellion, must they not fail when *divided,* and partialy paralized, by a political war among themselves?
>
> But the election was a necessity.
>
> We can not have free government without elections; and if the rebellion could force us to forego, or postpone a national election, it might fairly claim to have already conquered and ruined us. The strife of the election is but human-nature practically applied to the facts of the case. What has occurred in this case, must ever recur in similar cases. Human-nature will not change . . . But the election, along with its incidental, and undesirable strife, has done good too. It has demonstrated that a people's government can sustain a national election, in the midst of a great civil war. Until now it has not been known to the world that this was a possibility.

"Not very graceful," Lincoln commented to Hay after reading the remarks, which he had prepared in some haste. But history may have a different and rather more favorable judgment.

By the time of his annual message to Congress, of December 6, 1864, Lincoln's description of the past presidential campaign had already taken on mythical tones that ignored, in obeisance to republican values, the suspicion, strife, and anxiety of the previous months:

> Judging by the recent canvass and its result, the purpose of the people, within the loyal States, to maintain the integrity of the Union, was never more firm, nor more nearly unanimous, than now. The

extraordinary calmness and good order with which the millions of voters met and mingled at the polls, give strong assurance of this. Not only all those who supported the Union ticket, so called, but a great majority of the opposing party also, may be fairly claimed to entertain, and to be actuated by, the same purpose. It is an unanswerable argument to this effect, that no candidate for any office whatever, high or low, has ventured to seek votes on the avowal that he was for giving up the Union. There have been much impugning of motives, and much heated controversy as to the proper means and best mode of advancing the Union cause; but on the distinct issue of Union or no Union, the politicians have shown their instinctive knowledge that there is no diversity among the people.

Election day was marked by no unusual disorder or violence, as the President said, but his analysis was not quite what a modern historian sees in the election.

Both parties did appeal to Union, and to liberty for that matter, and both Democrats and Republicans doubtless shared the republic's basic values. But both shared its basic anxieties, too. That explains their continuing participation in large numbers; voter turnout remained high. Lincoln received about 360,000 more votes than he had in 1860; but only one party was now in the field against him, and government control of certain disputed areas in the border states may have brought the Republicans unnaturally high totals there—through outright intimidation in some cases. Likewise, the soldier vote, where recorded separately from the civilian, as it was in states (Republican, of course; Democratic states blocked absentee voting) that allowed voting in the field, though freely given and exposed to appeals from both parties, was given under unusually controlled circumstances.

No dramatic new voting realignment appeared: that had all been sorted out in 1856 and 1860, and the same kinds of people—ethnic groups, economically motivated interest groups, religious groups— voted roughly the same way they had in the previous presidential election. Even the soldiers and sailors who were fighting the war followed what has been called the "tribal" alignments of American voters. Although the soldier vote was overwhelmingly Republican, the variable determining their votes may have been that soldiers were young. The Republicans had performed well among youthful voters back in 1860, too. And the *sailors'* vote, hardly ever mentioned, makes this point even more forcefully. Sailors, also young, tended to be men of foreign birth, particularly Irishmen recruited in the country's largest port, New York City; and Catholic Irishmen traditionally voted the Democratic ticket. Moreover, the reforming Republicans had, once they gained control of the Navy, brought an end to the traditional grog ration, the daily tot of strong Navy rum, and the ethnic sailors, more accustomed to drink than some other Americans, resented it. Sailors tended to vote Democratic in 1864.

The vote in the electoral college was overwhelming: Lincoln carried every state except New Jersey, Kentucky, and Delaware. But, as McClellan preferred to state the results, the popular vote was closer, the Democratic candidate receiving about 45 percent. A 2 percent change in key states would have given the election to McClellan.

If the Union strategy failed to change many minds, it at least got the faithful out once again for Lincoln and the Republicans. And it left the Democrats a bruising legacy, from which it took the party literally generations to recover. Indeed, hardly any presidential campaign has been more successful than the Republicans' in 1864 in labeling its opponents with a distorted image. The notion that the Democrats harbored a gigantic fifth-column movement during the Civil War was to rally Republican voters for many elections to come, in what came to be called "waving the bloody shirt." In truth, almost everyone in the North, Democrat and Republican alike, wanted the Union to survive.

Reconstructing the Union once the war was over—and it was over in many areas of the Confederacy well before the spring of 1865—was a problem vexing enough to tax even Lincoln's political skills to their limit. The fundamental problems were two. First, white racism was not radically changed by the war. No new scientific conclusions emerged to call the idea of race into question—far from it. Second, changes once the war was over required coercion by the army or the

federal government, and that was difficult or impossible in a constitutional democracy in peacetime. In the South only black votes could
ensure change by a process compatible with democratic ideals, and
black votes were not compatible with white racism, northern or southern, in the nineteenth century.

Lincoln ran up against the problem even in the initial phases of
Reconstruction that he oversaw. Because it was the first significant area
to fall, New Orleans and surrounding parishes under Union control
made Louisiana Abraham Lincoln's most important laboratory for
reuniting the country. The unfortunate incompatibility of the Union's
ends and the means available to a constitutional democracy became
apparent in Lincoln's Proclamation of Amnesty and Reconstruction,
of December 8, 1863, his first national pronouncement on the subject
and a document issued while he struggled with the problem of reconstructing Louisiana.

The proclamation embodied what is often called the "ten percent
plan." The President provided for the formation of a new state constitution when ten percent of those who had voted in 1860 took an
oath guaranteeing future loyalty to the Union. That remnant could
elect a constitutional convention, and the government formed under
that new constitution would be recognized and its representatives
admitted to Congress, Congress permitting. The President offered
amnesty and the restoration of property rights to all southerners who
took the oath of allegiance, excepting a few people of prominence like
high-ranking Confederate officials. Lincoln vowed "not to attempt to
retract or modify the emancipation proclamation; nor . . . return to
slavery any person who is free by the terms of that proclamation, or
by . . . acts of Congress," and the new state governments organized
under the amnesty proclamation had to recognize freedom of the
slaves and provide for their education. He would allow any other
policies "consistent, as a temporary arrangement, with their present
condition as a laboring, landless, and homeless class." Nicolay and
Hay reported that the proclamation was well received, passing muster
with conservatives like Reverdy Johnson of Maryland and radicals like
Charles Sumner.

The plan nevertheless was not a practical success, though based on a realistic recognition that secession had broad popular support. At first, Lincoln had not been willing to acknowledge that, saying in his annual message to Congress of 1861 that he doubted "whether . . . a majority of the legally qualified voters of any State, except perhaps South Carolina, . . . favor . . . disunion." Many Republicans continued throughout the war to use bitter rhetoric accusing the Confederacy of being a military despotism imposed by a tiny slaveholding elite (it was not, of course; it was a popular white democracy). But the ten percent plan seemingly acknowledged that it would be difficult to find even ten percent of the population in any state that seceded who would declare their loyalty to the Union. For any Louisianan, for example, to take such an oath could be dangerous. Who in Louisiana knew that Union forces occupying certain parishes would not be driven out by resurgent Confederate attack? And what would be the fate of the oath-takers then?

The plan was also undemocratic. On the surface it offered the prospect of imposing a government chosen by a little over five percent of the white voters (a majority of the remnant eligible to vote) on the rest of the population. The realistic alternatives for the southerners were even less democratic than the ten percent plan. Lincoln himself had appointed military governors over conquered areas in the Confederacy, and radical members of the Republican party talked of the South's reverting to territorial status or worse.

The great unknown in the equation was the possibility of enfranchising black people. In December of 1863, unimpressed by the speed with which local forces willing to work with free black people in Louisiana were organizing, Lincoln gave full political power to the commander of the military district, Nathaniel Banks, who had the support of the more conservative white Louisianans willing to take the oath. General Banks told Lincoln:

> Offer them a Government without slavery, and they will gladly accept it as a necessity resulting from the war. Other questions relating to the condition of the negro, may safely be deferred until this one is

secured. If he gains freedom, education, the right to bear arms, the highest privileges accorded to any race and which none has yet proved itself worthy unless it be our own, his best friend may rest content for another year.

Postponement of "other questions relating to the condition of the negro" would bring even worse problems, surely. How could Banks guarantee improvement in blacks' status after demobilized Confederates and white refugees returned to vote? Besides, democracy is process, and Banks was guaranteeing results that democratic process alone could not guarantee.

The next January Banks told the President that he was creating a government in Louisiana that would provide "for the gradual restoration of power to the people" but "in such manner as to leave the control of affairs still in the hands of the comm[an]ding General." Louisiana's citizens understood, Banks assured Lincoln in another letter, that the new governor elected in February, Michael Hahn, "represents a popular power entirely subordinate to the armed occupation of the state." "The election perilled nothing," Banks said. "Had it resulted in the election of an opponent, he would be without power." A state constitution adopted in September abolished slavery (before that, General Banks had simply suspended the slavery provisions of the Louisiana constitution by military order). The contradictions in Banks's letters to Lincoln embodied one of the two fundamental problems of Reconstruction: only force or the threat of it could attain the result Republicans desired.

For many Republicans in Congress it was bad enough that the President asserted control of Reconstruction. The fact that the practical result was the conservative Banks regime made it even more galling. Lincoln had written Hahn after his inauguration in March a gingerly letter, saying, "I barely suggest for your private consideration, whether some of the colored people may not be let in—as, for instance, the very intelligent, and especially those who have fought gallantly in our ranks. They would probably help, in some trying time to come, to keep the jewel of liberty within the family of freedom. But this is only a suggestion, not to the public, but to you alone." It may have been only a private hint, but it was an eloquent one, and Lincoln's pouring on the rhetorical oil was a sign that he cared. In the end the new constitution did not mandate black enfranchisement.

In the summer of 1864 Senator Benjamin F. Wade of Ohio and Representative Henry Winter Davis of Maryland sponsored a bill that presented the Reconstruction plan of Republicans in Congress. The process could begin only when a majority of the voters took an oath of allegiance, and the state constitutional convention would be selected only by voters who could take what was called the "Ironclad oath" that they had never aided the Confederacy. The bill was more vindictive than Lincoln's plan, excluding some classes of ex-Confederates from citizenship forever. Even the congressmen, led by radicals, would not demand black suffrage, however. Lincoln gave the bill a pocket veto (it would have made his government in Louisiana illegal, presumably, and undone all of Banks's work), and he also issued a veto statement questioning the "constitutional competency in Congress to abolish slavery in States." Wade and Davis issued a manifesto in protest, denouncing Lincoln as a military despot who imposed unpopular governments on states. The manifesto had no effect on Lincoln, while Davis failed to gain renomination to run for the House and Wade was denounced in Republican meetings in his home state.

The threat of Democratic resurgence in the presidential election kept the rift in Republican ranks from growing wider (Wade campaigned for Lincoln in the fall), but Louisiana had still not been reconstructed when Lincoln was inaugurated in March 1865. In what proved to be his last speech, the President discussed Louisiana on April 11. For the first time he publicly endorsed the franchise for "the very intelligent [Negroes], and . . . those who serve our cause as soldiers." He admitted that the base on which the Louisiana government rested, some 12,000 voters, was smaller than he would like, but he could not see that starting over would help it grow. He insisted again that he was not wed to any single plan.

An actor named John Wilkes Booth was in the audience that heard Lincoln's speech.

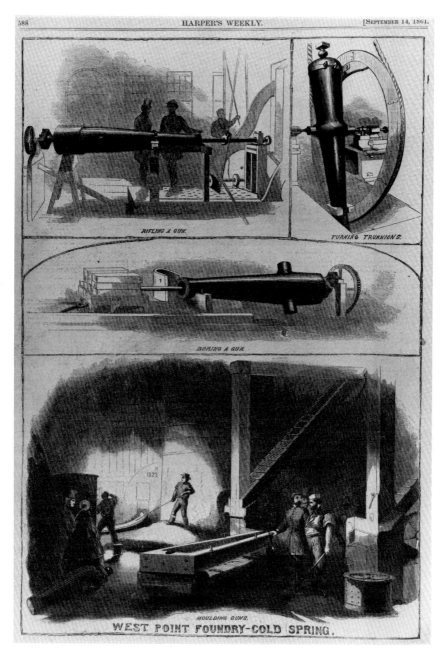

RIFLING A GUN.

TURNING TRUNNIONS.

BORING A GUN.

MOULDING GUNS.

WEST POINT FOUNDRY-COLD SPRING.

On June 24, 1862, the troubled commander in chief, on a visit to the great old soldier Winfield Scott at West Point, indulged his personal interest in technology by taking an excursion to Cold Spring, New York, where he visited the Parrott Foundry. There the most widely used rifled cannons in the Union army were made. [*Lincoln Museum*]

Like most recruiting posters, this one for a regiment of Zouaves (infantrymen whose uniforms and precision drilling were patterned after the Algerian recruits in the French infantry during the Crimean War) emphasized the practical aspects of soldiering: pay and rations. The Fire Zouaves, made up of New York City firemen, became the 11th New York Volunteer Infantry. They were mustered in May 1861 and fought at the First Battle of Bull Run, where they fled from a charge by Virginia's Black Horse Cavalry. The event traumatized the Union infantry long afterward, and was often depicted ignominiously in popular illustrations of that first great battle of the war. [*Illinois State Historical Library*]

THE BATTLE OF BULL'S RUN.

In this crude separate-sheet lithographed cartoon, the follies of the First Battle of Bull Run in July 1861 were memorialized. In the left center of the print (at no. 8) are the Fire Zouaves. The cartoon is quite rare for its expression of prosouthern sentiments. For example, in the upper left-hand corner the cobblers of Lynn, Massachusetts, who engaged in a famous strike before the war, are likened to the slaves of the South. [*Lincoln Museum*]

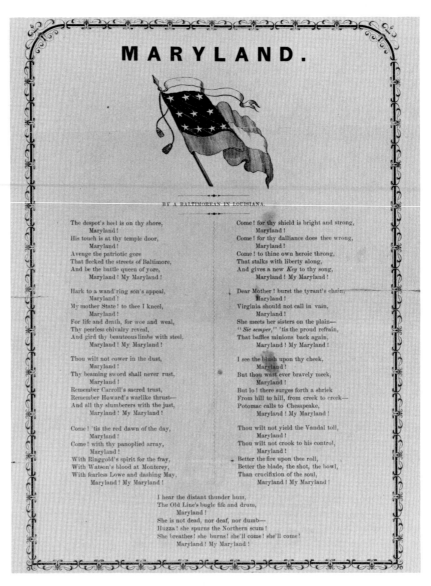

No single event prompted more protests during the war than the early suspension of the writ of habeas corpus in Maryland and the subsequent arrest of prominent Baltimore government officials. James Ryder Randall wrote what became the Maryland state song as one such protest, and an anonymous satirist took to the extreme an order of General John A. Dix, commander of the military district including Baltimore, forbidding the display of rebel emblems. Lincoln is identified as "His Majesty Abraham 1st." [*Lincoln Museum*]

Gen. Dix's
PROCLAMATION

Know all men by these presents: that I, John L. Dix, (no relation to the rebel " Dixie") knowing that the feeling excited in the breasts of our brave Union army by the combination of colors known as red, white and red, are by no means agreeable, do hereby, by virtue of the authority vested in me, by His Majesty Abraham 1st, require and command all police officers of the city of Baltimore in the pay of His Majesty's government to suppress and cause to disappear all substances, whether in the heavens above, or in the earth beneath, or in the waters under the earth, bearing the said combination of rebel colors. All babies having red, white and red stockings on will be sent to Fort Lafayette. All houses built of red brick and white mortar, must be removed, or painted red, white and blue, in alternate stripes. All water-melons must be painted blue on the rind; and all mint candy, and barber's poles so colored are forbidden. All red and white cows are required to change their spots or take the oath of allegiance. Red and white variegated flowers must be altered to include blue. All white persons having red hair and moustaches or whiskers are hereby warned to have the one or the other dyed blue. No sun-rises or sun-sets which exhibit such combinations will be permitted, on pain of suppression. Persons are forbidden to drink red and white wines alternately. His Majesty is, however, graciously pleased to make an exception in favor of red noses, these last being greatly in vogue among Federal officers, and additional *lustre* having recently been shed upon such noses, by one of my former predecessors in this command.

Done at the Baltimore Bastile, this 4th day of September, the 1st year of Abraham's glorious and peaceful reign.

(Signed),   JOHN L. DIX, Maj. Gen.

Striking the standard statesman's pose of the era, Mississippi's Jefferson Davis, hand on book and classical architectural element in background, made a rare appearance for a photographer. By far the most popular photograph of the Confederate President, this was actually a prewar portrait taken in the North while Davis was a Mississippi Senator. [*Lincoln Museum*]

The loyalty of Mr
Larrabee, as seen with-
in, is vouched by Gov:
Hicks— He wishes a
pass for himself and
driver, to cross and
recross the Potomac,
taking oysters to our
camps— I think he
should have the pass.

A. Lincoln
Oct. 25. 1861.

Although Jefferson Davis is frequently faulted for involving himself in minutiae that distracted him from more important duties, all nineteenth-century Presidents seem surprisingly occupied with petty details, as this note from Lincoln attests. This was partly due to the tiny staffs allowed the executives and partly because, in the absence of a protective bureaucracy, Presidents paid attention to the problems brought directly to them by politically important men. Governor Thomas H. Hicks of Maryland played a crucial role in keeping that slave state in the Union in the summer and autumn of 1861, and so an oysterman vouched for by Hicks could pass through the Union lines even along the precarious and sensitive border between Maryland and Virginia. [*Louise and Barry Taper Collection*]

TO THE LOYAL WOMEN OF AMERICA.

WASHINGTON, D. C., *October*, 1861.

COUNTRYWOMEN:

In the extraordinary enlargement of the whole structure of our National Government, which has this year been forced upon us, the wants of the sick and wounded of the Army and Navy cannot be at once fully provided for by the ordinary means.

Whatever aid is to be given from without, must, nevertheless, to be effective, be administered systematically, and in perfect subordination to the general system of administration of the government. To hold its agents in any degree responsible for the duties with which they are charged, government must protect them from the interference of irresponsible persons.

Hence, an intermediate agency becomes necessary, which, without taking any of the duties of the regular agents of government out of their hands, can, nevertheless, offer to them means of administering to the wants of the sick and wounded much beyond what could be obtained within the arbitrary limits of supply established by government, and in strict accordance with the regulations necessary for maintaining a proper accountability to it.

The Sanitary Commission, a volunteer and unpaid bureau of the War Department of the government, constitutes such an agency.

The Sanitary Commission has established its right to your confidence. The President, the Secretary of War, General Scott and General McClellan, have each recently acknowledged, in the warmest terms, the advantages which have already resulted from its labors, and the discretion and skill with which they have been directed. Its advice has been freely taken, and, in several important particulars, acted upon, favorably to the health of the army, by the government. There has scarcely been a company of volunteers in the field, with regard to which some special defect, error, or negligence, endangering health, has not been pointed out by its agents, and its removal or abatement effected. There has not been a single instance in which its services or advice, offered through all its various agencies, have been repulsed; not a single complaint has been received of its embarrassing any officer in his duty, or of its interfering with discipline in the slightest degree. Its labors have, to this time, been chiefly directed to induce precautions against a certain class of diseases which have scourged almost every modern European army, which decimated our army in Mexico, and which, at one time, rendered nearly half of one of our armies in the war of 1812 unfit for service. It is a ground for national gratitude that our present armies have passed through the most trying season of the year wonderfully escaping this danger. That there are grander causes for this than the labors of a Commission cannot be doubted, but that, among human agencies, a large share of credit for it should be given to those labors, it is neither arrogant nor unreasonable to assert. In this assurance, what contribution that has hitherto been made to the treasury or the store of the Commission is not received back again ten fold in value?

After full and confidential conference with the Secretary of War, the Commander of the Army of the Potomac, and the Quarter master General, there is reason to ask with urgency for a large increase of the resources of the Commission, especially of that class of its resources upon which it must chiefly draw for the relief of the sick and wounded.

The experience of the Commission has so well acquainted it with the earnest desire of their loyal countrywomen to be allowed to work in the national cause, that it is deemed unnecessary to do more than announce that there is a real and immediate occasion for their best exertions, and to indicate convenient arrangements for the end in view.

It is, therefore, suggested that societies be at once formed in every neighborhood where they are not already established, and that existing societies of suitable organization, as Dorcas Societies, Sewing Societies, Reading Clubs, and Sociables, devote themselves for a time, to the sacred service of their country; that energetic and respectable committees be appointed to call from house to house and store to store, to obtain contributions in materials suitable to be made up, or money for the purchase of such materials; that collections be made in churches and schools and factories and shops, for the same purpose; that contribution boxes be placed in post offices, newspaper offices, railroad and telegraph offices, public houses, steamboats and ferry boats, and in all other suitable places, labelled "FOR OUR SICK AND WOUNDED;" and that all loyal women meet at such convenient times and places as may be agreed upon in each neighborhood or social circle, to work upon the material which shall be so procured.

DESCRIPTION OF ARTICLES WANTED.

QUILTS, of cheap material, about seven feet long by fifty inches wide;

WOOLLEN or CANTON FLANNEL BED-GOWNS, WRAPPERS, UNDERSHIRTS, and DRAWERS;

SMALL HAIR and FEATHER PILLOWS and CUSHIONS FOR WOUNDED LIMBS;

KNIT WOOLLEN SOCKS;

SLIPPERS.

All articles should be closely packed in wooden boxes, or in very strongly wrapped bales, and clearly directed. On the top of the contents of each box, under the cover, a list of what it contains should be placed; a duplicate of this list should be sent by mail. Arrangements for free transportation should be made, or freight paid in advance. (The express companies will generally convey goods for this purpose, at a reduction on the usual rates.) Packages may be directed and sent, as is most economical, from any point to any of the addresses below, ("For the U. S. Sanitary Commission:")

Office of the Woman's Central Relief Association, Cooper Union, No. 10, Third Avenue, New York;

Care of Samuel, and William Welsh, No. 218 South Delaware Avenue, Philadelphia;

Care of Dr. S. G. Howe, 20 Bromfield street, Boston;

Care of Russell M. Larned, Providence, R. I.

Care of Dr. W. H. Massey, Cincinnati;

Office of Soldiers' Aid Society, 95 Bank street, Cleveland;

Care of Dr. C. D. Griswold, Wheeling, Virginia;

Care of Dr. J. V. Z. Blaney, Medical Purveyor, Chicago;

Care of F. L. Olmsted, 211 F street, Washington, D. C.

Acknowledgments will be made to all those who forward parcels, and a final report to the Secretary of War will be published, recording the names of all contributors, so far as they shall be known to the Commission.

HENRY W. BELLOWS, D. D., *President.*

PROF. A. D. BACHE, L. L. D.	PROF. WOLCOTT GIBBS, M. D.
GEORGE T. STRONG.	ELISHA HARRIS, M. D.
FRED. LAW OLMSTED.	SAMUEL G. HOWE, M. D.
GEORGE W. CULLUM, U. S. A.	CORNELIUS R. AGNEW, M. D.
ALEXANDER E. SHIRAS, U. S. A.	J. S. NEWBERRY, M. D.
ROBERT C. WOOD, M. D., U. S. A.	HORACE BINNEY, JR.
WILLIAM H. VAN BUREN, M. D.	RT. REV. THOS. M. CLARK, D. D.

Commissioners under authority of the Secretary of War.

The Sanitary Commission is doing a work of great humanity, and of direct practical value to the nation, in this time of its trial. It is entitled to the gratitude and the confidence of the people, and I trust it will be generously supported. There is no agency through which voluntary offerings of patriotism can be more effectively made.

A. LINCOLN.

WINFIELD SCOTT.

WASHINGTON, *September* 30, 1861.

CONTRIBUTIONS will be received at—

A male officer supervises the work of women making cartridges in a government arsenal in New York, in this sketch by Winslow Homer. This dangerous work was also exacting: poorly made cartridges could mean death for the individual soldier or defeat for the armies. [*Lincoln Museum*]

(*Left*) This rare United States Sanitary Commission broadside suggests some of the difficulties involved in organizing resources for a war. The commission had been informed by the Quarter Master General of the U.S. Army that blankets for the approaching cooler season were scarce and if the commission supplied blankets for hospitals, that would free the army to supply the soldiers in the field. The commission wanted to solicit blankets without announcing the shortage. The result was this sheet, which lacks the propaganda skills of twentieth-century war drives. Even Lincoln, in his appeal printed at the end of the sheet, experienced difficulty in sustaining eloquence while explaining the organizational purpose of the commission. [*Lincoln Museum*]

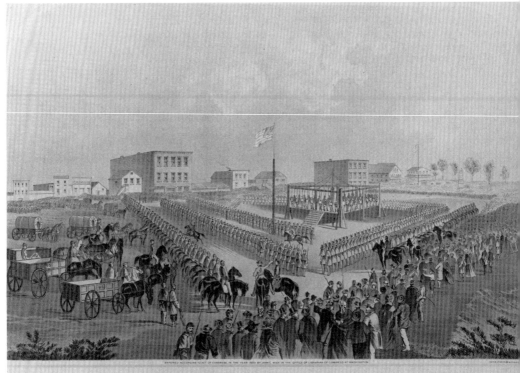

EXECUTION OF THE THIRTY-EIGHT SIOUX INDIANS
AT MANKATO MINNESOTA DECEMBER 26.1862.

This chromolithograph celebrating the sad ending of the Minnesota Sioux uprising of 1862 seems an unlikely subject for memorialization in a parlor print.
Not only was the subject a public execution but there also existed other sensational events to attract printmakers' attention—the great Civil War raged on.
The juxtaposition of different standards of justice prompted no reflection, high
or low. There was no similar mass execution of white Civil War soldiers who
engaged in atrocities, and white prisoners of war were not dispossessed of their
property rights after the war as were the Indians who were removed from Minnesota after the uprising. [*Lincoln Museum*]

The arrest of Clement Vallandigham on May 5, 1863, for giving a speech discouraging enlistments into the Union army, and his military trial and sentencing the next day, put Lincoln on the defensive and damaged his reputation with historians. The Ohio politician was arrested at night in his own bedroom by U.S. soldiers, as shown in this woodcut. [*Lincoln Museum*]

THE MEETING OF THE FRIENDS,
CITY HALL PARK.

A Friendly Voice.—GOVERNOR, WE WANT YOU TO STAY HERE.
Horatio Seymour.—I AM GOING TO STAY HERE, "MY FRIENDS."
Second Rioter.—FAITH, AND THE GOVERNOR WILL STAY BY US.
Horatio Seymour.—I AM YOUR "FRIEND," AND THE "FRIEND" OF YOUR FAMILIES.
Third Rioter.—ARRAH, JEMMY, AND WHO SAID HE CARED ABOUT THE "DIRTY NAGURS"?
Fourth Rioter.—HOW ABOUT THE DRAFT, SAYMERE?
Governor.—I HAVE ORDERED THE PRESIDENT TO STOP THE DRAFT!
Chorus—BE JABERS, HE'S A "BROTH OF A BOY."

This cartoon about the New York City draft riots of July 13–17, 1863, mixes sympathy for victimized black people with rank anti-Irish prejudice. [*Lincoln Museum*]

EXECUTIVE MANSION,

Washington, D. C., *Aug 10th,* 1863.

I, ABRAHAM LINCOLN, President of the United States of America, and Commander=in=chief of the Army and Navy thereof, having taken into consid=eration the number of volunteers and militia furnished by and from the several States, including the State of *New York* , and the period of service of said volunteers and militia since the commencement of the present rebellion, in order to equalize the numbers among the Districts of the said States, and having considered and allowed for the number already furnished as aforesaid, and the time of their service aforesaid, do hereby assign *Two Thousand and Fifty (2050)* as the first proportional part of the quota of troops to be furnished by the *2nd* DISTRICT OF THE STATE OF *New York* under this, the first call made by me on the State of *New York* , under the act approved March 3, 1863, entitled "An Act for Enrolling and Calling out the National Forces, and for other purposes," and, in pursuance of the act aforesaid, I order that a draft be made in the said *2nd* DISTRICT OF THE STATE OF *New York* for the number of men herein assigned to said District, and FIFTY PER CENT. IN ADDITION.

IN WITNESS WHEREOF, I have hereunto set my hand and caused the seal of the United States to be affixed.

Done at the City of Washington, this *tenth* day of *August* , in the year of our Lord one thousand eight hundred and sixty-three, and of the independence of the United States, the eighty-eighth.

Abraham Lincoln

After the New York City draft riots, Democratic Governor Horatio Seymour asked for a suspension of conscription in New York, arguing that half the people in the country thought the draft unconstitutional and that further action should await a Supreme Court decision on its legality. Lincoln was determined to go forward with the draft and on August 10, 1863, issued the draft call reproduced here. The draft resumed without incident on August 19. [*Louise and Barry Taper Collection*]

57

Four score and seven years ago our fathers brought forth upon this continent, a new nation, conceived in Liberty, and dedicated to the proposition that all men are created equal.

Now we are engaged in a great civil war, testing whether that nation, or any nation so conceived, and so dedicated, can long endure. We are met on a great battle-field of that war. We have come to dedicate a portion of that field, as a final resting place for those who here gave their lives, that that nation might live. It is altogether fitting and proper that we should do this.

But, in a larger sense, we can not dedicate—we can not consecrate—we can not hallow—this ground. The brave men, living and dead, who struggled here, have consecrated it, far above our poor power to add or detract. The world will little note, nor long remember, what we say here, but it can never forget what they did here. It is for us, the living, rather, to be dedicated here to the unfinished work which they who fought here, have, thus far, so nobly advanced. It is rather for us to be here dedicated to the great task remaining before

Of the five known drafts of the Gettysburg Address written in Lincoln's hand, this neatly transcribed version was likely written for Edward Everett, to be included in a patriotic volume. The volume was to be offered at a charity auction by the women directing the great Metropolitan Fair for the U.S. Sanitary Commission in New York City in 1864. It was not put together in time to be sold, however, and the original materials were later dispersed. [*Illinois State Historical Library*]

us— that from these honored dead we take increased devotion to that cause for which they here gave
the last full measure of devotion— that we here
highly resolve that these dead shall not have
died in vain— that this nation, under God,
shall have a new birth of freedom— and that,
government of the people, by the people, for the
people, shall not perish from the earth.

This separate-sheet cartoon by "L.A.C." (monogram at lower left), probably issued for the presidential election campaign of 1864, showed Lincoln, Scots-plaid cap in hand and looking diabolical, asking a distraught soldier to sing a funny song. [*Lincoln Museum*]

(*Right*) The equivalent of Democratic charges that the President had asked to hear a vulgar song amid the carnage of the Antietam battlefield was the widespread Republican charge that General McClellan was a physical coward and a traitor. The slender basis of fact for this broadside was that McClellan, like other generals commanding the large armies of the Civil War, often needed to remain far to the rear of his troops to organize supplies and transportation. Here such a disposition of headquarters is depicted as skulking and as plotting treasonous surrender to the Confederates—all amidst European "Princes." McClellan, like many other American generals, had on his staff foreign military observers. [*Lincoln Museum*]

DEPLORABLE

Cowardice of M'Clellan,

During the Battle of Malvern!

THE GUNBOAT STORY AGAIN CONFIRMED!

[From the Detroit Advertiser and Tribune.]

We give below a letter from Dr. O. J. BISSELL, late Surgeon of the U. S. steamer "Jacob Bell," and a copy of a portion of his journal. The letter is addressed to one of the most prominent and respected citizens of this State, who knows the writer well, and vouches for his truth and respectability. More than this, the writer of the letter made the same statements to other gentlemen of high character in this State and elsewhere, very soon after the occurrence of the events to which it refers. Read this transcript from his journal carefully, and then say, if you can, that Fernando Wood is wrong in saying that "INTELLIGENT AND HONEST PEACE MEN DO NOT CONCUR IN THE OPINION THAT M'CLELLAN WILL CONTINUE THE WAR IF ELECTED."

Grand Rapids, October 3, 1864.

DEAR SIR: Agreeably to your request I have made a copy of my journal of June 30, 1862, which I read to you some days since. I cannot consent to let the original which you desired, to pass from my possession, although any person can have the privilege of seeing it by calling on me. All the material facts I wrote to my wife at the time, but the letter was handed to different persons and now it cannot be found, although those who read it recollect the facts.

I also in October, 1862, gave the leading facts to Gen. Garfield and Secretary Chase, and several others. I will make affidavit to the facts and statements made in the journal, and the log-book of the "Jacob Bell" contains the evidence of all the facts. I am, Sir, your most Obedient Servant,

O. J. BISSELL, Late Surgeon of U. S. S. S. "Jacob Bell."

[Extract from the Journal referred to in the foregoing letter.]

June 30, 1862. Soon after our arrival at City Point, we learned that Gen. McClellan, with his army had arrived at Turkey Bend, and we got under weigh and stood up the River, arriving at Turkey Bend about noon. The North Bank of the river was lined with soldiers washing, and bathing, or filling their canteens. In the distance was heard the thunder of cannon.

Lieut. McCrea inquired of some of the soldiers where Gen. McClellan was? He was informed that his headquarters were about half a mile distant. McCrea called for his gig and went on shore. In about an hour the coxswain returned and told the Steward the Captain wanted him to send a dozen bottles of whiskey. The whiskey was given the coxswain in a basket. At about 3 P. M., the firing became very brisk, and soon McCrea hailed the United States steamship "Galena," a boat was sent, and the Captain with Gen. McClellan, the Prince de Joinville, Prince de Paris (Count,) Duke de Chartres, and an officer who I understood was Chief of Artillery (he was not in uniform) came on board the "Galena." The United States steamship "Jacob Bell" at the time was turning the "Galena's" bow up stream, as we were about starting up the river to shell the Charles-city road.

The "Galena," "Jacob Bell," and "Aroostook," stood up the river to a point from which we could reach that road with our shell. The "Galena" occupied the centre of the stream, with the "Jacob Bell," lapping up her stern. All our guns were brought to bear upon the lookout of the "Galena," giving and receiving signals from the shore, in order to give the proper direction to our guns. Gen. McClellan was on the "Lookout" a short time. At about 4 1-2 P. M., the fire in that direction began to slacken, and the vessels stood down to the point from which we started, the old ferry. Before we got under weigh, Gen. McClellan with the Princes, came on board the "Jacob Bell."

After the introduction of the General and Staff to the officers of the "Jacob Bell" present, McClellan said, "MY ARMY IS DEMORALIZED AND I SHALL BE COMPELLED TO SURRENDER OR CAPITULATE THIS AFTERNOON OR TO-NIGHT, AND I MUST HAVE A GUNBOAT TO TAKE THE PRINCES TO FORTRESS MONROE IMMEDIATELY," that it would not be safe to send them on a Transport. McCrea replied that Capt. Rogers and he could not spare a Gunboat. The General and Princes insisted on a Gunboat. Much conversation took place between the General and the Princes and McCrea, myself being present and a part of the time a Correspondent of the New York Times, as I afterwards learned. M'CLELLAN AND THE PRINCES AGREED THAT THE FEDERAL CAUSE, AS THEY CALLED IT HAD FAILED, AND THE GOVERNMENT WOULD HAVE TO ACKNOWLEDGE THE SOUTHERN CONFEDERACY.

The result, if the Princes should be taken prisoners, owing to their European relations, was also discussed; and finally it was agreed to make another effort to induce Capt. Rogers to send a Gunboat with the Princes to Fortress Monroe. This was the more earnestly insisted on, as they all agreed that the surrender of the flotilla would certainly follow the surrender of the army; and Gen. McClellan said the authorities at Washington would be responsible for that result. At this time about 6 P. M., a letter was brought to Gen. McClellan, which he said was from his Chief of Staff, and gave its contents: "The enemy is repulsed and our army is safe." He then remarked, "He wished me to come to the front."

After reading the letter the General and the rest of the group left the hurricane-deck for the quarter-deck. The General, Prince de Joinville and McCrea went aft the deck and conversed some minute, and then returned, and the General left, after bidding the Prince farewell, for the army. The "Jacob Bell" then got under weigh and stood down to City Point to order up some of the transports, and then returned to Turkey Bend.

After our return, Prince de Joinville requested McCrea to go and persuade Rogers to send a Gunboat to carry them to Fortress Monroe. The Captain went and soon returned and said Capt. Rogers had ordered a Gunboat to go, and that he was going with his vessel. The Prince de Joinville said to him: That will interfere with your arrangements with Gen. McClellan. How is that, said the Captain? You know, said the Prince, YOU WERE TO KEEP YOUR VESSEL HERE AND A BOAT ON SHORE, so that the General could get on board if he should be attacked in the night. McCrea said he had arranged with another vessel to lie here.

About this time McCrea learned that there was a correspondent on board, and asked me if it was so? I told him a man came on board about the time the the General did. I did not, however, know his business. He said if there was any on board he must leave immediately, as he would have no correspondent on board his vessel.

We got under weigh after the Princes' baggage could be brought on board, and had a pleasant trip to Old Point, where we arrived at 8 P. M., July 1, and the Captain had the honor of the correspondent of the New York Times as a passenger in his gig from the vessel to the wharf.

There were some things connected with this day's events which surprised me very much. There seemed from the conversation of Gen. McClellan and the Princes, AN APPARENT DESIRE TO SURRENDER THE ARMY ON THE PRETEXT OF AN UNSUCCESSFUL CAMPAIGN, THROWING, HOWEVER, THE RESPONSIBILITY UPON THE AUTHORITIES AT WASHINGTON. I may be mistaken in this. But I could not otherwise interpret their conversation, especially as their remarks about surrendering the army were coupled with the acknowledgment of the Southern Confederacy, and the responsibility of the authorities at Washington.

Another fact which struck me was the free, not to say excessive use of whiskey. The whiskey-bottle was passed three times while they occupied the hurricane-deck, each time General McClellan, the Princes, and McCrea drinking. This struck me the more forcibly, as I had understood the General was strictly a temperance man.

The effect of the whiskey was quite manifest on the tall, slim Prince (Count), as he required material aid, in the shape of a man at each side, to pass from the hurricane to the quarter deck; and after a little time, being unable to keep his position in his chair, McCrea proposed that he occupy his bed in the cabin, which he did with the assistance of McCrea and one of the Princes.

THE MODERN BELISARIUS.

McClellan.—AFTER THE FIRST BATTLE OF BULL RUN, I RE-ORGANIZED YOUR SHATTERED FORCES; AFTER THE SECOND, I SAVED YOUR MENACED CAPITOL: I SIT BY THE WAYSIDE WAITING FOR JUSTICE FROM THE PEOPLE. SHALL I HAVE IT!

Two 1864 cartoons show contrasting views of Lincoln's rival for the Presidency. The "Belisarius" woodcut compared McClellan to the general of the late Roman empire, who repeatedly saved his homeland from enemies and was then put aside by his jealous sovereign. The "Harrison's Landing" lithograph portrayed the general lolling in safe luxury, sipping champagne, his saber ironically drawn, on shipboard, far from the battle lines where duty called. [*Lincoln Museum*]

HEAD QUARTERS AT HARRISON'S LANDING.

"See evidence before Committee on conduct of the War."

THE CHICAGO PLATFORM AND CANDIDATE.

A two-faced McClellan stands atop the rickety Democratic platform, held up by Jefferson Davis, the Devil, and Peace Democrats Clement Vallandigham and Fernando Wood. The Democratic party is also identified with the brutish Irish draft rioter at right, while the Republicans gain the support of the stalwart soldier at left. McClellan appears with two faces, one for his warlike letter accepting the nomination and the other for the peace plank of his party's platform. [*Lincoln Museum*]

Private

Executive Mansion.

Washington, July 25 , 1864.

Abram Wakeman, Esq

My dear Sir:

I feel that the subject which you pressed upon my attention in our recent conversation is an important one. The men of the South, recently (and perhaps still) at Niagara Falls, tell us distinctly that they _are_ in the confidential employment of the rebellion; and they tell us as distinctly that they are _not_ empowered to offer terms of peace. Does any one doubt that what they _are_ empowered to do, is to assist in selecting and arranging a candidate and a platform for the Chicago Convention? Who could have given them this confidential employment but he who only a week since declared to Jacques and Gilmore that he had no terms of peace but the independence of the South— the dissolution of the Union? Thus the present presidential contest will almost certainly be no other than a contest between a Union and a Disunion candidate, disunion certainly following the success of the latter. The issue is a mighty one for all people and all time; and whoever aids the right, will be appreciated and remembered.

Yours truly A. Lincoln.

This letter to a New York Republican, written in the troubled summer of 1864, was shown (and Lincoln apparently knew it would be) to James Gordon Bennett, owner of the New York *Herald*. Bennett had erratic political preferences but loathed the antislavery movement—hence, perhaps, this letter's emphasis on Union as the real issue in the presidential election. The statement that "whoever aids the right, will be appreciated and remembered" was almost surely a promise of an appointive office in exchange for support in the presidential race. [*Huntington Library*]

THE BEGINNING.

ELECTION OF M'CLELLAN!

PENDLETON, VALLANDIGHAM,
Vice-President.   Secretary of War.

ARMISTICE!

FALL OF WAGES!

NO MARKET FOR PRODUCE!

Pennsylvania a Border State!

INVASION! CIVIL WAR! ANARCHY!

DESPOTISM!!

THE END.

The election of 1864 was particularly hard fought in Pennsylvania, bringing to the polls 135,000 more voters than in 1860 and producing a great abundance of campaign items. These two broadsides followed the basic Union party strategy of not mentioning the issue of slavery. Instead they equated McClellan's election with loss of the Union and the creation of a hostile nation on Pennsylvania's southern border. [*Lincoln Museum*]

PEACE & DISUNION!

WHAT IS MEANT BY AN
IMMEDIATE CESSATION OF HOSTILITIES?

It means the withdrawal of our Armies from Louisiana, Mississippi, Arkansas, Alabama, Florida, Georgia, Tennessee, North Carolina, South Carolina and Virginia. It means the raising of the Blockade. It means allowing the Rebels to supply themselves with men and money, and munitions of war. It means the abandonment of all that we have gained; the acknowledgment that the war is a failure, that we are defeated, and that we cannot subdue the rebellion. In short, it means the

DISMEMBERMENT OF THE UNION!

WHAT IS MEANT BY A
CONVENTION OF THE STATES?

It means that we shall beg the South to grant us a treaty of peace, the first condition of which they have proclaimed to be the recognition of their independence. It means that we shall surrender to them half the territory of the Union, and hold the rest on such terms as they shall dictate.

WHAT IS MEANT BY A
SEPARATION OF THE UNION?

It means two or more military nations involved in perpetual war with each other. It means the destruction of our industry and the loss of our liberties. It means huge standing armies recruited by incessant drafts. It means the burden of unlimited expenditure without resources or credit to defray it. It means yearly invasions and desolation. It means anarchy and desolation.

Citizens, reflect that this is what you vote for if you vote

THE DEMOCRATIC TICKET.

King & Baird, Printers, 607 Sansom Street, Philadelphia.

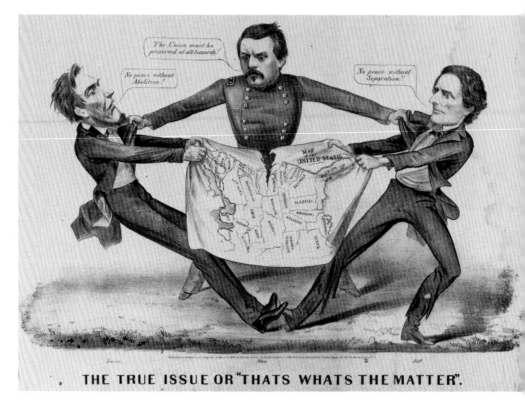

THE TRUE ISSUE OR "THATS WHATS THE MATTER".

Printmakers like Currier & Ives issued both pro- and anti-Lincoln cartoons. In this one McClellan is depicted as the true champion of Union while Lincoln's insistence on abolition of slavery provides the obstacle to reunion. Lithography was dominated by German immigrants (where the technique had been invented) and was characterized by commercial haste in production—hence the curious misspellings on the map "Indiana Territory" for "Indian Territory," "Pennsylvaina" for "Pennsylvania," and "Micigan" for "Michigan." [*Lincoln Museum*]

NATIONAL UNION TICKET

The Union forever, Hurrah boys, Hurrah!
Down with the Traitors, up with the Stars.

And we'll rally 'round the Flag boys,
rally once again.
Shouting the battlecry of freedom.

FOR PRESIDENT,

ABRAHAM LINCOLN

FOR VICE PRESIDENT,

ANDREW JOHNSON

☞ BE CAREFUL AND EXAMINE YOUR TICKETS.

ELECTORS.

MORTON McMICHAEL,	WILLIAM TAYLOR,	DAVID M'CONAUGHY,
THOMAS CUNNINGHAM,	JOHN A. HIESTAND,	DAVID W. WOODS,
ROBERT P. KING,	RICHARD H. CORYELL,	ISAAC BENSON,
G. MORRISON COATES,	EDWARD HALIDAY,	JOHN PATTON,
HENRY BUMM,	CHARLES F. READ,	SAMUEL B. DICK,
WILLIAM H. KERN,	ELIAS W. HALE,	EVERARD BIERER,
BARTON H. JENKS,	CHARLES H. SHRINER,	JOHN P. PENNEY,
CHARLES M. RUNK,	JOHN WISTER,	EBENEZER M'JUNKIN,

This broadside warns the voter to "examine your ticket" to avoid a fraudulent ballot printed by the opposition. Although paper ballots were standard in most elections in Lincoln's era, they were not genuinely secret because the parties rather than the government printed and distributed them. A voter's preference could be known by the printing format or color of his ballot, by the office or kiosk where he obtained it, or even by the glass bowl or wooden box in which his ballot was placed: there were two, usually, one for each party. [*Huntington Library*]

Estimated Electoral Vote 1864
Three weeks before Election

Supposed Copperhead Vote.		Union Vote. for President	
New York	33	New England States	39
Penn	26	Michigan	8
New Jersey	7	Wisconsin	8
Delaware	3	Minnesota	4
Maryland	7	Iowa	8
Missouri	11	Oregon	3
Kentucky	11	California	5
Illinois	16	Kansas	3
	114	Indiana	13
		Ohio	21
		W. Virginia	5
			117
		Nevada	3
			120

Having learned of the election returns from key states that held state elections in October, President Lincoln, cheerful about the news, made a "worst case" estimate of the electoral vote to be decided in some three weeks. The title, date, and column headings are in another hand. The time of deep pessimism, August 1864, was past, and Lincoln obviously thought he could win. [*Huntington Library*]

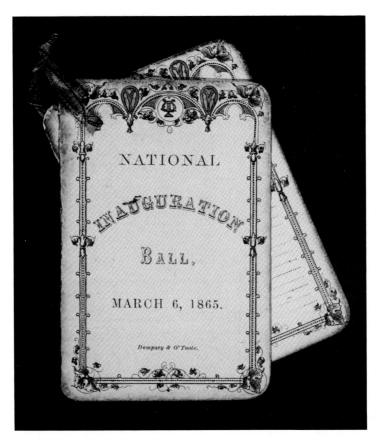

This example of the ornately printed dance programs in which
men signed up for dances with women at Lincoln's second inaugural ball exemplified the uninterrupted vigor of life behind the lines
in the North. While Richmond high society held "starvation parties" to conserve supplies for the Confederate army, Washington's
Republican revelers could indulge in giant sugar confections repre-
senting the military and naval events of the war. [*Louise and Barry
Taper Collection*]

Artists depicting the return of Union veterans usually chose as the setting a rural homestead rather than a teeming metropolis in a country transformed by the Republican program of industrialism and economic development. Such reunions with wife, children, aged parents, servants, and a faithful dog served to demilitarize the soldier's image and to symbolize the reuniting of the old pastoral Union. Patriotism is symbolized by the American flag and the Washington portrait, and the value of religious belief is suggested by the church steeple dimly visible through the window. [*Lincoln Museum*]

SATAN TEMPTING BOOTH TO THE MURDER OF THE PRESIDENT

This lithograph, published in Philadelphia in 1865, suggests the difficulties encountered in investigating the murder of Abraham Lincoln and prosecuting his murderers. The use to which such a picture would be put is difficult to imagine, but with dimensions of roughly six by eight inches plus margins, it clearly had decorative purpose—if not in the parlors of private homes then at least in semipublic places like saloons or hotel basements or meeting halls where political cartoons were frequently displayed. [*Lincoln Museum*]

SURRAT. BOOTH. HAROLD.

War Department, Washington, April 20, 1865,

 # $100,000 REWARD!

THE MURDERER

Of our late beloved President, Abraham Lincoln,

IS STILL AT LARGE.

$50,000 REWARD

Will be paid by this Department for his apprehension, in addition to any reward offered by Municipal Authorities or State Executives.

$25,000 REWARD

Will be paid for the apprehension of JOHN H. SURRATT, one of Booth's Accomplices.

$25,000 REWARD

Will be paid for the apprehension of David C. Harold, another of Booth's accomplices.

LIBERAL REWARDS will be paid for any information that shall conduce to the arrest of either of the above-named criminals, or their accomplices.

All persons harboring or secreting the said persons, or either of them, or aiding or assisting their concealment or escape, will be treated as accomplices in the murder of the President and the attempted assassination of the Secretary of State, and shall be subject to trial before a Military Commission and the punishment of DEATH.

Let the stain of innocent blood be removed from the land by the arrest and punishment of the murderers.

All good citizens are exhorted to aid public justice on this occasion. Every man should consider his own conscience charged with this solemn duty, and rest neither night nor day until it be accomplished.

EDWIN M. STANTON, Secretary of War.

DESCRIPTIONS.—BOOTH is Five Feet 7 or 8 inches high, slender build, high forehead, black hair, black eyes, and wears a heavy black moustache.

JOHN H. SURRAT is about 5 feet, 9 inches. Hair rather thin and dark; eyes rather light; no beard. Would weigh 145 or 150 pounds. Complexion rather pale and clear, with color in his cheeks. Wore light clothes of fine quality. Shoulders square; cheek bones rather prominent; chin narrow; ears projecting at the top; forehead rather low and square, but broad. Parts his hair on the right side; neck rather long. His lips are firmly set. A slim man.

DAVID C. HAROLD is five feet six inches high, hair dark, eyes dark, eyebrows rather heavy, full face, nose short, hand short and fleshy, feet small, instep high, round bodied, naturally quick and active, slightly closes his eyes when looking at a person.

NOTICE.—In addition to the above, State and other authorities have offered rewards amounting to almost one hundred thousand dollars, making an aggregate of about TWO HUNDRED THOUSAND DOLLARS.

A famous actor as well as a political fanatic, John Wilkes Booth was often photographed. The familiarity of his countenance caused him to wear a false beard on his escape after the assassination of Lincoln, and pursuit and eventual identification of his corpse were aided by popularly circulated photographs like this one. [*Huntington Library*]

(*Left*) The War Department's reward posters (there were several kinds) for the arrest of Lincoln's alleged assassins boldly announced that the fate of those arrested would be military trial. This one also referred to crimes unknown to federal law: harboring, aiding, or concealing the alleged murderers. [*Huntington Library*]

The sculptor Clark Mills made the second, and last, life mask of Lincoln on February 11, 1865. In the version seen here, Mills has molded hair and ears not present in the original cast. [*Louise and Barry Taper Collection*]

CHAPTER SEVEN

Fate

As party conflicts during the war aroused animosities to the levels reached in the days of the early republic, familiar symbols appeared. After the Emancipation Proclamation, for example, Lincoln was depicted with a crown on his head and given the title "Abraham Africanus I" in a Democratic pamphlet. Some took such allegations more seriously than others. In 1864 John Wilkes Booth told his brother Edwin that Lincoln's reelection meant that he would become king of America. John Wilkes Booth had the role of Brutus in his repertoire.

Fate began to stalk Lincoln even before he took the oath of office in 1861. On February 21, 1861, the President-elect, in Pennsylvania on his way to Washington, was warned by detective Allan Pinkerton, by political associate Norman Judd, and by railroad executive S. M. Felton that a plot to assassinate him had been uncovered in Baltimore. They advised him to abandon his published itinerary and travel through that notoriously riotous and prosouthern city in secret. Seward sent word that General-in-chief Winfield Scott had also heard of a plot brewing there. Lincoln insisted on making his scheduled appearances in Philadelphia and Harrisburg the next day, which was George Washington's birthday. He spoke first at Independence Hall, but his confidants must

have realized he was upset when they heard what he told the Philadelphia crowd:

> I can say . . . that all the political sentiments I entertain have been
> drawn . . . from the sentiments which originated, and were given to
> the world from this hall in which we stand. I have never had a feeling
> politically that did not spring from the . . . Declaration of Inde-
> pendence . . . I have often inquired of myself, what great principle
> or idea it was that kept this Confederacy so long together. It was not
> the mere matter of the separation of the colonies from the mother
> land; but something in that Declaration giving liberty, not alone to
> the people of this country, but hope to the world for all future time.
> It was that which gave promise that in due time the weights should
> be lifted from the shoulders of all men, and that *all* should have an
> equal chance . . . If this country cannot be saved without giving up
> that principle—I was about to say I would rather be assassinated on
> this spot than to surrender it.

This was "a wholly unprepared speech," Lincoln said, and he feared
he "may . . . have said something indiscreet."

It may not have been indiscreet, but it was revealing. Lincoln
traveled as planned to Harrisburg to appear with Governor Andrew J.
Curtin and to address the state legislature. Afterward he agreed to
travel to Washington, unannounced, in a night train. Posing as the
invalid brother of one of Pinkerton's female agents, Kate Warne,
Lincoln donned a soft hat and a long overcoat and arrived in Washington at 6 a.m. in the company of an Illinois crony, armed to the
teeth, burly Ward Hill Lamon.

The decision to sneak into Washington was probably a mistake. The
press, following the lead of Joseph J. Howard, an irresponsible *New
York Times* reporter, spread the story that Lincoln had skulked through
Baltimore disguised in "a Scotch plaid cap and a very long military
cloak." Cartoonists used the story for years, and southerners found
their contempt for Yankee cowardice vividly substantiated. South
Carolinian Mary Boykin Chesnut—with her husband in Montgomery,
Alabama, for the drafting of the Constitution of the Confederate States

of America—wrote in her diary: "Lincoln came through Baltimore locked up in [an] Adam's Express car! Noble entrance into the Government of a free people." She was amused to read in the *New York Herald* that Lincoln would "not drive in his carriage because it is not *bomb* proof."

The newspaper criticism surely stung Lincoln, and he would ever after attempt to avoid any appearance of physical timidity; he did not swagger, but he refused to pay much heed to those who warned him of personal danger.

For leaders of a country involved in a vast civil war, the members of the Lincoln administration showed remarkable unconcern about assassination. When the minister to Paris, John Bigelow, warned the Secretary of State that he heard rumors of assassination plots even in France, Seward replied that there were "no grounds for anxiety":

> Assassination is not an American practice or habit, and one so vicious and so desperate cannot be engrafted into our political system . . . This conviction of mine has steadily gained strength since the Civil War began. Every day's experience confirms it. The President, during the heated season, occupies a country house near the Soldiers' Home, two or three miles from the city. He goes to and . . . from that place on horseback, night and morning, unguarded. I go there unattended at all hours, by daylight and moonlight, by starlight and without any light.

Seward wrote that letter in 1862. Later Lincoln traveled by carriage accompanied by a small cavalry escort when on his daily trips to the Soldiers' Home in the hot Washington summertime, but Seward's attitude never changed.

Even if Lincoln felt moved by the warnings he received—especially from Secretary of War Edwin M. Stanton—he was prevented from employing elaborate security by memories of his humiliating arrival in Washington. Lincoln's fatalism played a role, too. Colonel Charles Halpine, a writer serving on General Henry W. Halleck's staff, recalled a conversation with the President in which Lincoln first attempted to shrug off serious consideration of his physical safety by describing his ardently antislavery Vice President, Hannibal Hamlin, as "an insurance on my life worth half the prairie land of Illinois"; surely no Confederate would plot Lincoln's assassination with Hamlin in the wings as successor. As the conversation wore on, Lincoln revealed a deeper fatalism: no vigilance could keep out determined southerners, for Lincoln met with southerners in his office regularly. Posting guards "would only . . . put the idea into their heads," and "as to the crazy folks," Lincoln added philosophically, "why I must only take my chances."

Of course, Lincoln did not mention memories of the "Baltimore plot," but when danger threatened Washington in 1864 the President conspicuously, and needlessly, exposed himself to gunfire. In July Confederate General Jubal A. Early led a small army up the Shenandoah Valley toward Washington. By July 11 he was in the District of Columbia. The next day, Lincoln stood atop the parapet of Fort Stevens, which guarded the northern approach to the capital, as Early's soldiers fired. General Horatio G. Wright, commanding the fort, noted with some exasperation that the President "took his position at my side on the parapet, and all my entreaties failed to move him, though in addition to the stray shots that were passing over, the spot was a favorite for sharp shooters."

That summer a reminder of the President's ignominious entry into Washington appeared in a poster cartoon entitled "The Commander in Chief Conciliating the Soldiers' Votes on the Battle Field." Recalling the incident from his visit to Antietam when, during a jolting ambulance ride over the field, the President had asked Lamon to sing, this bitter cartoon depicted the President on a field of wounded and dying soldiers. "Now, Marshal, sing us 'Picayune Butler' or something else that's funny," the President says. He wears a long cloak and carries a Scottish plaid cap.

Months later, when Richmond fell to Ulysses Grant's armies, Lincoln could not resist a visit—he even sat in Jefferson Davis's chair in the White House of the Confederacy. This was no doubt a delicious moment and Union soldiers cheered, but Secretary of War Stanton worried about Lincoln's taking chances by getting so close to Robert E. Lee's retreating armies. "I will take care of myself," Lincoln replied.

〜

There are many theories offered to explain the assassination of Abraham Lincoln, some irresponsible examples of purest prejudice (such as the allegation that it was a Roman Catholic plot) and others more plausibly alluring. Only four merit consideration. (1) Lincoln's assassin, the famed 27-year-old actor John Wilkes Booth, was insane. This was a theory strengthened by the testimony of other members of the Booth family. (2) Booth was the agent of Jefferson Davis or other members of the Confederate government. This was the theory followed by the prosecution at the trial of Booth's co-conspirators after the crime, and it has been revived recently. (3) Booth may have been the assassin, but the plot was more complicated than it seems from the evidence at the trial, and there were conspirators higher up, perhaps even in the President's cabinet. Maybe Edwin M. Stanton himself was involved, for he was as well placed to cover up the crime as to uncover it. (4) John Wilkes Booth plotted and committed a political crime quite like many other pre–World War I assassination attempts, from that of the Italian nationalist Orsini on Napoleon III in Paris in 1858, to the murder of Alexander II of Russia in 1881 by a group of anarchists or the fateful 1914 shooting of the Austrian archduke and duchess in Sarajevo by the Bosnian nationalist Gavrilo Princips.

"Crazy folks," as Lincoln knew, were always cause for concern. A house painter named Richard Lawrence had fired two pistols at President Andrew Jackson in 1835 because he thought Jackson thwarted his rightful claim to the British throne. (The guns misfired because the powder and shot had fallen out of the weapons into Lawrence's pockets while the guns were concealed there before the attempt.) But John Wilkes Booth was no Richard Lawrence. Booth had no difficulty attracting confederates to his risky plans. Naturally, other members of the Booth family wanted to depict their relative as different once the assassination occurred, but the real power of the argument for Booth's madness comes from a species of backward logic. Reasoning back from Lincoln's unequaled reputation in modern times, some find it difficult to think of killing him as a rational scheme on anyone's part. The irony of this wrongheaded thinking is that it was the assassination itself that guaranteed Lincoln much of his modern fame.

For in his own time the President received many threats against his life and endured the bitter newspaper criticism traditionally meted out to politicians in that era of unrestrained press partisanship. Lincoln's secretaries threw threatening letters away; they did not turn them over to the War Department or local authorities for routine investigation. Drunks and angry opponents of the administration sometimes swore aloud in saloons or in the streets that Lincoln should be shot or hanged.

It was natural to think at the time that the assassination was a plot concocted by the Richmond government. "Crazy folks" aside, that was the direction from which Lincoln and Seward had anticipated trouble. And when Secretary of the Navy Gideon Welles first heard of the crime, he exclaimed, "Damn the rebels. This is their work." Real tragedy lay in this mistaken assumption when it was held past the initial moment of shock. It became the prosecution theory at the trial of Booth's alleged accomplices. Because of that, justice was not done, and history was poorly served by the skewed and flawed investigation. Genuinely suspicious characters went uninterrogated while the prosecutors fell for perjured testimony that fit their preconceptions of the crime. Jefferson Davis was libeled, and seeds for a fundamental misunderstanding of the nature of the Civil War were sown in the propagation of the belief that either side in this restrained civil war was likely to embrace methods condemned by international law—like assassination.

There should be less cause than ever to believe in a theory that could not be proved by the prosecution in 1865 and that fed off the residual hatred bred of war. Yet modern adherents of the Confederate plot theory have seized on what they think was a powerful motive. On an aborted cavalry raid to Richmond to free Union prisoners of war early in March 1864, Union General Hugh Judson Kilpatrick had divided his force and sent Colonel Ulric Dahlgren with a separate column to attack from another direction. A treacherous guide caused Dahlgren's attempt to fail, and on his return, Confederates ambushed the Union cavalrymen, killing Dahlgren and taking many prisoners. When a thirteen-year-old boy rifled the colonel's pockets, he discovered documents that, according to Confederate authorities, ordered Dahlgren's men to burn Richmond and kill Jefferson Davis and his cabinet. Davis himself shrugged off the threat at first, but Robert E. Lee expressed outrage at the "unchristian & atrocious acts" contemplated in the documents. He demanded explanation from the commander of the Army of the Potomac, George Gordon Meade. Kilpatrick and Meade took the position that the Dahlgren Papers, if authentic and not clever Confederate forgeries, represented plans that the young colonel had devised on his own. Yet Meade told his wife, "I regret to say Kilpatrick's reputation and collateral evidence in my possession, rather go against that theory." Assassination theorists find Meade's comments tantalizing, but uncovering the evidence that would link this event to Lincoln's assassination a year later is more than anyone has been able to do. Besides, it ignores the purport of the Confederate reaction to the Dahlgren Papers. Lee, for example, found them unthinkably "unchristian," and neither he nor Davis seems likely to have embraced assassination as a method of war, even in retaliation. They were content to manipulate the documents, forged or authentic, for public opinion advantage.

As for locating a conspiracy to murder the President in the Washington government rather than Richmond, that is a fantastic enterprise that has never been given credence by any professional historian. As much as any of the false theories, this one libels conscientious men, like Stanton, and its theory of motivation hides the white supremacist motives of Lincoln's real killers. Booth and his Confederate-sympathizing fellow conspirators wanted to eliminate Lincoln in part because they hated the Emancipation Proclamation. In the fanciful theory, Lincoln becomes a victim because he would have protected southern whites from radical Republicans, like Stanton, bent on giving political power to the recently freed black men.

Disagreements over Reconstruction between Lincoln and Stanton were not deep enough to provide the latter a motive for assassination. Even if they disagreed on issues of revenge—retribution for Confederate leaders, for example, who the forgiving Lincoln hoped would flee the country without his knowledge—Lincoln and Stanton agreed on the necessity of guaranteeing the liberty of the recently freed slaves in the South.

Lincoln was easy to kill. The inadequacy of security and the flawed investigation afterward make more sense if it is remembered that this was the first presidential assassination in America and that few people thought a republic would be plagued with assassinations. Threats of assassination were the bane of czars and emperors, but republican leaders need not fear them. It was precisely that view that Seward expressed to calm Bigelow's anxiety back in 1862.

Yet the very example Seward cited as proof of the safety of the President and cabinet would in time offer the opportunity that enticed John Wilkes Booth to attempt his political crime. For while the President rode out to the Soldiers' Home in the hot Washington summers, he was vulnerable to assault or capture.

Like many other Marylanders, Booth believed that "this country was formed for the *white,* not for the black man. And looking upon *African slavery* from the same standpoint held by the noble framers of our Constitution, I, for one, have ever considered it one of the greatest blessings (both for themselves and for us) that God ever bestowed upon a favored nation. Witness heretofore our wealth and power; witness their elevation and enlightenment above their race elsewhere." He underlined "African" because of his belief in the sacredness of white liberty and the concomitant fear of enslavement by loss of political liberty. "People of the North," he warned, "to hate tyranny, to love liberty and justice, to strike at wrong and oppression, was the teaching of our fathers. The study of our early history will not let me forget it, and may it never." These sentiments, expressed in a letter written probably in the summer of 1864 and left with his sister, could have been matched by many a Maryland speech or editorial. This was the state, after all, where the Lincoln administration had arrested legislators on their way to the assembly hall. The first line of the state song retained the memory of Lincoln's act: "The despot's heel is on thy shore, Maryland, my Maryland."

Such views, though common, rarely led to desire for Confederate independence, let alone to direct action in the Confederacy's behalf. Jefferson Davis's agents in Canada had discovered this when they contacted Peace Democrats in the war-weary summer of 1864. The discontented elements in the North hated Republicans and loathed emancipation, but they did not long for southern independence or love the South. Booth said he did. "My love (as things stand today) is for the South alone," he wrote, and he pictured himself as *"A Confederate, doing duty upon his own responsibility."* Even Booth expressed a modicum of reservation about his method of winning the war for the South. "Nor do I deem it a dishonor," he wrote, "in attempting to make for her a prisoner of this man, to whom she owes so much of misery."

Excited, as most Americans were, by the political controversies of a presidential election summer, Booth began to scheme to kidnap the President while he rode with his escort to the Soldiers' Home. He would take Lincoln to Richmond and exchange him for Confederate prisoners of war. Booth needed help, of course, and he could find it readily enough in southern Maryland.

Booth was articulate, but the political views of his fellow conspirators, who were rougher, commoner men, are known mostly by their behavior rather than by expressions of their ideas. Their allegiances are nonetheless obvious. Booth's first two recruits were old school chums, Samuel Bland Arnold and Michael O'Laughlin, who had felt Confederate sentiments intensely enough to leave Maryland and join the Confederate army. They had returned by 1864. In December Booth recruited John Harrison Surratt, a Confederate spy who carried dispatches from Richmond into the North. The most powerful and violent man in the conspiracy joined rather late. Lewis Thornton Powell, the son of a Protestant minister from Florida, had enlisted in the Confederate army but was captured at Gettysburg. He had since escaped and in 1864 was in hiding in Baltimore. Booth and the ex-soldiers knew how to shoot and to ride, as did David Herold, a one-time Washington pharmacist's assistant from whom Booth had purchased medicines. Herold was a hunter who knew the back roads of southern Maryland, the conspirators' likely escape route. George Atzerodt, a Maryland coach painter, owned a boat; he became a valuable addition to the group because they would need to get across the Potomac into Virginia with Lincoln.

By the time Booth had assembled his conspiracy, he had lost his original opportunity, for it was now winter and the President no longer slept at the Soldiers' Home. In mid-March 1865 the group prepared to strike, but their information that Lincoln would be attending a performance at the Campbell Hospital proved erroneous, and the group scattered, never to be brought together again. Booth hoped to resurrect the kidnapping scheme, but Arnold and O'Laughlin were finished with him, and Surratt left on a mission for the Confederacy in early April. Booth now had too few men to kidnap the President, and when Richmond fell on April 2, there was no place to take him anyway. Very late, perhaps on the day of the crime, Booth decided to kill Lincoln, to have Atzerodt kill Vice President Andrew Johnson, and to send Powell to kill Secretary of State Seward. General Grant was supposed to accompany the Lincolns to Ford's Theatre in Washington that night, and the actor could realistically hope to eliminate many of the government's strong men in one evening of slaughter. Perhaps such a revolution would yet save the South.

He nearly succeeded. Grant decided not to attend and was thus saved, and Johnson was spared when Atzerodt lost his courage or his opportunity. Powell wounded Seward horribly with a knife. Booth, of course, succeeded completely in his part of the mission, shooting Lincoln fatally in the back of the head while he watched an English farce called *Our American Cousin* on the night of April 14, 1865. The President never regained consciousness, and died the next morning at 7:22.

The republic survived another test in this bloody event. Booth's hopes proved groundless. As Secretary of the Treasury Hugh McCulloch wrote on April 16, "My hope is, and my belief is, that this great National calamity will teach the world a lesson, which will be of the most beneficial character to our Republican form of Government; that it will show that the assassination of our Chief Magistrate does not affect in the slightest degree the permanence of our institutions, or the regular administration of the laws; that an event that would have shaken any other country to the centre does not even stagger for a moment a Government like ours."

McCulloch was correct. Booth's crime did not win the war for the Confederacy. Abraham Lincoln would surely have been pleased to know that "the last best hope of earth" survived this final test.

Notes

1. Peculiar Ambition

Abraham Lincoln on his "wandering" father appears in Roy Basler et al., eds., *The Collected Works of Abraham Lincoln*, 9 vols. (New Brunswick: Rutgers University Press, 1953–1955), IV, 61. On Henry Clay see Clement Eaton, *Henry Clay and the Art of American Politics* (Boston: Little, Brown, 1957), esp. 17. Louis A. Warren, *The Slavery Atmosphere of Lincoln's Youth* (Fort Wayne, Indiana: Lincolniana Publishers, 1933) helps set the scene. Lincoln to his "squirming" stepbrother is in *Coll. Works*, II, 111. William H. Herndon's unforgettable "little engine" is in Paul M. Angle, ed., *Herndon's Life of Lincoln* (New York: Albert & Charles Boni, 1930), 304. Lincoln on Indiana's "unbroken forest" and the sum book pages are in *Coll. Works*, IV, 62.

The most important book on Lincoln's early political life is Gabor S. Boritt's *Lincoln and the Economics of the American Dream* (Memphis, Tennessee: Memphis State University Press, 1978), and this chapter relies heavily on it for the depiction of Lincoln's sincere interest in economic development. Lincoln's first platform with its admission of "peculiar ambition" and discussion of navigation is in *Coll. Works*, I, 5–9. Early Illinois election returns are in Theodore Calvin Pease, ed., *Illinois Election Returns, 1818–1848* (Springfield: Illinois State Historical Library, 1923). Lincoln's 1836 "I go for all" platform is in *Coll. Works*, I, 48. The context of his slavery protest in the Illinois legislature is best described in Leonard Richards, *Gentlemen of Property and Standing: Anti-Abolition Mobs in Jacksonian America* (New York: Oxford University Press, 1970). The protest itself ("injustice and bad policy") and the first recorded speech ("these capitalists," "filled their pockets," "a politician myself") are in *Coll. Works*, I, 75, 64–66.

Edmund Wilson's *Patriotic Gore: Studies in the Literature of the American Civil War* (New York: Oxford University Press, 1962), esp. 106–108, put the Lyceum

Speech on the intellectual map of all Lincoln biographers. The address itself appears in *Coll. Works,* I, 108–115. On the political system of the era and the election of 1840 see William Nisbet Chambers, "Election of 1840," in Arthur M. Schlesinger, Jr., and Fred L. Israel, eds., *History of American Presidential Elections,* 4 vols. (New York: Chelsea House, 1971), I, 643–744. Lincoln on "organization," "removals," "excessive importations," and "right in itself" is in *Coll. Works,* I, 205, 221, 287, 314. Emphasis on the convention issue in the origins of the political parties in Illinois appears in Richard P. McCormick, *The Second American Party System: Party Formation in the Jacksonian Era* (Chapel Hill: University of North Carolina Press, 1966), and the statements denouncing conventions appear on page 284. Lincoln on "diamond rings," "like to go," "deist," "thunder," "little headway," and "protection . . . to American industry" is in *Coll. Works,* I, 311–312, 307, 320, 323, 289, 339. "Turn about," "Christian church," and "the Texas question" are in *Coll. Works,* I, 350, 382, 347–348. "Being elected," "Kings . . . and . . . wars," "distracting question," "purpose of extending slave territory," "a final crisis," and the Irishman's boots are in *Coll. Works,* I, 391, 451–452, 454, 476, 481, 487. "Me personally" is in Roy Basler, ed., *The Collected Works of Abraham Lincoln: Supplement, 1832–1865* (Westport, Connecticut: Greenwood, 1974), 14.

2. Republican Robe

The most important book for understanding this period of Abraham Lincoln's life is Don E. Fehrenbacher, *Prelude to Greatness: Lincoln in the 1850's* (orig. pub. 1962; New York: McGraw-Hill, 1964). Placing Lincoln's political development in proper context requires knowledge of Fehrenbacher, *The Dred Scott Case: Its Significance in American Law and Politics* (New York: Oxford University Press, 1978), which is actually a history of the slavery expansion issue in national politics. (This chapter follows his interpretation of the Kansas-Nebraska Act, for example.) Equally important is Eric Foner, *Free Soil, Free Labor, Free Men: The Ideology of the Republican Party before the Civil War* (New York: Oxford University Press, 1970), which emphasizes the capitalist critique of slavery. Both books are quite favorable to the Republicans, though Foner rather prefers the radical wing of the party. Also crucial and more balanced are David M. Potter, *The Impending Crisis, 1848–1861* (New York: Harper & Row, 1976), and William E. Gienapp, *The Origins of the Republican Party* (New York: Oxford University Press, 1987). Approaching neorevisionism in its likewise important insights is Michael F. Holt, *The Political Crisis of the 1850s* (New York: Wiley, 1978), which properly emphasizes Republican sectionalism. All shaped this chapter as well as G. S. Boritt's *Lincoln and the Economics of the American Dream,* which sees

Lincoln's capitalism tempered by his working-class origins. The "macho" side of political life is brought to our attention by Robert H. Wiebe's "Lincoln's Fraternal Democracy," in John L. Thomas, ed., *Abraham Lincoln and the American Political Tradition* (Amherst: University of Massachusetts Press, 1986), 11–30. Also useful was James Davidson *et al.*, *Nation of Nations: A Narrative History of the American Republic* (New York: McGraw-Hill, 1990).

Mary Owens's recollections of the "bad branch" are in Mark E. Neely, Jr., *The Abraham Lincoln Encyclopedia* (New York: McGraw-Hill, 1982), 230. For Lincoln's "anxious" statement on Richard Yates see *Coll. Works,* II, 228. "I am naturally anti-slavery," "his own country," "fresher days of the republic," "the author of the declaration," "spirit of seventy-six," "covert *real* zeal," "saving the Union," "republican robe," and "Pharoah's country" are in *Coll. Works,* VII, 281; II, 126, 249–250, 275, 255, 270, 276. On nationalism see David M. Potter, "The Historian's Use of Nationalism and Vice Versa," in *The South and the Sectional Conflict* (Baton Rouge: Louisiana State University Press, 1968), 34–83. Mrs. Lincoln on the "wild Irish" is in Justin G. and Linda Levitt Turner, *Mary Todd Lincoln: Her Life and Letters* (orig. pub. 1972; New York: Fromm International, 1987), 46. For "Russia," "purity of its principles," "Northern freemen," "a Kentuckian," and "old Whigs" see *Coll. Works,* II, 323, 341, 364, 379, 343. "Sacraficing us," "*all* one thing," "*cares* not," "result of preconcert," "*lie down*" are in *Coll. Works,* II, 430, 461, 463, 465–466, 467. "Celtic gentlemen," "wild boys," "sober reason," "natural disgust," "white and black races," "axioms" are in *Coll. Works,* III, 329–330; I, 491; II, 469, 405; III, 145–146, 375. "Ten thousand dollars" and "*first* choice" are in *Coll. Works,* IV, 33, 34.

3. Commander in Chief

Abraham Lincoln owes his twentieth-century reputation as an able commander in chief mostly to British writers. First among them was Colin R. Ballard, whose *Military Genius of Abraham Lincoln: An Essay* (London: Oxford University Press) appeared in 1926. I have relied more on another British work that appeared the same year, Frederick Maurice's *Statesmen and Soldiers of the Civil War: A Study of the Conduct of War* (Boston: Little, Brown); Maurice writes with welcome clarity. A more detailed American work, of great influence, is T. Harry Williams, *Lincoln and His Generals* (New York: Alfred A. Knopf, 1952). Most detailed of all is Kenneth Williams's five-volume *Lincoln Finds a General: A Military Study of the Civil War* (New York: Macmillan, 1949–1959). All four seem a bit dated now, and two scintillating modern interpretive military histories that have shaped this narrative heavily are Richard M. McMurry, *Two Great Rebel Armies: An Essay in Confederate Military History* (Chapel Hill: University of North Carolina Press,

1989), and Michael C. C. Adams, *Fighting for Defeat: Union Military Failure in the East, 1861–1865* (orig. pub. 1978 as *Our Masters the Rebels*; Lincoln: University of Nebraska Press, 1992).

For a sense of the larger geopolitical drama in the secession crisis see Daniel W. Crofts, *Reluctant Confederates: Upper South Unionists in the Secession Crisis* (Chapel Hill: University of North Carolina Press, 1989). In general this chapter follows David M. Potter, *Lincoln and His Party in the Secession Crisis* (New Haven: Yale University Press, 1942). For Lincoln's image in the secessionist South see Robert M. Johannsen, *Lincoln, the South, and Slavery: The Political Dimension* (Baton Rouge: Louisiana State University Press, 1991). Lincoln's letter to Trumbull ("no compromise"), the inaugural address texts ("reclaim" and "hold, occupy, and possess"), and his General War Order and subsequent orders are in *Coll. Works*, IV, 149–150, 254, 266; V, 111, 115. My description of the strategic significance of the Shenandoah Valley follows McMurry's *Two Great Rebel Armies*. On "Stonewall" Jackson see Frank E. Vandiver, *Mighty Stonewall* (New York: McGraw-Hill, 1957), and Charles Royster, *The Destructive War: William Tecumseh Sherman, Stonewall Jackson, and the Americans* (New York: Alfred A. Knopf, 1991). Archer Jones's essay, "Military Means, Political Ends: Strategy," in Gabor S. Boritt, ed., *Why the Confederacy Lost* (New York: Oxford University Press, 1992), 45–77, made me aware of the significance of Lincoln's letter to Gasparin; the letter itself is in *Coll. Works*, V, 355. Lincoln's "Destroy the rebel army" is in *Coll. Works*, V, 426; and McClellan's comment on it is in Stephen W. Sears, ed., *The Civil War Papers of George B. McClellan: Selected Correspondence, 1860–1865* (New York: Ticknor & Fields, 1989), 486. For "horses . . . broken down" and "very kind personally" see Sears, 488, 490. Halleck's "cross the Potomac" and Lincoln's letter to Thomas Clay are in *Coll. Works*, V, 452n, 452. Halleck on Stuart's ride is in Sears, 498n, and Lincoln's "unmanly" letter is in *Coll. Works*, V, 460–461. Maurice's comment is on page 157 of his book. The "sore tongued" horses correspondence appears in *Coll. Works*, V, 474, 479.

Grant's recollection of Lincoln's "Military Orders" is in his *Memoirs and Selected Letters* (New York: Library of America, 1990), 473. Lincoln's "you must act" is in *Coll. Works*, V, 185. Stoddard's recollection of the Fredericksburg aftermath appears in Gabor S. Boritt, *Lincoln and the Economics of the American Dream* (Memphis: Memphis State University Press, 1978), 271. On the merchant marine see James Russell Soley, *The Blockade and the Cruisers* (New York: Charles Scribner's Sons, 1883), and George W Dalzell, *The Flight from the Flag: The Continuing Effect of the Civil War upon the American Carrying Trade* (Chapel Hill: University of North Carolina Press, 1940). On Missouri see Michael Fellman's brilliant book, *Inside War: The Guerrilla Conflict in Missouri during the American Civil War* (New York: Oxford University Press, 1989);

Lincoln's letter about Missouri refugees is in *Coll. Works,* VI, 492. Halleck's significance is described in Adams, *Fighting for Defeat.* See *Coll. Works,* V, 98, for Lincoln to Buell; and VI, 326, for Lincoln to Grant on Vicksburg. For Grant on Lee see Horace Porter, *Campaigning with Grant* (orig. pub. 1897; New York: Bantam Books, 1991), 65. I rely on Adams's refinement of T. Harry Williams's interpretation of Meade here. For the Lincoln-Meade controversy after Gettysburg see *Coll. Works,* VI, 318n, 318, 319, 327. See (on failure to pursue, especially) also Richard E. Beringer, Herman Hattaway, Archer Jones, and William N. Still, Jr., *Why the South Lost the Civil War* (Athens: University of Georgia Press, 1986). Lincoln on "every soldier" is in *Coll. Works,* V, 355. Halleck's report is printed in *The War of the Rebellion: A Compilation of the Official Records of the Union and Confederate Armies,* 128 vols. (Washington, D.C.: Government Printing Office, 1880–1901), ser. I, vol. 19, pt. 1, pp. 6–7. Hereafter cited as *O.R.*

On Lincoln's predecessors as commander in chief see K. Jack Bauer, *The Mexican War, 1846–1848* (New York: Macmillan, 1974); Ernest R. May, "The President Shall Be Commander in Chief," and Marcus Cunliffe, "Madison," in Ernest R. May, ed., *The Ultimate Decision: The President as Commander in Chief* (New York: George Braziller, 1960); Donald R. Hickey, *The War of 1812: A Forgotten Conflict* (Urbana: University of Illinois Press, 1989).

On the cabinet and Pope's replacement see the *Diary of Gideon Welles: Secretary of the Navy under Lincoln and Johnson,* 3 vols. (Boston: Houghton Mifflin, 1911), I, 93–105. Lincoln's comments on Jackson and Taylor are in *Coll. Works,* II, 60. Lincoln's blunt letter on Halleck's "useless" skill is in *Coll. Works,* VI, 31. Halleck on Hooker's appointment is in Kenneth Williams, *Lincoln Finds a General: A Military Study of the Civil War,* 5 vols. (New York: Macmillan, 1949–1959), II, 549. Grant on councils of war is in Porter, *Campaigning with Grant,* 226. Lincoln on the "moral effect" of battle is in *Coll. Works,* V, 355. Grant on "snow" in Georgia appears in Porter, *Campaigning with Grant,* 224; and Beauregard is quoted in T. Harry Williams, *P. G. T. Beauregard: Napoleon in Gray* (Baton Rouge: Louisiana State University Press, 1954), 77. Horace Porter on Grant's "broader view" and launching "all his armies" is in *Campaigning with Grant,* 23, 33. Hay's recollection of Lincoln's "skinning" comment appears in Tyler Dennett, ed., *Lincoln and the Civil War in the Diaries and Letters of John Hay* (orig. pub. 1939; New York: DaCapo, 1988), 178–179.

On Sherman see Royster's work cited above and John F. Marszalek, *Sherman: A Soldier's Passion for Order* (New York: Free Press, 1993). Sherman's "doing vast damage" is in *O.R.,* I, 39, pt. 2, p. 412; "statesmanship" is in *O.R.,* I, 39, pt. 3, p. 660. Lincoln on Savannah is in *Coll. Works,* VIII, 181–182. On "house-burning" see *Coll. Works,* VII, 493. Lincoln's visit to Grant after Cold Harbor is described in Porter, *Campaigning with Grant,* 157. Lincoln to Grant on following the enemy "to the death" is in *Coll. Works,* VII, 476. Halleck's fear of draft resistance appears in Porter, *Campaigning with Grant,* 194–195; Lincoln's reaction is in *Coll. Works,* VII, 499. Lincoln on courage is in Dennett, *Diaries and Letters of John Hay,* 176. Lincoln to Sherman on the Indiana election is in *Coll. Works,* VIII, 11, and the general's recollection of his conference with the President appears in Sherman, *Memoirs* (New York: Library of America, 1990), 812. For Lincoln's surrender terms see *Coll. Works,* VII, 435, 517; VIII, 151–152, 250–251. Jefferson Davis's remarks appear in his *Rise and Fall of the Confederate Government,* 2 vols. (New York: Appleton, 1881), II, 611; Lee's are quoted in Alan T. Nolan, *Lee Considered: General Robert E. Lee in Civil War History* (Chapel Hill: University of North Carolina Press, 1991), 87–88. Davis's "give my life" is quoted in Larry Nelson, *Bullets, Ballots, and Rhetoric: Confederate Policy for the United States Presidential Contest of 1864* (University, Alabama: University of Alabama Press, 1976), 130.

4. Emancipation

The literature on the Emancipation Proclamation seems meager when measured against the importance of the document itself, which was both Declaration of Independence and Constitution for black Americans. Although there are at least five full-length books on the two-minute oration Lincoln delivered at Gettysburg, there is but one modern book on the Emancipation Proclamation, the slender volume written by John Hope Franklin for the centennial of the document: *The Emancipation Proclamation* (Garden City: Doubleday, 1963). In recent years historians have focused on the practical social results of the proclamation in such books as Leon F. Litwack, *Been in the Storm So Long: The Aftermath of Slavery* (New York: Alfred A. Knopf, 1980); Ira Berlin et al., eds., *Freedom: A Documentary History of Emancipation, 1861–1867, Series I, Volume I: The Destruction of Slavery* (Cambridge: Cambridge University Press, 1985); and Joseph T. Glatthaar, *Forged in Battle: The Civil War Alliance of Black Soldiers and White Officers* (New York: Free Press, 1990).

Important constitutional insights which I rely on in this chapter lie in Arthur M. Schlesinger, Jr., "War and the Constitution: Abraham Lincoln and Franklin Delano Roosevelt"; in Gabor S. Boritt, ed., *Lincoln, the War President: The Gettysburg Lectures* (New York: Oxford University Press, 1992). See also Charles A. Lofgren, *"Government from Reflection and Choice": Constitutional Essays on War, Foreign Relations, and Federalism* (New York: Oxford University Press, 1986). Lincoln on the question of "fatal weakness" in republics appears in *Coll. Works,* IV, 426; for "measures . . . legal or not" see 429. *The Lincoln Catechism Wherein the Eccentricities & Beauties of Despotism Are Fully Set Forth. A Guide to the Presidential Election of 1864*, first published in New York in 1864, is reprinted in Harold M. Hyman, "The Election of 1864," in Arthur M. Schlesinger, Jr., and Fred L. Israel, eds., *History of American Presidential Elections* (New York: Chelsea House, 1971), esp. 1238. K. C. Wheare's useful remark that Lincoln "was prepared to go much farther to prevent the break up of the Union than ever he proposed to go to prevent the extension of slavery" appears in *Abraham Lincoln and the United States* (London: English Universities Press, 1948), 158. Frederick Douglass's oration on Lincoln, perhaps the best speech on the sixteenth President ever given, was occasioned by the dedication of the Freedmen's Memorial Monument to Lincoln in Washington, April 14, 1876; quotations here are from the version reprinted in Waldo W. Braden, ed., *Building the Myth: Selected Speeches Memorializing Abraham Lincoln* (Urbana: University of Illinois Press, 1990), 95–97, 99.

Lincoln's letters to General Frémont and to Senator Browning on the Missouri proclamation are in *Coll. Works*, IV, 506, 531–532, and Beriah Magoffin is quoted at IV, 497n; Lowell ("self respect") is quoted in Reinhard H. Luthin, *The Real Abraham Lincoln* (Englewood Cliffs: Prentice-Hall, 1960), 337. General Hunter's proclamation and Lincoln's answer to it are in *Coll. Works*, V, 222–223. C. C. Jones is quoted in Litwack, *Been in the Storm So Long*, 54. Lincoln on "radical and extreme measures," on capital and labor, and on colonization are in *Coll. Works*, V, 49, 52–53, 48. Lincoln on "the side of the Union," on a "fair valuation," "four hundred dollars," "close the war in two weeks," and "punctillio" are in *Coll. Works*, V, 50, 145, 153, 304, and 318. Gideon Welles's recollection of the President's "new departure" appears in *Diary of Gideon Welles, Secretary of the Navy under Lincoln and Johnson*, 3 vols. (Boston: Houghton Mifflin, 1911), I, 71. Lincoln complaining that Congress could not free slaves "in a slave state" and apologizing for "intense engrossment" are in *Coll. Works*, V, 329 and 306. David Homer Bates describes the actual writing of the proclamation in *Lincoln in the Telegraph Office: Recollections of the United States Military Telegraph during the Civil War* (orig. pub. 1907; New York: D. Appleton-Century, 1939), esp. 138–141. Immediate contemporary sources for the origins of the proclamation are unfortunately very limited. Besides Bates's dubious account, Francis B. Carpenter's recollections in *Six Months at the White House with Abraham Lincoln: The Story of a Picture* (New York: Hurd and Houghton, 1866), came four years after the fact and from an ardent antislavery enthusiast; Gideon Welles started his famous diary only after the event and summarized his recollection of it considerably later.

William H. Seward's "destroyed years ago" is recalled in Tyler Dennett, ed., *Lincoln and the Civil War in the Diaries and Letters of John Hay* (orig. pub. 1939; New York: DaCapo, 1988), 197; his statement on "*paper*" proclamations is in Frederic Bancroft, *The Life of William H. Seward*, 2 vols. (New York: Harper &

Brothers, 1900), II, 335. Lincoln's letter to Greeley, his "different races" statement to the African Americans, his "silly affec[ta]tion" letter, his "bull against
the comet" disavowal, his expression of lack of fear of "insurrection and massacre," his worries about "50,000 bayonets," and the preliminary proclamation are
in *Coll. Works*, V, 388–389, 371, 420; IV, 129; V, 421, 423–424, 433. Karl
Marx's letter to Frederick Engels on "pettifogging" appears in Richard Enmale,
ed., *The Civil War in the United States by Karl Marx and Frederick Engels* (New
York: International Publishers, 1937), 258. "Acts to repress" appears in *Coll.
Works*, V, 434.

   On foreign reactions see John Hope Franklin, *The Emancipation Proclamation*,
esp. 71, 72, 73; James G. Randall, *Lincoln the President: Midstream* (New York:
Dodd, Mead, 1953); and E. D. Steele, *Palmerston and Liberalism, 1855–1865*
(Cambridge: Cambridge University Press, 1991). Books about foreign policy
vary wildly in their interpretations, and it is always a good idea to consult other
works, for example, David Brion Davis, *Slavery and Human Progress* (New York:
Oxford University Press, 1984), where the paradox of British public opinion is
well stated if not explained. All Lincoln biographies treat the Emancipation
Proclamation at some length, though none, probably, at greater proportionate
length than has been done here. Gladstone on Jefferson Davis is quoted in
Randall, *Lincoln the President: Midstream*, 342–343. Lincoln's letter to Manchester is in *Coll. Works*, VI, 64.

   Lincoln's letter about the "not very satisfactory" effect of the proclamation is
in *Coll. Works*, V, 444; "to garrison forts" and "labor faithfully" appear at VI,
30; "drilled black soldiers" is at VI, 149–150; the "heaviest blow" is at VI,
408–409; "act on motives" is at VII, 500; "200,000" is at VII, 507. For
Frederick Douglass on "squads of Slaves" and "not . . . a 'necessity,'" see
Douglass to Abraham Lincoln, August 29, 1864, Abraham Lincoln Papers,
Library of Congress, and the *Life and Times of Frederick Douglass Written by
Himself* (New York: Pathway Press, 1941). The statement about "white folks"
appears in Litwack, *Been in the Storm So Long*, 20.

5. A Free People Conduct a Long War

   One must look about widely to piece together a portrait of the North in the
Civil War. The best modern overview is Phillip Shaw Paludan, *"A People's
Contest": The Union and Civil War, 1861–1865* (New York: Harper & Row,
1988). James M. McPherson's *Battle Cry of Freedom: The Civil War Era* (New
York: Oxford University Press, 1988) is distinguished by its broad approach to
military history and contains much on economics and politics. Both shaped this
chapter considerably. For Abraham Lincoln's relationship to the "dark side" of

the nineteenth-century American economy see Phillip S. Paludan, "Commentary on 'Lincoln and the Economics of the American Dream,'" in Gabor S. Boritt, ed., *The Historian's Lincoln: Pseudohistory, Psychohistory, and History* (Urbana: University of Illinois Press, 1988), 116–123.

On conscription see Charles A. Lofgren, *"Government from Reflection and Choice": Constitutional Essays on War, Foreign Relations, and Federalism* (New York: Oxford University Press, 1986). For the reaction to conscription see Iver Bernstein, *The New York City Draft Riots: Their Significance for American Society and Politics in the Age of the Civil War* (New York: Oxford University Press, 1990). Lincoln on the value of replacements is in *Coll. Works*, V, 338, and the War Department orders of Aug. 8, 1862, are in *O.R.*, II, 4, 358–359. On dissent in 1812 see Marcus Cunliffe, "Madison," in Ernest R. May, ed., *The Ultimate Decision: The President as Commander in Chief* (New York: George Braziller, 1960), esp. 52. Lincoln to Gasparin is in *Coll. Works*, V, 355, and Webster is quoted in Cunliffe, "Madison," 28. Lincoln's Corning letter is in *Coll. Works*, VI, 266–267. On the importance of the Corning letter see Philip S. Paludan's book review, *Georgia History Quarterly*, XXV (Fall 1991), 644. Greeley is quoted in an essential source, James G. Randall, *Constitutional Problems under Lincoln* (rev. ed. 1951; Urbana: University of Illinois Press, 1964), 268n. The "first law" is from John G. Nicolay and John Hay, *Abraham Lincoln: A History*, 10 vols. (New York: Century, 1890), VII, 5. Lincoln's undated paper on the draft is in *Coll. Works*, VI, 446–448. "Why don't they come" is in Nicolay and Hay, *Abraham Lincoln: A History*, IV, 151–152. For "gone forever" see Wood Gray, *The Hidden Civil War: The Story of the Copperheads* (New York: Viking Press, 1942), 207. Eric L. McKitrick, describing what he calls the "lighter side" of party competition during the war, blithely states that the Republicans, "when in doubt [about loyalty] . . . could always round up the local Democrats, as many a time they did, and in case of error there was always a formula for saving face all around: it was 'just politics.'" See McKitrick, "Party Politics and the Union and Confederate War Efforts," in William Nisbet Chambers and Walter Dean Burnham, eds., *The American Party Systems: Stages of Political Development* (New York: Oxford University Press, 1967), 141. There were no such party "round-ups," and there was nothing light-hearted about military arrests of civilians: both the administration and those arrested acted in deadly earnest.

The Civil War was a modern war in that (1) it organized mass armies motivated more by ideology than by cruel discipline, and (2) it armed its soldiers with products of the industrial revolution. It was not a "total war" in which the gross domestic product of society was organized for the war effort and in which civilians were considered fair targets for military attack. The term "total war" is an imprecise cliché dismissed as a "literary" term by modern military authorities, like Edward Luttwak in *A Dictionary of Modern War* (New York: Harper & Row,

1971), 203. The Joint Chiefs of Staff's *Department of Defense Dictionary of Military Terms* (New York: Arco, 1988), 362, says it is "not to be used." For a view of the northern economy as "premodern," see Stanley Engerman, "The Economic Impact of the Civil War," in Ralph Andreano, ed., *The Economic Impact of the American Civil War,* 2nd ed. (Cambridge, Massachusetts: Schenkman Publishing, 1967), 188–209. See also J. Matthew Gallman, *Mastering Wartime: A Social History of Philadelphia during the Civil War* (Cambridge: Cambridge University Press, 1990), and a paper by Gallman and Engerman, "The Civil War Economy: A Modern View," presented at the conference "On the Road to Total War: The American Civil War and the German Wars of Unification, 1861–1871," German Historical Institute, Washington, D.C., April 1–4, 1992. This paper shaped this chapter's view of the economy decisively. See also Patrick K. O'Brien, *The Economic Effects of the American Civil War* (Atlantic Highlands, New Jersey: Humanities Press International, 1988). The work of the Republican Congress is described many places: I relied on the succinct coverage in James G. Randall and David Donald, *The Civil War and Reconstruction,* 2nd. ed. (Boston: D. C. Heath, 1961), 285–292. On the railroads see Thomas Webber, *The Northern Railroads in the Civil War, 1861–1865* (New York: King's Crown Press, 1952), 94–106, and, for comparison, K. Austin Kerr, *American Railroad Politics, 1914–1920: Rates, Wages, and Efficiency* (Pittsburgh: University of Pittsburgh Press, 1968), 59–71, and Walker D. Hines, *War History of American Railroads* (New Haven: Yale University Press, 1928), 145–149. General McClellan's letter to the B & O president is in *O. R.,* I, 19, pt. 2, 343. Lincoln on "inexhaustible" resources is in *Coll. Works,* VIII, 151.

The paragraphs on Lincoln and technology are based on Robert V. Bruce, *Lincoln and the Tools of War* (Indianapolis: Bobbs-Merrill, 1956), and *The Launching of Modern American Science, 1846–1876* (New York: Knopf, 1987). On dysfunctional technology in artillery and on buckshot—for a general view of the war as Napoleonic—see Paddy Griffith, *Battle Tactics of the Civil War* (orig. pub. 1987; New Haven: Yale University Press, 1989). Michael C. C. Adams's *Fighting for Defeat* brilliantly reminds us of the importance of agrarian virtues in the image of war held by nineteenth-century Americans. On naval technology in the Confederacy see Joseph T. Durkin, *Stephen R. Mallory: Confederate Navy Chief* (Chapel Hill: University of North Carolina Press, 1954). For Lincoln's racial theory of enterprise and his defense of Simon Cameron see *Coll. Works,* II, 437; III, 358; and V, 241–243. On Lincoln's "monomania" for honesty and on Cameron and Mrs. Lincoln, see Justin G. and Linda Levitt Turner, *Mary Todd Lincoln: Her Life and Letters* (orig. pub., 1972; New York: Fromm International, 1987), esp. 180. On fraud in Philadelphia, see Charles A. Dana, *Recollections of the Civil War: With the Leaders at Washington and in the Field in the Sixties* (New York: D. Appleton, 1902). I have followed McPherson's *Battle*

Cry of Freedom in discussing the illicit cotton trade, and Boritt's explanation in *Lincoln and the Economics of the American Dream* for Lincoln's willingness to license rather than to forbid the trade. For the Philadelphia seamstresses episode see *Coll. Works,* VII, 466–467, and 467n. Inflation is succinctly discussed in McPherson, *Battle Cry of Freedom,* esp. 447. On women see Kathryn Kish Sklar, "Victorian Women and Domestic Life: Mary Todd Lincoln, Elizabeth Cady Stanton, and Harriet Beecher Stowe," in Cullom Davis et al., eds. *The Public and Private Lincoln: Contemporary Perspectives* (Carbondale: Southern Illinois University Press, 1979), 20–37. The Lincoln-Stowe anecdote appears in Edmund Wilson, *Patriotic Gore: Studies in the Literature of the American Civil War* (New York: Oxford University Press, 1962), 3. Lincoln on "our red brethren" is in *Coll. Works,* VI, 151–152. The discussion of Ulysses S. Grant's notorious Order No. 11 is based on John Y. Simon, ed., *The Papers of Ulysses S. Grant,* 18 vols. to date (Carbondale: Southern Illinois University Press, 1967–), VII, 50, 51n–56n. Mrs. Lincoln's comment on her "tired & weary Husband" is in Turner, *Mary Todd Lincoln: Her Life and Letters,* 187. Lincoln's daily grind is best appreciated in Earl Schenck Miers, ed., *Lincoln Day by Day: A Chronology, 1809–1865* (orig. pub. 1960; Dayton, Ohio: Morningside, 1991). The classic description of it appears in the chapter called "Profile of a President" in the enduring work of Benjamin P. Thomas, *Abraham Lincoln: A Biography* (New York: Knopf, 1952).

Lincoln's response to the serenade appears in *Coll. Works,* VI, 319; the Gettysburg Address is at VII, 21, and the Second Inaugural Address, at VIII, 332–333 of the same work. His letter about the inaugural address is in *Coll. Works,* VIII, 356, and the 1862 annual message is at V, 537.

6. Politics as Usual

There is no standard one-volume political history of the Lincoln administration or the Civil War era in the United States. James G. Randall's *Lincoln the President,* 2 vols. (New York: Dodd, Mead, 1945); *Lincoln the President: Midstream* (New York: Dodd, Mead, 1953) and, with Richard N. Current, *Lincoln the President: Last Full Measure* (New York: Dodd, Mead, 1955) contain the most political lore but are marred by a distaste for and consequent misunderstanding of political parties. It is extremely difficult to see Lincoln as the opposition saw him, though the place to start is Joel H. Silbey's *A Respectable Minority: The Democratic Party in the Civil War Era, 1860–1868* (New York: W. W. Norton, 1977). William E. Gienapp's "Who Voted for Lincoln?" is valuable, and Michael F. Holt's flawed "Abraham Lincoln and the Politics of Union" is the only work on the idea of the Union party; both appear in John L. Thomas, ed., *Abraham Lincoln and the*

American Political Tradition (Amherst: University of Massachusetts Press, 1986). The previous chapter's title comes from Charles Janeway Stillé, *How a Free People Conduct a Long War,* first printed in Philadelphia in 1862 and available to modern readers in Frank Freidel, ed., *Union Pamphlets of the Civil War, 1861–1865,* 2 vols. (Cambridge: Harvard University Press, 1967), 381–403, esp. 384.

For Lincoln on political parties and the letter to Carl Schurz see *Coll. Works,* II, 126; V, 494–495, 510. Michael C. C. Adams's *Fighting for Defeat* detects the murmur of Caesarism abroad in the land but fails to link it with party politics. For "despot" see C. Vann Woodward and Elisabeth Muhlenfeld, eds., *The Private Mary Chesnut: The Unpublished Civil War Diaries* (New York: Oxford University Press, 1984), 146. McClellan's comments on losing the election of 1864 are in Sears, ed., *The Civil War Papers of George B. McClellan,* 622, 618. The Hooker letter is in *Coll. Works,* VI, 78–79. Lincoln's exasperation with General Meade is described in *Diary of Gideon Welles, Secretary of the Navy under Lincoln and Johnson,* 3 vols. (Boston: Houghton Mifflin, 1911), I, 370. Lincoln's judgment on the "power of congress" appears in *Coll. Works,* VI, 446. On Missouri see Michael Fellman, *Inside War: The Guerrilla Conflict in Missouri during the American Civil War* (New York: Oxford University Press, 1989); on Indiana see Emma Lou Thornbrough, *Indiana in the Civil War Era, 1850–1880* (Indianapolis: Indiana Historical Bureau & Indiana Historical Society, 1965), esp. 186–190; and on Illinois see Mark E. Neely, Jr., *The Abraham Lincoln Encyclopedia* (New York: McGraw-Hill, 1982), 340–341.

On the election of 1864 see William Frank Zornow, *Lincoln & the Party Divided* (Norman: University of Oklahoma Press, 1964), and Harold M. Hyman, "Election of 1864," in Arthur M. Schlesinger, Jr., and Fred L. Israel, eds., *History of American Presidential Elections,* 4 vols. (New York: Chelsea House, 1971), II, 1155–1244. I have found Zornow's account the most useful and rely on it here for the narrative thread. Thurlow Weed's recollection of the episode of cabinet formation appears in Harriet A. Weed, ed., *Life of Thurlow Weed,* 2 vols. (Boston: Houghton Mifflin, 1883–1884), I, 606–610. For the cabinet crisis of December 1862 and "now I can ride" see James G. Randall, *Lincoln the President,* 2 vols. (New York: Dodd, Mead, 1945), II, *Springfield to Gettysburg,* 241–248. On Lincoln as a politician see especially David Donald, *Lincoln Reconsidered: Essays on the Civil War Era* (rev. ed.; New York: Vintage, 1956). Lincoln on "Union" and "Disunion" candidates, "one term," and "being a candidate for re-election" is in *Coll. Works,* VII, 461; I, 339; VIII, 2. The blind memorandum, the response to the serenade of October 19, 1864, the remarks to the post-election serenade, and the annual message of 1864 appear in *Coll. Works,* VII, 514; VIII, 52–53, 100–101, 102n, and 149–150. On "tribal" voting see Joel H. Silbey, *The Partisan Imperative: The Dynamics of American Politics* (New York: Oxford

University Press, 1985). William Gienapp correlates youth with Republican voting in "Who Voted for Lincoln?"

Lincoln's amnesty proclamation is in *Coll. Works*, VII, 53–56. The key book is Herman Belz, *Reconstructing the Union: Theory and Policy during the Civil War* (Ithaca: Cornell University Press, 1969), which I have followed here. For General Banks's views see Neely, *Abraham Lincoln Encyclopedia*, 18–19. The "jewel of liberty," the Wade-Davis veto message, and the last speech are in *Coll. Works*, VII, 243, 433–434; VIII, 399–405.

7. Fate

The most important work on the assassination is William Hanchett, *The Lincoln Murder Conspiracies* (Urbana: University of Illinois Press, 1983). Also useful are George S. Bryan, *The Great American Myth* (New York: Carrick & Evans, 1940), and, for broad context, Franklin L. Ford, *Political Murder: From Tyrannicide to Terrorism* (Cambridge: Harvard University Press, 1985). Most readers probably want no more than a succinct summary, and that is available in Reinhard H. Luthin, *The Real Abraham Lincoln* (Englewood Cliffs, New Jersey: Prentice-Hall, 1960), 606–676.

Abraham Africanus I: His Secret Life, as Revealed under the Mesmeric Influence. Mysteries of the White House was published in New York by T. R. Dawley in 1864. Lincoln's "indiscreet" statement is in *Coll. Works*, IV, 240. Mrs. Chesnut's comments are in C. Vann Woodward and Elisabeth Muhlenfeld, eds., *The Private Mary Chesnut: The Unpublished Civil War Diaries* (New York: Oxford University Press, 1984), 34, 22. Seward on assassination appears in Bryan, *The Great American Myth*, 59, as is his interview with Charles Halpine (at 61–62). General Wright is quoted in Luthin, *The Real Abraham Lincoln*, 523–524. "I will take care" is quoted in *Coll. Works*, VIII, 385. General Lee and General Meade are quoted on the Dahlgren Papers in Hanchett, *The Lincoln Murder Conspiracies*, 33–34. Booth's letter is quoted in Bryan, *The Great American Myth*, 241–242. Hugh McCulloch commented on the assassination in a letter quoted in *Lincoln Lore*, No. 1661 (July 1976), 4.

Index

Abolitionism, 14–15, 42, 44, 97; Lincoln and, 15, 42, 119; antiabolition violence, 16–17
Alabama (ship), 75
American Colonization Society, 43
American party. *See* Know Nothing party
American Revolution, 125, 132
American System, 11
Amnesty, 179
Anaconda Plan, 76
Anglo-African Institute for the Encouragement of Industry, 11
Anti-Catholicism, 18, 22, 56
Antietam, Battle of, 69, 70–71, 72, 79, 112
Anti-Semitism, 151
Arnold, Samuel Bland, 191, 192
Assassination: plot against Lincoln, 183–186, 187–188, 189, 190–193; plot against Davis, 189
Atlanta, 83, 87, 94, 122
Atzerodt, George, 192

Baker, Edward D., 21, 22, 31
Balloon corps, 143
Baltimore plot, 183–185, 186
Banking/banks: state, 10; central, 13–14, 19, 20; national, 140
Banks, Nathaniel, 102, 180–181, 182
Bank War, 141
Bates, Edward, 57, 164, 167, 168
Beauregard, P. G. T., 84
Bell, John, 58
Berry, William F., 9
Bigelow, John, 185, 190

Bingham, George Caleb, 76
Black Hawk Indian War, 8, 61
Blair, Francis P., Jr., 75
Blair, Montgomery, 64, 109, 164, 168, 171
Booth, Edwin, 183
Booth, John Wilkes, 182, 183, 187, 190–192
Border slave states, 112, 116–117
Brady, Mathew, 153
Breckinridge, John C., 58
Browning, Orville Hickman, 63, 99, 100
Buchanan, James, 48–51, 58, 63, 145, 164, 166–167
Buell, Don Carlos, 77
Bull Run: First Battle of, 65, 81, 84; Second Battle of, 81, 162
Burnside, Ambrose, 72, 74, 82, 162
Butler, Benjamin F., 102, 103

Cabinet crisis of 1862, 168–170
California gold rush, 35
Cameron, Simon, 57, 145, 146, 167, 168
Carolinas campaign, 87
Carpenter, Francis B., 153
Cartwright, Peter, 23
Catholicism, 18, 44
Chase, Salmon P., 36, 57, 81–82, 164, 167, 168, 169–171
Chesapeake Bay, 66, 67
Chesnut, Mary Boykin, 161, 162, 184–185
Chicago Christians, 111, 112, 115
Christian issues and politics, 21, 23